*Race, Rape, and Lynching*

RACE AND AMERICAN CULTURE
Arnold Rampersad and Shelley Fisher Fishkin
  General Editors

Love and Theft
Blackface Minstrelsy and the American Working Class
  Eric Lott

The Dialect of Modernism
Race, Language, and Twentieth-Century Literature
  Michael North

Bordering on the Body
The Racial Matrix of Modern Fiction and Culture
  Laura Doyle

"Who Set You Flowin'? "
The African-American Migration Narrative
  Farah Jasmine Griffin

"Doers of the Word"
African-American Women Speakers
and Writers in the North (1830–1880)
  Carla L. Peterson

Race, Rape, and Lynching: The Red Record
of American Literature, 1890–1912
  Sandra Gunning

# Race, Rape, and Lynching

The Red Record of American

Literature, 1890–1912

SANDRA GUNNING

*New York    Oxford*

OXFORD UNIVERSITY PRESS

1996

Oxford University Press
Oxford    New York
Athens    Auckland    Bangkok    Bogota    Bombay
Buenos Aires    Calcutta    Cape Town    Dar es Salaam
Delhi    Florence    Hong Kong    Istanbul    Karachi
Kuala Lumpur    Madras    Madrid    Melbourne
Mexico City    Nairobi    Paris    Singapore
Taipei    Tokyo    Toronto

and associated companies in
Berlin    Ibadan

Published by Oxford University Press, Inc.
198 Madison Avenue, New York, New York 10016

Oxford is a registered trademark of Oxford University Press, Inc.

Library of Congress Cataloging-in-Publication Data

Gunning, Sandra.
Race, rape, and lynching: the red record of American literature,
1890–1912 / Sandra Gunning.
p.    cm. — (Race and American culture)
Includes bibliographical references (p.    ) and index.
ISBN 0-19-509990-7
1. American literature—20th century—History and criticism.
2. American literature—19th century—History and criticism.
3. Afro-Americans in literature.    4. Violence in literature.
5. Lynching in literature.    6. Rape in literature.    7. Race in
literature.    I. Title.    II. Series.
PS173.N4G86    1996
810.9'3520396073—dc20        95–36520

9    8    7    6    5    4    3    2    1
Printed in the United States of America
on acid-free paper

*To Marguerite and Jacqueline,*
*and in memory of Rymund*

# Preface

IN 1895 the militant African American woman journalist Ida B. Wells published *A Red Record: Tabulated Statistics and Alleged Causes of Lynchings in the United States, 1892–1893–1894* to discredit the widespread belief in the threat of black rape and to alert audiences at home and abroad about the scandal of lynching in the United States enabled by this belief. In naming my study *Race, Rape, and Lynching: The Red Record of American Literature, 1890–1912*, I deliberately echo Wells's title in order to call attention to and problematize discursive "records" on turn-of-the-century racial violence as primary moments of a complex literary engagement with the questions of race, rape, and lynching.

In this study I read American literature on racial violence as a broad construct that must include black and white, male and female writers utilizing a host of genres, and I offer a critical narrative that includes expected and unexpected names: Thomas Dixon, Jr., Mark Twain, Charles W. Chesnutt, and Ida B. Wells; but also Pauline E. Hopkins, David Bryant Fulton, and Kate Chopin. My purpose here is to engage neither in a chronological study nor an exhaustive examination of how differing camps drew up battle lines for or against lynching. Rather, I consider the similar and dissimilar ways in which, as these writers addressed the phenomena of lynching and white mob violence for which the trope of the black-male-as-rapist was a precondition, they simultaneously referenced post-Reconstruction anxieties about identity, sexuality, citizenship, and social change.

Chapter 1 addresses the novels of Thomas Dixon, Jr., the most famous propagator of the trope of the black rapist. I argue here that this figure mediates Dixon's merged anxieties about African American demands for citizenship, white femininity, and the Southern tradition of miscegenation. In this chapter I also consider Dixon's conflicted attitude toward racial violence as, paradoxically, a necessary tool of white supremacy but also an indicator of white racial degeneration, at a time when white supremacists appeared especially forceful in arguing for African American disenfranchisement on the basis of racial inferiority. In Chapter 2 I discuss similar moments of conflict around gender and racial identities in turn-of-the-century literature, in Mark Twain's *Pudd'nhead Wilson* (1894) and Charles W. Chesnutt's *The Marrow of Tradition* (1901). Both Twain and Chesnutt take stands against white supremacy by imagining white male culpability and black resistance to racial domination. However, their attempts to refigure black community, black masculinity, and black aggression necessarily achieve only a partial response to white supremacy; and at some moments they replicate the kinds of race and gender representations they seek to refute. Thus the examples of Dixon, Twain, and Chesnutt reveal the uneasy correlations between "racist" and "anti-racist" discourses at the turn of the century, as they drew on commonly derived definitions of gender, domesticity, and power.

Several writers offer important but hitherto neglected counterpoints to the examples of Dixon, Twain, and Chesnutt. In Chapters 3 and 4, I address black writers Ida B. Wells, David Bryant Fulton, and Pauline E. Hopkins; and the white feminist writer Kate Chopin. Equally in dialogue with the late-nineteenth-century gender and race discourses that shape the work of Dixon, Twain, and Chesnutt, these writers explore the problems of female subjectivity and community history, specifically in the context of rape and lynching. As such, their work offers crucial moments for considering how a whole range of black and white writers variously addressed not just the criminalization of black masculinity and the reinvigoration of white masculinity through retributive violence, but also the figuration of silenced womanhood as a crucial component in turn-of-the-century discourses of rape and lynching.

# Acknowledgments

M Y FIRST WORDS of thanks are to Stephanie A. Smith, who graciously read virtually every word of this work and who provided me with encouragement and crucial commentary at every step; and to Anne E. Goldman and M. Giulia Fabi for always being ready to read and believe in my work. Also, this book might not have been completed without the intellectual and emotional support provided by my old and new friends Betty Louise Bell, Barbara Christian, Frances Smith Foster, Peter Logan, Fred Moten, Adela Pinch, Carolyn Porter, Rei Terada, Terri Tinkle, Richard Yarborough, and Rafia Zafar.

I have also been fortunate in having other friends and colleagues who have extended themselves and supported me in innumerable ways: Michael Awkward, Linda Deitert, Jonathan Freedman, Rosemary M. George, the late James Gindin, Veronica Marie Gregg, June Howard, Lemuel Johnson, Kerry Larson, Lisa Lowe, Kate McCullough, Anita Norich, Bill Paul, Yopie Prins, Marlon Ross, Judith Rosen, Michael Schoenfeldt, Eric J. Sundquist, Sherley Anne Williams, Winifred Woodhull, Martha Vicinus, Robert Wiesbuch, and Patsy Yeager. Thanks also to my research assistants Janice Koistinen, David Shih, and Delia Coleman in the English Department at the University of Michigan, Ann Arbor. And I must express my gratitude to the anonymous reader at Oxford University Press for his valuable criticisms, and especially to senior editor Elizabeth Maguire, to her assistant Elda Rotor, and to the Race and American Culture series editors Shelley Fisher Fishkin and Arnold Rampersad for ushering this work into print. Also, I will be forever indebted to my friends and copyeditors Steve Gray and Madeleine Clark for their careful attention to the preparation of my manuscript.

Much of the work in the following pages would have taken considerably longer had it not been for the following institutional support: a University of California Affirmative Action 1990–1991 Dissertation Year Fellowship; a University of California President's Postdoctoral Fellowship for 1992–1993, held in residence at UC San Diego, Department of Literature and Language; and funds from the Office of the Vice Provost for Academic and Multicultural Affairs and from the Office of the Vice President for Research, both at the University of Michigan, Ann Arbor.

Finally, I thank my mother Marguerite Gunning and my sister Jacqueline Hicks, her husband Dan, and their sons, Dan, Jr., and Wesley, all of whom show me what really matters; my aunt Dulce Gunning, and my uncle Elon Gunning who take the time to listen; my dear friends Francene Rutlin and Janice Stephenson who have never been deterred by great distances; and Keith L. T. Alexander, whose love, patience, and much appreciated humor have sustained us both through many moments of trial.

A shorter version of Chapter 4, entitled "Kate Chopin's Local Color Fiction and the Politics of White Supremacy," appeared in *Arizona Quarterly* 51 (Autumn 1995).

# Contents

*Race, Rape, and Lynching*

*INTRODUCTION*

# On Literary Records
# and Discursive Possibilities

> Because these things are bound up with their notion of chaos it is al-
> most impossible for many whites to consider questions of sex,
> women, economic opportunity, the national identity, historic
> change, social justice—even the "criminality" implicit in the broaden-
> ing of freedom itself—without summoning malignant images of
> black men into consciousness.
>
> Ralph Ellison,
> "Change the Joke and Slip the Yoke"

THE BLACK MALE BODY, hypersexualized and criminalized, has always functioned as a crucial and heavily overdetermined metaphor in an evolving national discourse on the nature of a multiethnic, multiracial American
society. And whether it was the burning of Sam Hose in 1899 on suspicion of
rape and murder, the lynching of Emmett Till in 1955 for whistling at a white
woman shopkeeper, the 1989 murder by a white mob of Yusuf Hawkins for
being a black man in an Italian-American neighborhood, or finally the beating
of Rodney King in 1991 for allegedly menacing white police officers, "malignant
images" of black masculinity have been accompanied by some of the most
horrific eruptions of white violence this country has ever known.

Present-day impulses to map out the history, meaning, and consequences of
the figure of the criminalized black male body—as well as the white violence
through which that figure is produced—have consistently driven cultural histo-
rians to trace its roots back to slavery and post-Reconstruction American culture. In *Race, Rape, and Lynching* I direct this tracing within the specific context
of American literature's confrontation with the figure of the black as beast and
the American tradition of lynching in the 1890s and early 1900s. I have selected
these particular years because they mark the intersection of several historical
and cultural events: an unprecedented rise in the number of lynchings and
white race riots directed specifically at African American communities; an outpouring of distinctive narratives concerned with white supremacy and alleged
black degeneration in the wake of Reconstruction; the continuing expansion of
the movement for Woman Suffrage and a growing demand among various

groups of white women for higher education and an increased level of sexual and social freedom; the flowering of a small but active postslavery generation of African American male and female writers intent upon making their political and artistic mark on the American literary scene.

The frightening drama of lynching, of black rape and white victimhood, the endless questions about the moral and legal nature of lynching itself: these issues made their imprint on American literature at the turn of the century. But with the exception of Trudier Harris in *Exorcising Blackness: Historical and Literary Lynching and Burning Rituals* (1984) and Hazel V. Carby in *Reconstructing Womanhood: The Emergence of the Afro-American Woman Novelist* (1987), few literary critics have attempted to come to terms with how writers of the 1890s and early 1900s might have engaged with the discourses of race and violence that would preoccupy Americans for decades to come.[1] As a continuation of the kinds of critical conversations initiated by Harris and Carby on literature and racial violence, I undertake in *Race, Rape, and Lynching* a selective study of literature by black and white men and women as a means of uncovering ways in which Americans of both races contributed to a continual renegotiation and redefinition of the terms and boundaries of a sectional and ultimately national dialogue on racial violence in the 1890s and early 1900s.

While not exhaustive (many will note, for instance, that I do not discuss black novelist Sutton E. Griggs), *Race, Rape, and Lynching* does bring together expected and unexpected names: Thomas Dixon, Jr., Mark Twain, Charles W. Chesnutt, Ida B. Wells, David Bryant Fulton, Pauline E. Hopkins, and Kate Chopin. Thus I define American literature as a multiplicity of dependent traditions that include the work of black and white, male and female writers.[2] I am especially concerned in this study with how, within texts normally segregated in present-day American literary scholarship by canon, or as male and female "modes" of writing, the trope of black rape functions as a multilayered metaphor to structure and articulate latent anxieties over black and white self-construction in terms of gender, class, and citizenship roles.

Though this is a literary study of writers on the subject of black criminality and white violence at the specific moment of the post-Reconstruction era, attention must be paid to the rapidly changing world in which the texts under study were produced and to the evolution of national and community attitudes and assumptions that shaped the writers' interpretations of events. A number of scholars have attempted to track the historical, sociological, and psychological underpinnings of white supremacist violence and black responses to it in the post-Reconstruction era—in particular, George M. Fredrickson, *The Black Image in the White Mind: The Debate on Afro-American Character and Destiny, 1817–1914* (1971); Joel Williamson, *The Crucible of Race: Black-White Relations in the American South Since Emancipation* (1984); Herbert Shapiro, *White Violence and Black Response: From Reconstruction to Montgomery* (1988); and most recently, W. Fitzhugh Brundage, *Lynching in the New South: Georgia and Virginia, 1880–1930* (1993). As these studies have suggested, while the figure of blackness as the epitome of animalism and sexual energy has always been an overriding preoccupation for white Americans, the dangerously pervasive stereotype of the black rapist—the black as beast—fully emerged in the post–Civil War era.

During this period lynching and white mob violence aimed at African American individuals and communities alike achieved their highest levels. The lynching of African Americans (a practice that often included torture, burning, dismemberment, and, in the case of black men, ritual castration), began as early as the 1870s during Reconstruction, while bloody white race riots were a standard feature of American life throughout the rest of the century, in a variety of locations including St. Landry Parish, Louisiana (1868); Colfax, Louisiana (1873); Clinton, Mississippi (1875); Carrollton, Mississippi (1886); Wilmington, North Carolina (1898); New Orleans (1900); Atlanta (1906); East St. Louis (1917); and Chicago (1919). Figures on the number of blacks killed by lynch mobs during this period vary widely; estimates made by the NAACP and by anti-lynching activists such as James Elbert Cutler and Ida B. Wells suggest that the number of black victims ranged from 3,337 to 10,000.[3]

In any era in American history, lynching and white mob violence were produced by numerous interrelated factors; however, white violence against African Americans persisted at the turn of the century in part because many white Americans had come to believe that, notwithstanding the disregard for legal process that attended white violence, severe and immediate retribution was the only means of disciplining the accused black man, specifically when he was alleged to have committed the crime of rape.[4] According to the celebrated Virginia novelist Thomas Nelson Page, "such barbarity as burning at the stake" shocked "the South and . . . even the sense of those [white] men who, in their frenzy, have been guilty of it"; but "a deeper shock than this is at the bottom of their ferocious rage—the shock which comes from the ravishing and butchery of their women and children."[5] In a speech on lynching and law before the U.S. Senate in 1907, South Carolina's Ben Tillman put things more bluntly:

> And shall such a creature [the black rapist] . . . appeal to the law? Shall men coldbloodedly stand up and demand for him the right to have a fair trial and be punished in the regular course of justice? So far as I am concerned he has put himself outside the pale of the law, human and divine. . . . Civilization peels off us, any and all of us who are men, and we revert to the original savage type whose impulses under any and all circumstances has always been to "kill! kill! kill!"[6]

The Southern historian Wilbur Cash has commented that in the postbellum era "the actual danger of the Southern white woman's being violated by the negro . . . was much less, for instance, than the chance that she would be struck by lightning."[7] However, this circumstance, coupled with the fact that many lynchings did not involve black men charged with rape, but rather aimed to punish African American women and children for any number of petty "crimes," made little impact on white Americans enthralled by the more compelling narrative of their nation in racial danger.

After Reconstruction the idea of the black rapist proved particularly useful for white Americans seeking to come to terms with post–Civil War anxieties over national unity, black emancipation, altered gender roles, growing labor unrest, European immigration, and the continued evolution of the United States into an increasingly multiethnic nation.[8] Thus we need to see the figuration of the rapist as *one of a number* of intertwined responses many white Americans enacted in the face of social upheaval.[9] For many white supremacists, the stereotype of the black male as sexual beast functioned as an externalized symbol of social chaos against which all whites, regardless of class, could begin to unite for the purpose of national renewal. As a result, whereas the years prior to Emancipation were marked (often, though not exclusively, in the South) by organized white violence against African Americans under the rubric of punishments necessary for slave discipline, after 1865 white-on-black violence came to be seen as urgently self-defensive. As Southern whites grappled with the reality that they were no longer masters, while their Northern counterparts watched fearfully a steady migration of newly freed blacks to cities above the Mason-Dixon line, many white Americans perceived themselves as a race potentially under siege once millions of ex-slaves were now (presumably) free to act on their own impulses.

Although little occurred after Reconstruction to ensure black political or economic success, many African American leaders at the turn of the century did exude a certain sense of optimism that they hoped might spur on their communities. In 1903, despite decades of unprecedented racial hostility exhibited by white Americans, the editor of the black *New York Age,* T. Thomas Fortune, was hopeful enough to declare: "[t]hat the Negro is destined . . . to be the landlord and master agriculturalist of the Southern states is a probability sustained by all the facts in the situation." Even the usually cautious words of accommodationist Booker T. Washington expressed the possibility of a revolution in the racial status quo:

> I would set no limits on the attainments of the Negro in arts, in letters or statesmanship . . . . I plead for industrial education and development for the Negro not because I want to cramp him, but because I want to free him. I want to see him enter the all-powerful business and commercial world.[10]

Such ambitions undoubtedly pitted ex-slaves against former masters and underscored the altered patterns of social relations, which alienated the ex-slaveholder from his property, the white man from the former image of himself as master. Not only had blacks literally shifted from the category of property, but black men were now to be considered as citizens and social equals—or so the Fourteenth (1868) and Fifteenth (1870) Amendments implied. And this shift in identities was marked by an epidemic of violence that lasted throughout the post–Civil War era and well into the early decades of the twentieth century.

Martha Hodes has effectively argued that "the violence of Reconstruction" and of the years beyond "can only be explained by a definition of politics that is broad enough to encompass traditional acts of citizenship and authority such as voting and economic independence, and, at the same time, the power of sexual agency." Sexual and political agency became increasingly linked in the figure of the black rapist precisely because of the dependent definition of citizenship on definitions of (white) manhood. According to Hodes, "the idea of manhood, which had long implied the rights and responsibilities of citizenship in American political thought, now took on connotations, in white minds, of black male sexual agency, and specifically of sexual transgression with white women." [11] This translation of the freedman's impulse toward democracy into ultimately a threat against the most personal, most sacred aspect of white life meant that what might have begun in the late 1860s and 1870s as a political struggle was increasingly characterized by the 1890s as a social rape, an encroachment on the sacred Anglo-Saxon male right to everything in American society and civilization. In turn, American society and civilization came increasingly to be figured as the white female body: silent, helpless, in immediate need of protection from the black beast. Thus the projection of feminized whiteness in danger functioned as a primary argument of white supremacists to justify terrorism against black communities. Because whites could allege that the struggle was really one of racial survival, not democracy, black men would not simply be disenfranchised, they would rightfully be exterminated. [12]

Outbreaks of white violence such as the 1898 Wilmington, North Carolina, race riot in which eleven blacks were killed and hundreds terrorized by white mobs, must be read at least in part in the context of this fantasy of white male loss and recovery through aggression. The Wilmington riot was provoked not by a rape, but by the participation in local elections of the town's majority black population. In justifying their violent actions, however, Wilmington's white Democrats echoed the coalesced rhetoric of nationalism, eugenics, domestic protection, and what they saw as the exclusive white right of citizenship, when they declared that "North Carolina shall not be negroized. It is of all the States of the Union particularly the home of the Anglo-Saxon, and the Anglo-Saxon shall govern it." [13]

Such outbursts in Wilmington occurred in conjunction with the "legal" maneuvering of white-controlled Southern state legislatures to disenfranchise former slaves and their descendents. The 1896 Supreme Court decision in *Plessy v.*

*Ferguson* provided legal support for state-mandated segregation, so by the end of the century white supremacists had already set up barriers to the very social contact between races they themselves argued encouraged black rape. However, these white political gains seemed to make no difference: enacting a self-fulfilling prophesy, white supremacists continued to point to the rise in the number of lynchings in the South as evidence that the black male threat was ever-present, with or without legal stays. After all, according to popular notions of the African American character, the accused black men had to be guilty, because they were by their very "nature" barbaric.

Although they variously advocated the extension or cessation of racial hostility, I do not argue that black and white writers actually effected a rise or decline in lynching, or that their work chronicled group opinions—an idea that might seem to be suggested by my subtitle *The Red Record of American Literature*. In fact, my subtitle echoes that of Ida B. Wells's 1895 anti-lynching pamphlet, *A Red Record: Tabulated Statistics and Alleged Causes of Lynchings in the United States, 1892–1893–1894*, and the juxtaposition of texts and traditions that I outlined earlier must necessarily problematize the very merger of the literary and the historical suggested in use of the word *record*. Although at times I undoubtedly engage in such discussions, my purpose here is not to attempt a recuperation of realistic images of black people or to enumerate which authors created racist depictions of blacks and which authors retaliated. Indeed, I view such literature neither as a historical record nor as a narrative of authoritative fact about what racial groups believed at the turn of the century. Rather, my interpretation of the term *record* as a discursive trope comes out of my reading of the politics of narrative, best exemplified in the career of Ida B. Wells.

When Wells published her pamphlet *A Red Record*, she envisioned her text as an urgent attack on what she saw as a "new system of intimidation" that had begun to evolve by the last decade of the nineteenth century.[14] As a black female protest writer, Wells adopted the signal strategy of gathering together for the sake of moral impact disparate white accounts of horrific scenes of violence, and then juxtaposing these accounts with overwhelming statistics on lynchings that had occurred, often in the absence of rape, to contradict the "fact" that lynching was an expression of white chivalry or that black men were naturally driven to rape white women. Thus Wells's goal was to call into question white supremacist narratives of nation, history, and community by providing an alternative reading of events for the purpose of influencing public opinion.[15]

As I see it, the compelling significance of Wells's pamphlet *A Red Record* was not only that it provided crucial information about racial violence at the turn of the century, but that it also functioned as a site of interpretive intervention within public discourse for a doubly disenfranchised black woman who, even momentarily, might challenge the dominant readings of history and culture in her own age. Thus, according to my definition of the term in this study, Wells's pamphlet functions as a record of discursive possibilities at the moment in which it engages the problems of audience and narrative stance, language, genre, gender, and power. My selection of authors, then, is based on my identification of their texts as moments of such discursive possibility that rupture what we too often think of as a seamless body of American attitudes at the turn of the century about race, violence, and black criminality.

One way to begin thinking about these issues is to revise the modern critical assumption that, despite the presence of figures like Ida B. Wells, turn-of-the-century literature on lynching was produced only when white and black male novelists, essayists, and journalists engaged in heated exchanges over black male/white female miscegenation, white rule, or black humanity—a phenomenon that resulted in what Trudier Harris calls, particularly for black writers, a "literature of emasculation."[16] If we limited our reading to literature on lynching, often by black and white men, we might be left with the linked "plots" of black rape and white lynching as the basis for a homosocial, interracial triangle of desire in which the body of the white female victim mediates between the oppositional pairing of the black beast and the white protector.[17] But like the stereotype of the rapist, such a view obscures other issues and distracts from more meaningful analyses. For one thing, we tend to ignore automatically the very different manner of participation engaged in by black and white women writers when they approached the subject of lynching. Indeed, the very figuration of black women in relationship to white, within the ideology supporting white racial violence gets lost in the shuffle over black and white male articulations.

In a recent attempt to address the role of black women in the lynching ritual, Robyn Wiegman argues rightly that the practice "carries an inherent negation of the African American woman through the very absence of her significatory role in the psychosexual drama of masculinity that underwrites the lynching and castration of black men." According to Wiegman, the black woman registers as an emphatic "absence," evacuated and expelled from lynching's ritual, so that she seems to drop out of "the cultural narrativity that defines and sanctions lynching."[18] Wiegman provides readers with an analysis of Mary Dalton and Bessie in Richard Wright's 1940 novel of lynching and rape, *Native Son*, ably demonstrating the ways in which Wright, even as he explores the agony and injustice of black male suffering, "find[s] it necessary to deny the gendered dimension of rape . . . to see only the black male as rape's social and sexual victim," a consequence that appears "to displace the category of woman altogether."[19]

While I agree with Wiegman generally, I would argue for a reconfiguration of the meaning of this displacement. In particular, are black women necessarily (to use Wiegman's choice of verbs) negated, absented, evacuated, expelled, and displaced from the ritual of lynching, or are they in fact profoundly present in the dimension of the symbolic, since they speak not only (as Wiegman says) to the sexual excess of white women, but also the sexual excess of white men themselves? After all, black women were regularly victims of white sexual aggression. This fact was consistently masked by the ancient charge that, because she was the female equivalent of the black rapist, the black woman could never be raped.[20]

In the case of the stereotype of lascivious black womanhood, the symbolic absence of the black woman is balanced by the symbolic presence of the white, since the primary construction of white femininity as a masculine prize (a construction that enables the ritual of lynching, since she is the "cause" of the struggle) is predicated on black femininity's sexual and social devaluation. Also, because the stereotype functions to thwart dangerous sexual passion and the disruptive crossing of racial boundaries, the white lyncher as the moral opposite of the black rapist signifies a suppression of the long American tradition of white male/black female sexual contact. A study of the representations of the black rapist and of white violence, then, would entail a study of interrelations among all four stereotypes. If we accept Hazel Carby's premise that "the objective of stereotypes is not to reflect or represent a reality but to function as a disguise, or mystification, of objective social relations," then we recognize the stereotype of the black rapist as a site from which to theorize about the full range of other "social relations" embedded in, crossed out, and crossed over by a continuing national obsession with the oversexualized black male.[21] A shift away from the notion of literature on racial violence as primarily a body of male homosocial narratives would allow for a rereading of a body of literature that might reveal a number of participants and a rich variety of political strategies and points of view.

Recent scholarship on black and white women's culture in the context of turn-of-the-century American lynching has been promising. In her discussion of turn-of-the-century gender politics, Bettina Aptheker has argued that even when black women's activism and protest writing were directed in response to the lynching of black men, as in the case of Ida B. Wells and Mary Church Terrell, such work functioned as a response to the apparent absence of black women from the discussion of white violence as themselves victims of rape and lynching. And in their recent books, Elizabeth Ammons and Claudia Tate have both argued for a recognition of how the political dimension of black women's novels of domesticity also worked to engage African American women in national debates about race, violence, and rape.[22] On the subject of white women, Jacquelyn Dowd Hall's *Revolt Against Chivalry: Jessie Daniel Ames and the Women's Campaign Against Lynching* (1974) and Katherine M. Blee's *Women of the Klan: Racism and Gender in the 1920s* (1991) represent major white feminist attempts to come to terms with racial violence as a political practice that included white women as participants, architects, and resisters.

Still, especially within the field of literary studies, Hazel Carby's call for "more feminist work that interrogates sexual ideologies for their racial specificity and acknowledges whiteness, not just blackness, as a racial categorization" has yet to be fully answered.[23] When we begin consistently to examine turn-of-the-century white women writers as female subjects already racialized (as indeed black women writers have always been considered), the question of how such women and their contemporaries might have participated—overtly or not—in discussions of race may become answerable. Without a concerted effort to envision the decidedly different dimensions of white female responses to lynching and mob violence, we are left with the impression that, outside of a small number of highly visible and controversial figures such as Women's Christian Temperance Union president Frances Willard, who believed Southern claims that lynching was a necessary act of domestic protection, and Rebecca Latimer Felton, who urged the lynching of black men "a thousand times a week if necessary," white women had little to say about racial violence until 1930, when Jesse Daniel Ames founded the Association of Southern Women for the Prevention of Lynching. Yet in the 1880s and 1890s, the years of greatest violence (and thus the years of the highest number of assaults on white women, if white supremacists are to be believed), white women certainly had something to say about racial violence and its impact on their communities; however, we need to recognize that, as was the case for black women, their angle of vision and, therefore, their very mode of address would necessarily have been different from those of their men.

In the texts on lynching and race riots by white and black men examined in this study, the black rapist, the white rape victim, the white avenger, and the black woman as prostitute operate together with differing resonances. These stereotypes also operate together in texts by black and white women, but here the definitions of what constitute racial violence and its consequences are at times profoundly different. For example, women's texts engage not with male access to citizenship and property, but rather with the problem of establishing female subjectivity within a public debate whose terms are universally established by men; with the political and personal consequences of rape; with the attraction and repulsion of fantasies of sexual desire; and with the need for sexual recovery. Thus we must reimagine the discourse on racial violence as including not just men *and* women writing, but men and women writing in different tonalities, with different strategies, and with different concerns.

While the discussions in this book are meant to point to the gendered nature of turn-of-the-century American literature on racial violence, they are also meant to direct readers away from attempts to categorize some writers as necessarily more "progressive" than others. For one thing, we need to be careful when considering the differences between so-called "racist" and "anti-racist" white and black discourses. For example, instead of defining turn-of-the-century literature on racial violence as polemical exchanges between pro- and anti-lynching factions, I argue that opposing discourses by black and white men might fracture in similar ways around the construction of gender and around notions of class and political action, precisely because both groups often utilized similarly constructed categories of masculinity and of the power relations between victim and victimizer to represent opposing sides in a race war. The point here is not to suggest that anti-racist narratives are always already co-opted by the discursive patterns of dominant racist ideology, but to suggest a more subtle way of reading the "progressivism" always ascribed to or hoped for in writing by people of color, when compared to "mainstream" white literary history.

I also attempt to show that various "sides"—white supremacist versus black protest fiction, for instance—hardly represented monolithic camps. This idea becomes clearer when we try to define the very complex category of "white supremacy" as a philosophy or a political faction. As both George M. Fredrickson and Joel Williamson have demonstrated in their scholarship, white supremacists were anything but a unified group, and this is never more evident than in the variety of white racist responses to the practice of lynching itself.[24] Robyn Wiegman reminds us that "[a]bove all, lynching is about the law"; this statement is correct, of course, in the sense that lynching fulfills the "symbolic" law of racial struggle as expressed in general by white supremacist ideology.[25] But in novels such as Dixon's *The Leopard's Spots* (1902) and *The Clansman* (1905), precisely because lynching was an experience outside traditional civil law, the practice enabled a state of liminality where white torture and dismemberment of the black male body allowed for the political reinvigoration of Southern masculinity, through a transference of what Wiegman calls the black male's imagined hypermasculinity.[26] Yet the recognition that the violence behind lynching, however "justified" or invigorating, was itself an expression of white lawlessness, of a perceived breakdown of white civilization (even as it supposedly worked to preserve the latter) was troubling for many who advocated such aggressive white domination. Lynching might have a "desired" effect on black men, but its very bloody execution drew the white avenger too close to the offender.

Inevitably, under the rubric of white supremacy we must include some unlikely candidates: certainly Thomas Dixon; but also Kate Chopin and even Mark Twain abided by certain tenets of white supremacy, albeit to vastly differing degrees. Yet the value they bring as subjects of study lies not in tracking the conservatism of their vision, but in analyzing the meaning of their struggle to work through the moral contradictions of the racial and literary politics of their era. Thus, while Chopin and Dixon rely on the same root fantasy of black male sexuality as a site from which to construct very different representations of white female sexuality or idealized white manhood, their final visions complicate easy pronouncements of what a white supremacist writer should look like. Part of the anxiety around racializing whiteness with respect to newly canonized writers like Chopin comes in the fear for some that she might be labeled as either a "racist" or a "nonracist," and might therefore either be condemned or praised because, in a humanist reading of literature, "racist" literature is automatically labled artistically "bad" literature. But for me the value of Chopin as a middle-class white woman writing primarily about the South comes precisely in the complexity and contradiction of her position on race, specifically on whiteness as a racialized category, and in the ways in which that complexity and that contradiction texture and shape her considerable literary achievements.

As a necessarily present figuration in the work of Dixon, in Twain's *Pudd'nhead Wilson,* as well as in Chopin's stories, whiteness itself begins to signify social disorder, as class war threatens to break out in the very ranks of the Klan, or as white men from pre– and post–Civil War generations, from the North and the South, struggle against their own differences by imposing a sense of racial unity through violence against the black male body. And within such chaotic situations, white femininity becomes as threatening as blackness because of its significations: the threat of black rape or of black male/white female miscegenation renders the white womb the site of race vulnerability, of suppressed white sexual unruliness as the myth of black rape becomes the mirrored image of the literal white rape of black women. In works by Dixon and Twain there surfaces a need to silence female utterance both black and white, as a means of curtailing opportunities for disruption, as a means of reducing to a manageable simplicity the public focus on the criminalized black male body. In Chopin's local color stories about post-Reconstruction white violence in Louisiana, however, while on the one hand the racist notion of white superiority is rarely challenged, on the other a severe judgment is passed on a male habit of bloodletting, because such a practice denies the supposed cultural values of white civilization and disrupts communal peace.

In their re-presentation of blackness for turn-of-the-century white Americans, African American writers register a similarly complex field for interpretation. Many African American male writers are quick to observe the dilemma of white masculine self-construction, and they respond with what seems to be their own reconstruction of black masculinity as the central, unified symbol of the true American man: hardworking, brave, solicitous of women black or white, peace-loving, but never passive. Yet as the examples of Charles Chesnutt in *The Marrow of Tradition* (1901) and David Bryant Fulton in *Hanover: or The Persecution of the Lowly* (1900) demonstrate, their signification of the role and experiences of black women varied dramatically, since Fulton's representation of white violence is almost completely located within the world of African American women. In challenging public discourse, black women writers Ida B. Wells and Pauline Hopkins add further diversity to the notion of turn-of-the-century African American literature on racial violence by addressing the impact of white violence on the body of the black community itself, through the figures of black men and women. Thus, to theorize on black literary responses to lynching and rape is to reference a host of political positions that represent a diversity of black opinion, based on region, class, and gender.

The chapters in *Race, Rape, and Lynching* have been formulated to emphasize the thematic overlaps and differences among writers, their novelistic subgenres, and their political locations. As such, I am concerned less with following a chronology of literary history than with mapping out particular discursive moments or culminations within the brief twenty-two-year period covered by this study. Chapter 1, "Re-Membering Blackness After Reconstruction: Race, Rape, and Political Desire in the Work of Thomas Dixon, Jr.," focuses on how, in *The Leopard's Spots: A Romance of the White Man's Burden—1865–1900* (1902) and *The Clansman* (1905), when his heroes find their masculinity threatened by the very space of white domesticity they have vowed to protect, Dixon enlists proscribed uses of violence to resolve white male confusion and conflict over the changing definitions of gender roles. At the same time, the ideal of white masculinity in Dixon's narratives is in danger of capitulating to a white male erotic obsession with monstrous blackness, as is his 1912 novel, *The Sins of the Father*. Considering that Dixon's plots manifest both a fascination for and a terror of white savagery unleashed by the ritual of lynching, what underlies his fiction is a struggle with contradictions that jeopardize the creation and maintenance of a coherent vision of white masculinity as the embodiment of social and sexual authority.

Shifting to Anglo-American and African American male opponents of white supremacy in Chapter 2, "Mark Twain, Charles Chesnutt, and the Politics of Literary Anti-Racism," I discuss *Pudd'nhead Wilson* (1894) and *The Marrow of Tradition* (1901). As a historical novel of slavery that calls into question the bases for white hysteria over the black rapist in the 1890s, Twain's *Pudd'nhead Wilson* details the consequences of a long tradition of sexual liaisons between Southern white patriarchs and their female slaves. In particular, I argue that Twain's text targets the complacency of popular plantation fiction's depiction of the happy darky by revealing, in a farcical "plantation fiction" novel, the suppressed white fear of black anger over disenfranchisement. Yet in the process of issuing a scathing indictment, Twain reaches for metaphors of malignant blackness similar to those subsequently developed and exploited by Thomas Dixon.

Written at the very moment of a new century, Charles W. Chesnutt's *The Marrow of Tradition* (1901) seeks to address the kinds of plot deficiencies that result in *Pudd'nhead Wilson*'s failure, by inventing new racial models and new codes of racial behavior. In his novelistic re-creation of the causes and consequences of the 1898 Wilmington, North Carolina, race riot, Chesnutt uses a moment of national tragedy to demonstrate the linked white worlds of domesticity and politics as the site of black oppression. By this means, on the one hand he rehabilitates black manhood, and on the other he implicates white women as well as white men in the economic rape of black communities. As in *Pudd'nhead Wilson*, the mulatto in *The Marrow of Tradition* becomes a metaphoric expression of the inevitability of racial union, but within that racial framework, class affiliation across racial lines becomes a crucial factor determining success for whites and blacks alike. However, Chesnutt stumbles on the very consequences of his recuperation of the black male, a recuperation that necessitates at times a violent silencing of black and white women in his text. Ironically, the very myth of the black rapist—the myth Chesnutt dedicated his book to disproving—had been traditionally built on this silencing.

As members of a politically and racially diverse triptych, Dixon, Twain, and Chesnutt are engaged in a fierce struggle to define black/white male heroism. As such, they exemplify a traditional discourse on lynching centered on figurations of black or white male criminality. The second half of *Race, Rape, and Lynching* demonstrates how this naturalized discourse could be challenged repeatedly and variously in contemporaneous texts by or about women in the context of the racial tensions of the 1890s. Beginning with the figuration of a narrative self in Ida B. Wells's 1892 pamphlet, *Southern Horrors: Lynch Law in All Its Phases,* as an introduction to the black female presence in public discourse on lynching, Chapter 3, "Black Women and White Terrorism: Ida B. Wells, David Bryant Fulton, Pauline E. Hopkins, and the Politics of Representation," presents a comparative study of two largely ignored black novels that explore the suppressed presence of black women within the economy of racial violence. Written as a tribute to Wells, David Bryant Fulton's *Hanover: or the Persecution of the Lowly* (1900) retells the story of the 1898 Wilmington riot largely through the eyes and experiences of black women. Rather than depicting female characters as silent victims, Fulton distills black communal bravery into the figure of the black woman, uniting his narrative around a tribute that deliberately attempts to cut across lines of complexion, class, and region—elements that sharply divide African Americans in *The Marrow of Tradition.*

Pauline E. Hopkins's *Contending Forces: A Romance Illustrative of Negro Life North and South* (1900) offers a unique commentary on Fulton's idealized attempt to counteract the negation of black femininity within the context of racial violence. In a "hybrid" text that melds traditional genres of women's writing (the sentimental novel, the melodrama, the seduction novel) with elements of gender representation characteristic of the slave narrative, Hopkins crafts a darker, subtler tale of the effects of the white rape of black women on the history of an "enlightened" group of Boston blacks. Within this community, the private space of black domesticity is both a shield and a prison for rape victims, whom Hopkins suggests cannot automatically find a voice within the black masculine world of anti-lynching discourse. While Fulton refers to but does not engage in a discussion of the rape of black women, Hopkins repeatedly seeks to test the limits of representing black female sexuality in the aftermath of rape, weaving a tale of bodily and spiritual redemption, community betrayals, and finally sexual and maternal fulfillment for her heroine.

Chapter 4, "Rethinking White Female Silences: Kate Chopin's Local Color Fiction and the Politics of White Supremacy" continues this reading of the female "script" by locating Kate Chopin's local color fiction of the 1890s within the context of post-Reconstruction traditions of white supremacy. Looking beyond *The Awakening* (1899) or the oft-anthologized "Désirée's Baby" (1893), this chapter begins by examining Chopin's first novel *At Fault* (1890) and the short stories "In Sabine" (1893) and "A No-Account Creole" (1894). Historically, the ethnically and racially diverse New Orleans and Cane River regions of Louisiana about which Chopin wrote were marked by a record level of racial violence during Reconstruction, and both Chopin's husband and her male acquaintances from the region were avid participants in the unrest. Historically and culturally located within in the context of white-on-black violence of the 1890s, Chopin looks back to the equally bloody days of Reconstruction; and in her depiction of post–Civil War white French creole society, white male aggression targets both people of color and white outsiders.

The discussion of Chopin concludes with readings of "A Lady of Bayou St. John" (1893) and "La Belle Zoraïde" (1894), both of which challenge restrictive notions of white female sexuality traditionally enabled by the alternate stereotype of the "immoral" black woman. The primary argument behind the lynching of black men was the need to protect white women from sexual contamination, but in both of these stories Chopin explores the possibility of white female sexual freedom through a deliberate flirtation with the stereotype of black male sexuality, going so far as to designate in "La Belle Zoraïde" the forbidden black male body as the idealized object of white female desire. By entertaining fantasies of white sexual liberation though an engagement with criminalized blackness, Chopin repudiates white supremacist constructions of black sexuality as monstrous and, in effect, voices what is suppressed in Thomas Dixon's fiction.

As a study of literary responses to a particular historical issue (racial violence after Reconstruction), this book aims to challenge the ways in which canonical boundaries have traditionally been defined, as well as the manner in which American discourses on "race" and "gender" have traditionally been mapped.[27]

Although scholars have long demonstrated how African American literature works to reveal American cultural preoccupation with blackness, this book stresses that the conception of whiteness as a racialized category has always been crucial for white as well as black writers, and that these conceptions in turn provide crucial contexts for any consideration of gendered literary traditions. Ultimately, with *Race, Rape, and Lynching* I hope to contribute to the ongoing attempt to shift critical attention from moments of linear traditionalism to moments of more problematic, contradictory convergences among American literatures.

### CHAPTER ONE

# Re-Membering Blackness
# After Reconstruction:
# Race, Rape, and Political Desire
# in the Work of Thomas Dixon, Jr.

It will probably be asked, Why not retain and incorporate the blacks
into the state, and thus save the expence of supplying, by importa-
tion of white settlers, the vacancies they will leave? Deep rooted prejudices entertained by the whites; ten thousand recollections, by the
blacks, of the injuries they have sustained; new provocations; the
real distinctions which nature has made; and many other circum-
stances, will divide us into parties, and produce convulsions which
will probably never end but in the extermination of the one or the
other race.

Thomas Jefferson,
*Notes on the State of Virginia*

Like many another person who had read of lynching in the South, I
had accepted the idea meant to be conveyed---that although
lynching was irregular and contrary to law and order, unreasoning
anger over the terrible crime of rape led to the lynching; that perhaps the brute deserved death anyhow and the mob was justified in
taking his life.

Ida B. Wells,
*Crusade for Justice*

IN THE 1890S MEMOIR *A Boy's Town,* William Dean Howells recalls a
rather singular occurrence of his childhood in Hamilton, Ohio:

One night, out of pure zeal for the common good, . . . [a group of white
boys] wished to mob the negro quarter of the town, because the "Dumb
Negro" (a deaf-mute of color who was a very prominent personage in
their eyes) was said to have hit a white boy. I believe the mob never came
to anything. I only know that my boy ran a long way with the other
fellows, and, when he gave out, had to come home alone through the

dark, and was so afraid of ghosts that he would have been glad of the company of the lowest-down black boy in town.

Looking back some forty years after this incident, Howells could afford to urge compassion rather than condemnation for youthful missteps: after all he had been born into a family of staunch abolitionists; as an influential editor and man of letters, he encouraged the careers of black writers Charles W. Chesnutt and Paul Laurence Dunbar; in 1909 he would participate in the founding of the National Association for the Advancement of Colored People. But while Howells the child sensed intuitively "the impassible gulf" between races established by custom even in the obscure reaches of an antebellum small midwestern town, he would have to wait for the adult writer to imagine other possibilities for racial intercourse.[1]

In his 1891 novel *An Imperative Duty*, Howells fancied he could make more palatable through the mediating figure of the passing mulatto the blackness that marked the "Dumb Negro" of early memory. But the white hero Dr. Olney is drawn to the octoroon-in-hiding Rhoda Algate precisely because of the threat of her submerged Africanity; the more she is camouflaged in white society, the more he longs for her hidden racial markers:

> [Rhoda's] splendor dazzled him from the sable cloud of her attire, and in Mrs. Atherton's blond presence, . . . he felt the tameness of the Northern type. It was the elder world, the beauty of antiquity, which appealed to him in the lustre and sparkle of this girl; and the remote tint of her servile and savage origin gave her a kind of fascination which refuses to let itself be put in words: it was like the grace of a limp, the occult, indefinable lovableness of a deformity, but transcending these by its allurement in infinite degree, and going for the reason of its effect deep into mysterious places of being where the spirit and the animal meet and part in us.[2]

In this very different scene of arousal, blackness becomes an alluring "deformity" instead of the mark of Cain; though "the elder world" of slavery and the interracial sexual economy of the plantation have been distilled to the point of historical and physical erasure in the beautiful octoroon body of Rhoda, the knowledge of her imperceptible "otherness" generates a sexual excitement that at once defies and affirms the laws of American racial custom. Thus, as the accounts of his own childhood bloodlust and of Olney's aching desire for the exotic Rhoda demonstrate, Howells never "lose[s] sight of the fact that boys and men respond with their pulses to the matter of race."[3]

Both the animal nature of Howells's autobiographical persona in *A Boy's Town* and Olney's equally visceral appreciation of American race relations in *An Imperative Duty* reference a simultaneous white loathing of and appetite for blackness, inevitably translated into a fascination with and a fear of racial mixing, which have been represented primarily as white male prerogatives in American culture. The notion of the black body as the uneasy subject of patriarchal discipline and desire was of course embedded in both Northern antebellum abolitionist rhetoric and Southern plantation ideology. In abolitionist literature especially, the visibly scarred and morally violated slave was feminized as the "erotic sign of servitude" under the power of a masculine plantocracy which raped and tortured with impunity.[4]

But after Emancipation, once the polemics of abolition and pro-slavery were no longer needed, how were narratives of white male desire for the black structured?[5] As with American writers before and after the Civil War, Howells's *Imperative Duty* drew on the stock figure of the tragic mulatto, especially in its female expression, as a figure who, according to Hortense J. Spillers, allowed "the dominant culture to say without parting its lips that 'we have willed to sin,' the puritan recoil at the sight and site of the genitals."[6] Yet the mulatto's mediation of this "recoil" was only partial: by its side the stereotype of the black rapist, the black-as-beast, functioned for decades after Reconstruction and into the twentieth century as yet another referent for the impact of race on evolving representations of gender, desire, and citizenship.[7]

By the time Howells published *A Boy's Town* and *An Imperative Duty*, American whites had already foisted onto blacks the age's most famous negative abstract: the "Negro Problem" referred to the dilemma of imagining a race apparently socially and biologically unfit for Americanization after slavery; indeed, this conceptualization of blacks as a problem, rather than as social individuals, was guaranteed to distance whites from their national duty to fulfill the social and political promises of the Fourteenth and Fifteenth Amendments. And of equal importance, in light of the traditional merger of the political, the social, and the sexual within American culture, the concept of the "Negro Problem" manifested itself as a white concern that blacks in search of citizenship must also desire to invade all other aspects of white life, including the white home. As one man in Reconstruction Georgia put it, speaking of his fellow whites, "if you talk about equality they at once conclude that you must take the negro into your parlor or into your bed—everywhere that you would take your wife."[8] Thus, the interracial male struggle over the terrain of the public would always be figured finally within the terms of the domestic—the privatized expression of the nation's political anxieties.

White Americans' conflation of the public and the private as the twin targets of black designs meant that the figure of the black as beast threatened to become a totalizing symbol of a race war many felt was already in progress.[9] In his 1889 study *The Plantation Negro as Freeman*, historian Philip A. Bruce alleged a dangerous moral (and by later implications, physical) regression among postemancipation African Americans, evidenced in what he saw as a sharp increase in the number of white women raped by black men. According to

Bruce, "rape . . . . is marked, in the instance of its perpetration by the negro, by a diabolical persistence and a malignant atrocity of detail that have no reflection in the whole extent of the natural history of the most bestial and ferocious animals." For Bruce, black rape was not simply an act of masculine aggression; it was the freedman's brutal attempt to annihilate a superior civilization:

> He is not content merely with the consummation of his purpose, but takes that fiendish delight in the degradation of his victim which he always shows when he can reek revenge upon one whom he has hitherto been compelled to fear; and here, the white woman in his power is, for the time being, the representative of that race which has always over-awed him.[10]

By arguing that the assault of white women was a new feature of black activity after slavery, Bruce and others could argue that black emancipation was tantamount to an initial breach of white national defenses. Not surprisingly, the institutionalization of such images served both to justify the disenfranchisement of blacks and to inaugurate a particularly barbarous period of widespread lynching and race rioting.

One way of coming to terms with the cultural power behind the stereotype of the black as beast is to analyze its deployment as a metaphor in the construction of racial identities in literature of the late nineteenth and early twentieth centuries. My concern here is primarily with how the stereotype mediated representations of white masculinity in the triple arenas of the domestic, the political, and the national. Because so many cultural producers (those for and against white supremacy) were compelled to reinvent the South after Reconstruction by re-visioning race relations for a new era, they engaged fully with the figure of the black rapist in order to delineate the post–Civil War identities of blacks and whites. Late-nineteenth-century American writers did not create the stereotype of the rapist, but their work became a forum for the playing out of what was virtually a national obsession with the black male body.

The stereotype of the black rapist—or at least the stereotype of a potent black masculinity—was evoked with all its multiple significations whenever American writers tried to imagine a black entrance into something like equality. Thus the dominating figure in George Washington Cable's pro-black historical novel *The Grandissimes: A Story of Creole Life* (1880) is the immensely virile, but enslaved African prince Bras-Coupé. Importantly the story begins some years after Bras-Coupé's death, so the slave is safely contained within the novel's temporal framework, surfacing as a memory that haunts primarily Cable's male characters; in fact, we actually only hear his story when it is performed by the novel's men as a merged narrative, a group recitation of interracial masculine envy, admiration, and terror.

When the newly enslaved African's refusal to work precipitates a confrontation between himself and the white master Don José, the result is a meeting of equals: "The dauntless captive and fearless master stood looking into each other's eyes until each recognized in the other his peer in physical courage, and each was struck with an admiration for the other which no after difference was sufficient entirely to destroy" (G, 172–73).[11] Bras-Coupé, the personification of a fallen African race, is named for a black patriarchal diminishment enacted under Western slavery: "his tribe, in losing him, had lost its strong right arm close off at the shoulder" (G, 171). But a more overtly sexualized vision of black manhood is destined to appear, ironically at the merged moments of naked dispossession and abjection, precisely when Bras-Coupé encounters white womanhood:

> his attire . . . [was] a single gaudy garment tightly enveloping the waist and thighs. As his eyes fell upon the beautiful white lady, he prostrated himself upon the ground, his arms outstretched before him. He would not move till she was gone. Then he arose like a hermit who has seen a vision. "*Bras-Coupé 'n pas oulé oir zombis* (Bras-Coupé dares not look upon a spirit)." From that hour he worshipped. He saw her often; every time, after one glance at her countenance, he would prostrate his gigantic length with his face in the dirt.   (G, 176–77)

Echoing Harriet Beecher Stowe's sanitized coupling of black male/white female in Tom and Eva of *Uncle Tom's Cabin* (1852), Cable tantalizes us with images of Bras-Coupé's dangerously "gigantic length" waiting passively for the command of white female desire, a desire Cable feels compelled to imagine at the moment of its denied possibility. But Bras-Coupé has no desire for white womanhood; rather, his danger lies in an aggressive assertion of his equality and free will. Though his ultimate refusal to submit to white male rule results in the savage mutilation of his body, the final legacy of Bras-Coupé's enslavement is the white anxiety and guilt produced by that punishment and the anger his death inspires in the blacks who survive him.

While allegedly pro-black novels such as Cable's *The Grandissimes* only subtextually registered anxiety over disciplining black male sexuality, the merged discourse of race, rights, and domestic survival made manifest in the figure of endangered white womanhood was exemplified in such popular novels as Thomas Nelson Page's *Red Rock: A Chronicle of Reconstruction* (1898). *Red Rock*'s elaborate narrative features dispossessed white men who struggle to regain control of their homes, a struggle symbolized by the novel's very title: the "red rock" is in fact a blood-stained crag on which the white hero's colonial ancestor established his claim on American soil, by killing the American Indian who had murdered (after presumably raping) his wife. Thus the imagined assault on white women expands to become a figuration of the struggles of white nation-building in the face of an uncivilized Other's racial threat; as a result, violent white male retaliation can be writ manageably as the protective concern for domestic spaces. This theme of white communal/white domestic recovery through violence is replayed throughout the novel, as when, wounded, disarmed, swindled by Reconstruction governments, the novel's Southern white heroes return as an organized Ku Klux Klan just in time to prevent the inevitable effects of Emancipation:

> It was well for Mrs. Deals that the young men arrived when they did, for the [black] troopers were tired of merely destroying property, and just as the white men rode up they had seized her. Her scream hastened the rescuing party. No one knew for a long time who composed the party; for in five minutes every one of the raiders were stretched on the ground.[12]

Incorporated into the very myths of the white hero's conquest of the Other, the black rapist would become a staple metaphor for social disorder and injustice, even for many white writers dedicated to changing the status quo. Whereas the conservative Page employed the rapist to recuperate the fallen South, the muckraker novelist Upton Sinclair later employed the same figure to epitomize the corruption of company bosses. In a particularly arresting moment in Sinclair's socialist novel *The Jungle* (1906), racist discourse around the figure of corrupting black male presence is made to validate class protest when striking white workers at the Chicago stock yards find themselves replaced by a frightening Southern import:

> [A]nd any night, in the big open space in front of Brown's, one might see brawny Negroes stripped to the waist and pounding each other for money, while a howling throng of three or four thousand surged about, men and women, young white girls from the country rubbing elbows with big buck Negroes with daggers in their boots, while rows of wooly heads peered down from every window of the surrounding factories. The ancestors of these black people had been savages in Africa; and since then they had been chattel slaves, or had been held down by a community ruled by the traditions of slavery. Now for the first time they were free—free to gratify every passion, free to wreck themselves. . . . They lodged men and women on the same floor; and with the night there began a saturnalia of debauchery—scenes such as never before had been witnessed in America.

*The Jungle*'s outraged narrator concludes this description by reminding readers that all this occurred "where food was being handled which was sent out to every corner of the civilized world."[13] In this (for modern readers, almost comical) collapsing of the contamination of food with the contamination of innocent white womanhood, Sinclair echoes Page's totalizing evocation of black Emancipation as a complete threat to all aspects of white life. In this passage the identity of post–Civil War blacks as themselves *wage* workers, gives way to the image of Emancipation as simply the release of barbaric Africans in a permanent state of arrested development. As racially and morally foreign after the Civil War as they were at the moment they were brought to American shores, Sinclair's black strikebreakers are presented as doubly unfit to participate in any social reconfiguration of the United States, however radical that reconfiguration might be in terms of class politics.[14]

The anxieties expressed in Sinclair's novel demonstrate that even white Americans who did not consider themselves to be radical white supremacists had become used to translating black post–Civil War freedom into a synonym for widespread criminality, debauchery, and contagion that could prove just as threatening as the evils of capitalism. Thus, to talk "rationally" of black and white social and political integration in the face of what blacks had come to represent was indeed to talk about effecting an annihilation of the basic tenets of civilizations the white race presumably signified.

In his 1908 collection of essays, *Following the Color Line*, white journalist Ray Stannard Baker seemed to proclaim this dangerous incompatibility when, in attempting to describe the African American "as a plain human being," he nevertheless suggests at one point that

> [m]any of the crimes committed by Negroes are marked with almost animal-like ferocity. Once roused to a murderous rage, the Negro does not stop with mere killing; he bruises and batters his victim out of all semblance to humanity. For the moment, under the stress of passion, he seems to revert wholly to savagery.[15]

Baker's collection of essays was meant to address "objectively" the problem of race division; yet not surprisingly, the journalist merely seemed to reproduce the very anxieties about blacks' alleged alien nature that he set out to interrogate.

It is crucial to recognize that such validations of the stereotype of the black as beast reveal more than merely the success of turn-of-the-century white supremacy's influence on public thought. White supremacist fabrication of the black beast served to resolve tensions over the racialization of power, but simultaneously it animated just as many debates over the state and progress of white civilization itself. Challenging the notion of white superiority in her militant anti-lynching pamphlets *Southern Horrors: Lynch Law in All Its Phases* (1892), *A Red Record: Tabulated Statistics and Alleged Causes of Lynchings in the United States, 1892–1893–1894* (1895), and *Mob Rule in New Orleans: Robert Charles and His Fight to the Death* (1900), Ida B. Wells could defend herself against charges that she was exaggerating the complete collapse of white self-control during lynching, because she drew so many accounts of violence from the white press itself.[16] For instance, using "a white man's description . . . published in the white journals of this country," Wells relates a particularly horrifying execution in Paris, Texas, of Henry Smith in 1893, who was accused of raping a white child:

> The negro was placed upon a carnival float in mockery of a king upon his throne, and, followed by an immense crowd, was escorted through the city so that all might see the most inhuman monster known in current history. . . . [Then] Smith was placed upon a scaffold, six feet square and ten feet high, securely bound, within the view of all beholders. Here the victim was tortured for fifty minutes by red-hot iron brands thrust against his quivering body. Commencing at the feet the brands were placed against him inch by inch until they were thrust against the face. Then, being apparently dead, kerosene was poured upon him, cottonseed hulls placed beneath him and set on fire. . . .
>
> Curiosity seekers have carried away already all that was left of the memorable event, even to pieces of charcoal.[17]

Even for Americans who supported lynching, such accounts were deeply shocking precisely because they presented to an international community white men barely distinguishable from their supposed foes, white men who were "coarse, . . . beastly, and drunk, mad with the terrible blood lust that wild beasts know, . . . hunting a human prey." [18]

Matters were further compounded by the ways in which, as white supremacist violence seemed to present whites of all classes as united around a common cause, the maintenance of class distinctions became threatened by the very rituals of violence. Thus in "Nigger Jeff" (1901), a story that never questions the occurrence of black rape, Theodore Dreiser exemplifies a popular white disgust with the act of lynching itself partly because, in its enactment of vengeful aggression, it presaged a breakdown of white moral and class order. Thus the middle-class journalist who witnesses a lynching in a small country town is subsequently challenged with the fact of his own presence in the mob that defied the efforts of the local sheriff and brutally murdered the accused rapist. The ritual of lynching, then, seemed to create even firmer ties between "civilized" whites and their class, as well as racial, inferiors.[19]

The threat of the black rapist also figured into white American responses to changing gender roles. The fear of uncontrollable white womanhood was already a point of contention for intellectuals and politicians of the period. In his 1890 article "Two Perils of the Indo-European," the distinguished scientist E. D. Cope identified "the masculinization of women" as a major threat to America's survival:

Should the nation have an attack of this kind, like a disease, it would leave its traces in many after-generations. During its time "a man's foes would be those of his own household." How many such households have been already created by the woman's-suffrage movement, and its attendant discussions cannot be well determined. . . . Woman's stronghold is the sex character of her mind. With that she is the mistress of the world; but if she once abdicates it, she becomes the slave of the man, who will then regard her for her body only.

In a pattern reminiscent of black men who attempted to remake themselves from slaves to freedmen and were suddenly afflicted with the "disease" of sexual passion, turn-of-the-century white women who asserted identities beyond the domestic space were figured both as race traitors and as diseased bodies, perhaps equally capable of spreading infection in their midst; as such, they threatened to transform the site of white domesticity into the very definition of instability.[20]

This figuration of the independent-minded white woman as traitor was echoed by Theodore Roosevelt in a 1908 speech: "the woman who, whether from cowardice or selfishness, from having a false and vacuous ideal shirks her duty as wife and mother, earns the right of our contempt, just as does the man who, from any motive, fears to do his duty in battle when the country calls him."[21] Thus the advent of the New Woman and its attendant discourse on birth control and female independence proved the need for greater surveillance of white women, especially in the context of sexual desire. As Ida B. Wells reported in *Southern Horrors,* many so-called "rapes" were really interracial love affairs that had been detected by whites in the community, or when "poor blind Afro-American Sampsons . . . suffer themselves to be betrayed by white Delilahs."[22] Consequently, a white belief in black male desire for these women was in part also a response to the idea of white female lust, especially with regard to miscegenation; the figure of the black rapist therefore supported "the comforting fiction that at least in relation to black men, white women were always objects and never agents of sexual desire."[23]

The anxiety generated by the stereotype of the black rapist also distracted attention from white men's dual horror and excitement over their own acts of race betrayal, embodied through the tradition of miscegenation. In *An Imperative Duty* Howells sought to mitigate the impropriety of Olney's eventual marriage to Rhoda by having the couple emigrate to Italy, but extramarital interracial coupling was still standard practice among many young white men in the post-Reconstruction era. Louisiana writer Lafcadio Hearn was both terrified and excited by his interracial love affair with a New Orleans quadroon: "I have suffered the tortures of a thousand damned souls. I went too near the flame and got cruelly burned. . . . I got caught in a terrible net. . . . I became

passionately in love before I knew it." [24] But while Hearn identified himself as
the victim rather than the willing participant in an interracial love affair, such
readings of white male passivity denied the fact that black women were regularly raped by white men as part of a larger attempt to assert social control
over African American communities. Under slavery, the master's management
of the slave body had always included the use of rape. After the Civil War, the
early Ku Klux Klan borrowed this practice to serve new political conditions:
when dealing with black and white foes alike, "Klansmen routinely raped and
sexually tortured women, especially black women, during 'kluxing' raids on
their households." [25] Conveniently, the stereotype of the black rapist, coupled
with the general assumption of black women's "natural" capacity for sexual
promiscuity, helped to distance white men from their own sexual transgressions. Still, white supremacists continued to be uneasy about a tradition of
interracial sex that remained virtually unabated, despite the arguments in favor
of racial separation.

These anxieties over racial contamination, black citizenship, a threatened
revision in traditional class and gender roles, and white barbarism surface repeatedly in any number of late-nineteenth-century texts; but the literary figure
most closely associated with the stereotype of the black rapist is probably
Thomas Dixon, Jr., a prolific novelist alternately celebrated and vilified by his
contemporaries as the ultimate literary spokesperson for white supremacy. Dixon's figurations of black men as lustful Negro beasts propelled his novels to
instant notoriety. In estimating the power of Dixon's white supremacist fiction,
historian Joel Williamson suggests that "his work said in a total way what his
audience had been thinking in fragments. His grand themes educed precisely
what a vast number of people were instinctively and passionately certain was
true." [26] But Dixon's work did more than simply codify racist images of African
Americans; his primary concern increasingly became the very problem of successful white self-management in an interracial context. In its articulation of
the horror of lynching and of white class and gender conflicts, Dixon's fiction
is less a register of popular white supremacy's triumph over African Americans,
than an expression of a profound anxiety over the maintenance of a stable
white identity. Thus, more than any other writer, Dixon becomes a register for
both the complexity and internal contradictions of radical white supremacist
thought.

Dixon's role in the shaping of post-Reconstruction American racist discourse
has often been overshadowed by that of D. W. Griffith and Griffith's landmark
film *The Birth of a Nation* (1915). Dixon in fact predates Griffith on the very subject of transferring the black rapist from the page to the stage: after the success in
1905 of his third novel *The Clansman: An Historical Romance of the Ku Klux Klan*,
he formed two production companies to tour the country simultaneously performing a play version of the novel, complete with fiery crosses and hooded Ku

Klux Klansmen bounding across the stage on horseback, to the delight of national audiences.[27] In part, the very image of heroic Klansmen in Dixon's fiction inspired Griffith to conceive of a historical film about white American racial "liberation"; and he recruited the novelist to write the movie's screenplay. Dixon obliged by merging his two most successful race novels, *The Leopard's Spots* (1902) and *The Clansman* to create the movie's plot, and reportedly he also provided *The Birth of a Nation* with its title.[28] By depicting race war and by celebrating the early Ku Klux Klan as a heroic organization, *The Birth of a Nation* reintroduced the image of the black rapist to national and international audiences. During its eleven-month run, the movie was seen by 5 million Americans, and its opening in Atlanta marked the reorganization of the Ku Klux Klan in the twentieth century.[29] The film was the first ever to be screened at the White House; after reviewing it, President Woodrow Wilson declared: "It is like writing history with lightning. And my only regret is that it is all so terribly true."[30]

As a transitional figure in terms of his links to popular fiction, theater, and film, Dixon has much in common with another early icon of American popular culture, Harriet Beecher Stowe, a cultural producer with seemingly a very different characterization of American race relations. Dixon's race novels functioned in much the same way as Stowe's *Uncle Tom's Cabin* in the history of America's racial culture: the work of both writers galvanized whites around severely limiting but ultimately enduring myths concerning the nature of race. And since Dixon's *The Leopard's Spots* was written especially as an aggressive anti-black response to Stowe's novel, it is ironic, and yet not so, that exactly fifty years after the introduction of the saintly, effeminate Uncle Tom waiting for a white God's salvation, Dixon would counter with an equally powerful vision of the black man as monster. Just as in Stowe's *Uncle Tom's Cabin,* the black male in Dixon's work becomes a crucial figure of multiple gender, racial, and class signification that binds as much as it distances black and white.

THOMAS DIXON AND THE CHALLENGE
OF WHITE MASCULINE RESCUE

Thomas Dixon, Jr. was born in 1864 near Shelby, North Carolina, to a family of humble farmers. At twenty he was one of the youngest men to be elected to his state's legislature. Two years later Dixon left the South for Boston and then New York to pursue a highly successful career in the Baptist ministry; by 1889 his reputation as an electrifying speaker gained him the largest Protestant congregation in the nation. Forever restless, the Reverend Dixon then doubled his visibility with an exhausting but highly profitable six-year stint on the national lecture circuit. Maxwell Bloomfield reads Dixon in these early years as a social activist "aligned . . . with the liberal reformers of the Social Gospel Movement in demanding justice for the immigrant, the slum-dweller, the 'weak and helpless.' " According to Bloomfield, Dixon's vision of progress was "traced to the development of character in man." Says Bloomfield: "Every man had the power to choose between good and evil, because every man was endowed with free will. Thus, in Dixon's hands, the theory of evolution took on a broadly democratic form, implying the preservation and uplift of the masses."[31] But while Dixon's philosophy challenged the notion of class as a determination of biology, his liberalism would ultimately not be extended to include African Americans. When Dixon finally left the ministry in 1899, his vision of America's democratic destiny included a message of absolute incompatibility between races and thus of the final inevitability of a racial war for territory and resources.

In 1902 he published the best-selling *The Leopard's Spots,* which sold 100,000 copies in its first few months of publication. Eventually 1 million copies were sold, with foreign translations appearing within the first year.[32] Conceived as a direct response to Stowe's ever-popular *Uncle Tom's Cabin, The Leopard's Spots* appealed to Americans who had always regarded Reconstruction as a process of economic and political victimization aimed at white Southerners. And for radical white supremacists who argued that the white South had to defend itself in the post-Reconstruction era against a savage black population on the rampage, Dixon's novel dramatized in lurid detail the acts of violence allegedly committed by freedmen. Claiming that "the North as a class is totally ignorant . . . [of] the negro in his relation to the white population of the South," *Saturday Evening Post* reviewer Lilian Lida Bell praised the novel as a truthful, historically accurate account of atrocities committed during Reconstruction: "I, for one, from absolute knowledge of my facts, do not hesitate to say that the book is moderate in tone considering what might have been written."[33] In 1905 Dixon repeated the successful race formula he used in *The Leopard's Spots,* presenting to the public what he claimed to be a carefully researched historical novel entitled *The Clansman.* His third novel, but the second in what was to become a trilogy of novels on the Ku Klux Klan, *The Clansman* easily surpassed *The Leopard's Spots* in sales.

Ironically, the years of Dixon's greatest success as a writer also saw the rise of the New York–based NAACP; meanwhile, the National League on Urban Conditions Among Negroes, and black schools, notably Booker T. Washington's Tuskegee Institute, were securing benefits from wealthy Northern white philanthropists.[34] In the face of these African American efforts toward self-improvement, Dixon continually waged war on the belief in the possibility of Negro progress. In a 1905 *Saturday Evening Post* article on "Booker T. Washington and the Negro," he echoed Frederick Jackson Turner's description of the white American national character:

> Our Republic is great not by reason of the amount of dirt we possess, or the size of our census roll, but because of the genius of the race of pioneer

white freemen who settled this continent, dared the might of kings, and blazed the way through our wilderness for the trembling feet of liberty.

American blacks on the other hand, no matter how well they trained, were not originators of ideas; they were not and could not be the spearhead of progress:

> Education is the development of that which *is*. The Negro has held the Continent of Africa since the dawn of history, crunching acres of diamonds beneath his feet. Yet he never picked one up from the dust until a white man showed to him its light.[35]

The duty of white America, then, was to guard against social and political unity with this inferior human species that could not be assimilated or "Americanized."

In its location of an anti-black message in the context of what many felt should be an exclusively white American destiny, Dixon's work, especially *The Leopard's Spots,* capitalized on the hostility expressed by many white Americans toward nonwhites who, after the annexation of Hawaii and the imperialistic gains of Cuba and the Philippines in Spanish-American War, had recently become part of the American "democratic" empire. By 1899 Theodore Roosevelt was referring to the Filipino patriot Emilio Aquinaldo as "the typical representative of savagery, the typical foe of civilization of the American people."[36] Against the backdrop of this perceived international struggle with the "darker races," Dixon's *The Leopard's Spots* and *The Clansman* packaged the South as the producer of a successful formula for race control (Southern race extremists argued that lynching was the only way to keep blacks in line), reintroducing Americans not only to a living example of what to expect from "lesser races" but also to neglected methodologies for their subjugation. As Michael Rogin has commented, Dixon's subtitle for *The Leopard's Spots, A Romance of the White Man's Burden,* "tied the racial question at home to America's world mission abroad." Thus, as "the [S]outhern race problem became national, the national problem was displaced back onto the South in a way that made the South not a defeated part of the American past but a prophecy of its future."[37]

Not surprisingly, then, in September 1905 during the intermission of his play *The Clansman* in Norfolk, Virginia, Dixon walked out on stage and declared that the play's objective was to situate the South's experience within the context of national destiny. After all, the South had previously been the national site of racial conflict and white suffering; logically then, it would be the site of national white healing and (especially) white unification, regardless of class or section: "I believe that Almighty God anointed the white men of the [S]outh by their suffering during that time immediately after the Civil [W]ar to demonstrate to the world that the white man must and shall be supreme."[38]

But this almost hysterical confidence in the white American's ability to sur-

vive against all odds underscored Dixon's complex definition of what he perceived to be the racial dangers facing his nation: "If allowed to remain here the
Negro race in the United States will number 60,000,000 at the end of this
century by their present rate of increase. Think of what this means for a moment and you face the gravest problem." The meaning of these figures translated into the certainty of the black freedman exercising his rights as citizen
and capitalist:

> And then the real tragedy will begin. Does any sane man believe that
> when the Negro ceases to work under the direction of the Southern white
> man, this . . . race will allow the Negro to master his industrial system,
> take the bread from his mouth, crowd him to the wall and place a mort-
> gage on his house? Competition is war—the most fierce and brutal of all
> its forms. Could fatuity reach a sublimer height than the idea that the
> white man will stand idly by and see this performance? What will he do
> when put to the test? He will do exactly what his white neighbor in the
> North does when the Negro threatens his bread—kill him![39]

A battle-cry for race war, Dixon's warning of a general black economic invasion is expressed in terms of domesticity and reproduction. Moving back and
forth between white control of capital production and uncontrollable black
reproduction, Dixon's rhetoric acknowledges the new signification of the black
body after slavery. Before the Civil War, "black women gave birth to property
and, directly to capital itself in the form of slaves"; after Emancipation, however, blackness metamorphosed into a sign of white poverty and political disenfranchisement.[40] Importantly, this threat of white alienation from traditional
bases of political and economic (but not sexual) power is acknowledged only
to be displaced later and then mystified in Dixon's race novels, through the
metaphor of black male/white female sex. Thus, Dixon's white heroes can evade
their anxiety over the seemingly unresolvable presence of 60 million blacks in
American economic and communal life by focusing instead on the (apparently)
more containable problem of miscegenation. In *The Leopard's Spots* one of Dixon's characters obsessively poses the question about the social/sexual violation
of the white nation/family with the slogan "*the future American must be either
an Anglo-Saxon or Mulatto*" (*LS*, 336).[41] Thus the threat of blacks' voting, working, buying property, and thereby inevitably achieving full American citizenship
must be reimagined as, and thus contained by, the threat of black rape.

In Dixon's novels, the resulting struggle to achieve the rescue of the endangered white nation, now refigured as the white home, in turn masks the white
supremacist preoccupation with control of the white female body. In his anti-
socialist novel *The One Woman* (1904), Dixon attacked the notion of the independent female intellectual, styling her as part of a socialist plot that if left

unchecked, would eventually ruin the very institutions of marriage and the patriarchal family. Dixon's own particular preoccupation with the dangers of white femininity is evident in a 1905 interview with the *Atlanta Constitution* that he gave while touring with the stage adaptation of *The Clansman*. (The interview appears side-by-side in the *Constitution* with an article on the local search for a black railroad worker turned rapist.) In relating a scene he witnessed in New York, Dixon evokes the familiar fragmented image of the white woman as either sexual aggressor or passive sexual object:

> I have lived in New York sixteen years. It is only within the past twelve months that I have se[e]n big buck negroes parading up and down Broadway with white girls hanging on their arms. The day before I left for Atlanta I saw a coal black negro of about thirty years of age walking on Broadway with a white girl of sixteen, clinging to him—a girl of radiant beauty, a perfect blond with golden hair and soft childlike blue eyes. Twenty years from today such a thing will not be permitted in New York if our race is preserved from the degradation of mulatto mongrelism.[42]

Dixon's vague reference to "such a thing as this" suggests both black men's impudence in seeking out white women, but also white women's disorderliness in choosing black paramours. While the notion of aggressive women (especially sexually aggressive women who prefer black men) is undercut by the vision of the fragile, clinging young blond "with childlike blue eyes" whom Dixon casts ambivalently as a victim unable to protect herself from the older black man, both stereotypes of white women—the whore and the frail child—represent them as being ultimately treacherous in either their state of sexual assertiveness or their state of sexual helplessness.

On the question of white male/black female miscegenation in *The Leopard's Spots*, Dixon suggested that "[t]his mixture . . . has no social significance [at all]" and is merely "the surviving polygamous and lawless instincts of the white male" (*LS*, 336). However, as one of the only moments in *The Leopard's Spots* when Dixon considers black women, this statement seems strangely at odds with the widely held belief that the black woman was essentially a sexual being who enticed the white male away from his better self. Dixon's rationalizations regarding white men's waning "lawless instinct" not only emphasize white male control over sexual relations with black women, but seem to confirm white attraction to degenerate sexuality—a suggestion that had dangerous potential for what it might reveal about the falsity of the racial distinctions on which Dixon's philosophy depended. Given that an acknowledgment of the presence of black women would automatically alter the racial construction of white masculinity, it is not surprising that black women are, in large measure, absent from Dixon's fiction. If they were referenced in too much detail, the reader would have to confront white male desire for the black within the plot of rescuing the domestic, and as such reveal the white man to be the foe of his own household.

Dixon did in fact feel compelled to confront the problem of white male/ black female miscegenation, briefly in *The Clansman* but more centrally in his 1912 novel *The Sins of the Father*. But in *The Leopard's Spots* and *The Clansman*, the engagement with black sexuality resurfaces ironically as what Dixon would certainly have styled "monstrous" homoerotic desire for black men.[43] Leslie A. Fiedler long ago contrasted narratives where "the concept of the white man's sexual envy of the Negro male . . . [is produced by] the ambivalent horror of miscegenation," with narratives articulating white male refuge from the domestic in the form of "the ennobling love of a white man and a colored one."[44] Dixon voices this desire as an ennobling race hatred, since his heroes achieve deification through their violent punishment of the alleged black rapist.[45]

The continual attempt to escape from and return to the black male body is played out whenever Dixon's narratives dramatize the detection, capture, and dismemberment of a black rapist, and even in his general descriptions of offending black male bodies. In *The Leopard's Spots* Dixon is fascinated with the effluvia of black males (the dangerous blood/semen of the deceptively white mulatto, one drop of which "will suddenly breed . . . a pure Negro child, thick-lipped, kinky-headed, flat-nosed, black-skinned") and with "the unmistakable odour of perspiring Negroes" (LS, 398, 139). His account of a bloody lynching in *The Leopard's Spots* styles the white hero's success as a mutilation of the black male body when the offender's "thick lips" are "split with a sharp knife" (*LS*, 151). In one scene in *The Clansman*, white men are mesmerized by the abnormally large footprints left at the scene of a rape. The elongated print lacks evidence of an arch; this monstrous sign of primitive physical development fixes the rapist as a black man. But one monstrous limb denotes another, so that Dixon can suggest the mark of black lust—the (apparently) abnormally large black genitalia—as the unmistakable symbol of the primitive black body at the scene of the crime.

When his white heroes face an invasion of the domestic space made vulnerable by unreliable white femininity, Dixon's men are doubly constructed as the true victims of black male penetration, emasculated by the more "potent" rapist. As a result, the masculine space of ritualized white violence (lynching) in which the black body becomes the object of "desire" must logically become the site on which to construct a powerful ideal of white manhood. The method of white regeneration worked through in Dixon's novels finds resonance in *The Birth of a Nation* when Griffith "displaces sexuality from white men to women to blacks in order, by subjugation and dismemberment of blacks, to reempower white men."[46] The conquest of the so-called renegade black beast through lynching also affirms white male communal power, since it is often a group action.

In the following discussion of selected scenes in *The Leopard's Spots* and *The Clansmen,* I hope to demonstrate how Dixon's use of the black rapist, together with the necessity of lynching that the stereotype's existence inspires, works in precarious and contradictory ways to contain the threat of white female vulnerability, to structure white male desire for the black, and to construct the myth of white male unity. Dixon's acknowledgment of and terror over aberrant white-authored miscegenation will be the subject of my closing discussion of his 1912 novel, *The Sins of the Father* in which the entire white supremacist schema founded on the myth of the black rapist threatens to disintegrate when the latter is feminized as the quadroon seductress.

### Class, Race, and Sexuality in *The Leopard's Spots* and *The Clansman*

Dixon's popular race novels achieve their success because they explore a fantasy of white male rescue enacted through the subordination of black men and white women. *The Leopard's Spots* follows the fate of Charles Gaston of North Carolina. A fatherless boy of eleven at the end of the Civil War, Gaston reaches manhood during the "Negro Domination" of Reconstruction; but together with the Ku Klux Klan and enterprising white citizens, he reclaims power for a white South and a white America. *The Clansman* traces the "education" of Ben and Elsie Stoneman, the children of a powerful pro-black Northern politician. When they move South after the war, their association with Margaret and Phil Cameron helps them recognize the folly of the North's support of Negro rule, and they develop a growing appreciation of the early Ku Klux Klan as the last line of defense for white civilization.

As historical romances of Reconstruction, *The Leopard's Spots* and *The Clansman* emphasize black gains during this period as short-lived, and they insist on the rise of a renegade black male sexuality representing the distillation of early attempts in the 1870s by African Americans to achieve citizenship into a single desire to rape. As Ben Cameron prophesies, when black men get the vote and economic opportunity, the next step "will be a black hand on a white woman's throat" (*C,* 262).[47] Thus, both novels present Southern whites in the popular heroic mode of disenfranchised freedom fighters struggling for economic freedom and the safety of wives and families.[48] Indeed *The Leopard's Spots'* chapter headings ("How Civilization was Saved," "The New America," "Another Declaration of Independence") point to a white supremacist project of national salvation. Dixon undoubtedly drew on the memory of economic suffering endured by his own family after the war; but in the 1900s—a time when the most acute victims of poverty and disenfranchisement were African American—Dixon shifted public attention away from the contemporary reality of black persecution and economic oppression.

In *The Leopard's Spots,* Dixon explicitly figures blacks past and present as the national plague that would spread through time and space if left unchecked:

> this towering figure of the freed Negro had been growing more and more ominous, until its menace overshadowed the poverty, the hunger, the sorrow and the devastation of the South, throwing the blight of its shadow over future generations, a veritable Black Death for the land and its people. (*LS,* 33)

Dixon further buttresses this image of the postwar black as disease(d) by drawing on the plantation fiction darky stereotype to suggest a deceptive duality in the character of the black population. Literally the last of their kind, the "good" blacks are those faithful to pre-emancipation race relations. For example, old Nelse, the Gastons' servant is a "giant negro" whose potential for terror is erased by his complete devotion to slavery's status quo. Nelse forgoes his freedom and its potential empowerment; instead, he returns from the battlefield with his late master's sword, to pass on the symbol of phallic strength to young Charles Gaston, Jr. (*LS,* 6–11). As a surrogate "mammy" to the young Gaston, Nelse's feminized submission helps perpetuate a Southern patriarchal power structure that the Civil War was fought in part to destroy.

But blacks like Nelse are scarce, and they are destined to be replaced by young black boys such as Gaston's childhood friend Dick. Born into violence, Dick narrowly escapes being decapitated by his father, and bears a scar on his neck that will mark him as a lynch victim later in the novel. Ironically, Dixon introduces Dick (who is supposedly based on his own real-life boyhood playmate) as a male version of Stowe's Topsy, although Dixon's character grows up to be a rapist, not a black missionary to Africa.[49] Gaston's friendship with Dick is figured almost as a seduction that dulls the white boy's better senses. More knowing adults recognize Dick's inherent imperfectibility ("the very rudimentary foundations of morals seem lacking. I believe you could take a young ape and teach him quicker"), but Gaston is enamored with the black child whose "rolling, mischievous eyes, his cunning fingers and his wayward imagination [are] . . . unfailing fountains of life" (*LS,* 179). When Dick's violent antics anger even black adults, he runs off, leaving a heartbroken Gaston.

Though styled as a desexualized boyhood friendship, this homosexual/homosocial union of black and white is desired but conveniently rendered impossible precisely because of the black male's inevitable "development" toward criminality—a development that, when cast in terms of a failed interracial male relationship, suggests the inevitability of black betrayal of white trust. As the novel progresses, Dick returns to the boyhood haunt he shared with Gaston (and where Dixon tells us Gaston returns as a child to pine and cry for his lost friend). But instead of finding Gaston, he finds—and rapes—a little white girl. The homosexual contact gestured to in the boyhood friendship is fulfilled at last, though in the containable context of the white female body. And as a rape, this sexual contact is given appropriate meaning as a sign of betrayal produced by aberrant black sexual desire for the white (wo)man.

Though useful on the one hand as a means of distancing white men's own imagined rape, on the other, white women's bodies provoke their own misogynous discourse in Dixon's narratives. As with the violence of lynching in the case of black men, rape in Dixon's texts functions as a punishment for white womanhood that by its nature seems to put the patriarchal family at risk. When the corrupt authorities dominated by "Negro rule" swindle the widow Gaston and young Charles out of their home, Mrs. Gaston immediately succumbs to her misfortunes. The very act of black appraisers entering the house is figured as a fatal violation of the submissive white maternal body:

> When she saw a great herd of Negroes trampling down her flowers . . . and swarming over the porches, she sank feebly into her chair, buried her face in her hands and gave way to a passionate flood of tears. She was roused by the thumping of heavy feet in the hall and the unmistakable odour of perspiring Negroes. They had begun to ransack the house on tours of inspection. The poor woman's head drooped and she fell to the floor in a dead swoon. . . . Her heart fluttered on for awhile, but she never spoke again.   (*LS*, 139–141)

No errant woman, Mrs. Gaston is condemned anyway: mental and physical fragility mark her as unfit to be the mother of her race. Indeed, the trademark vulnerability of the Southern belle is represented in the context of a degenerative disease when, on learning of her husband's death in battle she immediately falls into "a violent delirium," leaving her son virtually an orphan, betrayed by her dependency: "It seemed to him [Charles Gaston] some one was strangling him to death, and a great stone was piled on his little prostrate body" (*LS*, 14, 31).[50] In this context, Mrs. Gaston's own bodily torture now becomes her son's, as he is feminized and raped figuratively in her place.

All white women, simply by virtue of their being women, put their men in danger. It is precisely in their rape and their death that white women can redeem themselves because their vulnerability enables their refiguration as icons in a white male culture of violence. For example, when the old Confederate veteran Tom Camp witnesses the kidnapping of his older daughter Annie on her wedding night by a band of armed black soldiers, the men of the bridal party shoot the bride as well as her abductors. Camp responds with gratitude: "You've saved my little gal. . . . My God, I can't think of what would 'a' happened! Now it's all right. She's safe in God's hands" (*LS*, 127). As the vulnerable virgin, Annie's fate is either to be deflowered by a Negro rapist or be killed by her menfolk. In either situation she can only be truly made "safe" when penetrated and reclaimed through male violence:

They laid her [dead body] across the bed in the room that had been made
sweet and tidy for the bride and groom. The mother bent over her quickly
with a light. Just where the blue veins crossed in her delicate temple there
was a round hole from which a scarlet stream was running down her
white throat.    (*LS,* 127)

Besides making them safe, the rape and death of white women in Dixon's
novels facilitate a ritual of purification and white male triumph over black
rivals, thereby redressing the racial balance of power. This is made clear in the
case of the novel's principal rape victim, Camp's second daughter Flora, whom
Dixon fashions in the image of Stowe's blond, blue-eyed child, angelic little
Eva.[51] Ever fearful of another rape attempt, Camp arrives at the spring where
Flora has been playing just in time to see "the form of a negro man passing
over the opposite hill, going along the spring path that led in that direction"
(*LS,* 369). In her own response to Camp's upbraiding, Flora's innocence gives
way to impudence: " 'Yes, I said "Howdy!" when he stopped to get a drink of
water, and he gave me a whistle,' she replied, with a pout of her pretty lips and
a frown" (*LS,* 369). Flora's naiveté translates into an immodesty that shocks her
father: "She don't seem any more afraid of 'em than she is of a cat" (*LS,* 370).
The female upstart Flora is of course the stand-in for young Gaston. The physical landscape of her childish play is identical to that inhabited by Gaston and
Dick, although Gaston's potentially dangerous desire for Dick's presence is now
contained as white female immodesty in the face the threat of the black rapist.
Predictably the black figure spotted by Camp is indeed Dick, who returns to
commit the dreaded deed.

Apart from resolving the discomfort over the homoerotic, Flora's assault has
several other functions. First, as mentioned before, simply because she is an
exposed female in need of protection, the victim herself is already to blame; so
the rape becomes a method of imagining the removal of the unstable feminine.
Second, the assault provides the needed catalyst to call to action the heretofore
generally impotent white male community; thus the union of black male and
white female bodies becomes a mediating structure through which white masculinity can simultaneously punish transgressions and regenerate itself. Third,
because the rape victim and her family are lower class, Dixon can acknowledge
and at the same time insulate his middle-class readers from closer association
with the larger problem of desire for and violence against the black.

Some critics have suggested that Dixon identified himself with "the new
forces in Southern life: the rising industrialist, the reform-minded lawyer, the
poor white farmer of the back country," and that Dixon appealed to Americans
because he was "a democrat par excellence."[52] I would suggest just the opposite.
Dixon's popularity rests not on his support of egalitarianism, but precisely on
his ability to generate images of white violence that bring about racial unity,

while at the same time respecting and sustaining class divisions that had existed before the war. Dixon does not dwell on the crop lien system that oppressed both blacks and whites of the so-called New South, so Camp's poverty is not treated as the product of his status as a poor white. Rather Camp blames the ambiguously sketched black "presence" for his economic troubles: "I always hated a nigger since I was knee high. . . . Somehow, we always felt like they was crowdin' us to death on them big plantations, and the little ones, too" (*LS*, 28). Interestingly, Flora's rape in *The Leopard's Spots*, which is supposedly brought on by her lack of judgment (that is, her lack of a middle-class morality) enforces the traditional distinction between lower- and middle-class women: for all their faults as belles, the latter are nevertheless "impelled by some resistless instinct" that warns them of approaching trouble from black men (*LS*, 150). In contrast, as a lower-class figure, Flora Camp has a less developed feminine sense, and so most obviously presents herself as the appropriate sacrificial rape victim in the novel.

But it is in the idealized yeoman figure of Tom Camp that Dixon finally cordons off the image of white male impotence, white male savagery, and desire for the black. An aging amputee unable to move to a safer community (Dixon's dephallicization of the white male is hardly subtle here), Camp epitomizes the disempowered white male at a loss to control either the blacks or the women around him. Eventually the rape of his daughter propels him to join a lynch mob, but since the transformation into potent white manhood involves a process of feminization (as the white man occupies the space of the rape victim) and reincarnation before masculine empowerment can be achieved, the process is comfortably distanced in the bodily experience of a poor white.

When Flora is first declared missing, the frantic Camp waits at home where grief transforms him into a helpless maternal figure akin to Mrs. Gaston: "Through every hour of this awful night Tom Camp was in his room praying— his face now streaming with tears, now dry and white with the unspoken terror that could stop the beat of his heart" (*LS*, 373). As anguish over Flora's disappearance aggravates his old war wound, Camp's own body mirrors both the offstage deflowering of his daughter and her eventual death: "From the pain of his wound and the exhaustion of soul and body he fainted once with his lips still moving in prayer. For more than an hour he lay as one dead." (*LS*, 373). When Flora is finally brought home, her body has already been displaced by that of her powerless father/protector, her wounds are manifested on his form, ending with his melodramatic collapse (also like Mrs. Gaston) into hysteria and temporary madness to signify his complete feminization.

Dixon uses the lower-class Tom Camp similarly to acknowledge and then contain the horror of white violence; thus Camp prefigures the eventual character of a white mob—the "thousand-legged beast" as Dixon calls it: "Oh! if I only had him [the black rapist] here before me now, and God Almighty would give me strength with these hands to tear his breast open and rip his heart out! I—could—eat—it—like—a—wolf!" (*LS*, 380). At this point Camp achieves his wish: he rushes out to join in Dick's lynching, and he and the mob burn the black rapist.

While Dixon may be disturbed enough by the transformation of his law-abiding white heroes into violent men to suggest, as other Southerners did, that mob violence was a lower-class phenomenon, he nevertheless flashes before the reader scenes of classless racial solidarity inspired by Flora's assault:

> In a moment the white race had fused into a homogeneous mass of love, sympathy, hate and revenge. The rich and the poor, the learned and the ignorant, the banker and the blacksmith, the great and the small, they were all one now. The sorrow of that old one-legged soldier was the sorrow of all; every heart beat with his, and his life was their life, and his child their child. (*LS*, 372)

Yet even the supposedly righteous violence unleashed by the crowd threatens to move toward savagery, expressed in the text as a physical transformation, an erasure of the identifiably racial characteristics belying the purer character, intellect, and compassion that allegedly distinguish white from black:

> the crowd seemed to melt into a great crawling, swaying creature, half reptile, half beast, half dragon, half man, with a thousand legs, and a thousand eyes, and ten thousand gleaming teeth, and with no ear to hear and no heart to pity! (*LS*, 384)

Imaged as a demonic (albeit retributive) presence, the white mob comes closest here to resembling the equally demonic freedmen who manifest themselves like a "black cloud . . . on the horizon" (*LS*, 63). Like the threat of both miscegenation and interracial male contact, then, regenerative violence against blacks not only threatens to taint white morality and humanity, but also resembles the very bodily distortions threatened by black rape as the white avengers merge with the beast they originally set out to destroy.

As a register of this ambivalence (and to support the mythology that ennobling leadership in the eradication of blacks is ultimately a middle-class duty), the novel's hero Charles Gaston appeals to the mob, not to consider the possibility of Dick's innocence (even blacks know "him guilty of the crime charged against him"), but to reconsider the method of execution: "Don't disgrace our town, our country, our state and our claims to humanity by this insane brutality. A beast wouldn't do this. . . . If you will kill him, shoot him or knock him in the head with a rock—don't burn him alive!" (*LS*, 383) As it turns out, Gaston's appeal is unsuccessful, and in fact he himself falls victim to the crowd's uncontrollable fury, further signifying the potential for white self-destruction embodied by mob violence:

"Knock the fool in the head!" one shouted. "Pin his arms behind him!" said another. Some one quickly pinioned his [Gaston's] arms with a cord. He stood in helpless rage and pity, and as he saw the match applied [to Dick], bowed his head and burst into tears.    (*LS*, 383–84)

Whereas *The Leopard's Spots* evinces a conflicted search for an appropriate stance in the face of the imagined black peril, Dixon uses the *The Clansman* to work out a clearer vision of racial control that is less problematic than mob violence—namely, the organization of the early Ku Klux Klan. Dixon's boyhood memories of his adored uncle Colonel Leroy McAfee, Grand Titan of the Cleveland County Klan of North Carolina, shaped his presentation of the early Klansmen as the Anglo-American link with a European past of chivalric glory. Only in the highly ritualized, controlled executions performed by the Ku Klux Klan does white male violence become a fully liberating, purifying experience that absolves whites of guilt and restores the "natural" order. Equally important, Dixon represents the violence of the Klan as the chosen mode of resistance specifically for middle-class white men, feeding the myth of the Klan's original 1865 birth as a brotherhood of well-to-do white youths.[53]

The Klansmen make a brief appearance in *The Leopard's Spots* ("On those horses sat two hundred white-robed silent men whose close-fitting hood disguises looked like the mail helmets of ancient knights"), but they ride in full force into the pages of *The Clansman* (*LS*, 151).[54] Major Dameron in *The Leopard's Spots* and Phil Cameron in *The Clansman* are united with Camp in their natural instincts as white men to hate blacks; yet as leaders of the community, they are responsible for channeling male fury into honorable, chivalric modes as a solution to the horror of their own bloodletting. *The Clansman* seeks to present an idealized image of the early Klan as the institution of white male violence perpetrated by the middle-class; and while the method of corralling white womanhood and avenging white (fe)male violation is consistent with that of *The Leopard's Spots*, the assault against blacks finally rises to the level of a holy crusade.

As in *The Leopard's Spots*, the catalyst for male intervention in *The Clansman* is black rape. Dixon's contention that "the young Southern woman was the divinity that claimed and received the chief worship of man" (*C*, 210) is once more an ironic statement at best, since his female characters achieve apotheosis only after either literal death or the symbolic "death" of rape, when they function to inspire white violence. Dixon's handling of the symbolic significance of rape changes dramatically when the victims are middle class, however, as in the case of the assault on genteel Marion Lenoir. When black Gus and his henchmen break in on the defenseless Marion and her widowed mother, Mrs. Lenoir is forced to watch her daughter's violation, underscoring the helplessness of Southern white women. But unlike Flora in *The Leopard's Spots*, these women are self-policing. When Marion regains consciousness hours later, she knows instinctively the route of the fallen woman:

> "No one must ever know. We will hide quickly every trace of the crime. They will think we strolled to Lover's Leap and fell over the cliff, and my name will always be sweet and clean. . . . Only those who hate me could wish that I live." (C, 305–6)

Finally, in a double suicide, mother and daughter jump from Lover's Leap.

White supremacy once more puts the white woman in an impossible dilemma: alive, her own proscribed physical and emotional weakness renders her indefensible and so a liability to her man in his battle against blacks; dead, she can finally epitomize a racial purity and chastity unencumbered by the physical. As such, in death she safely approximates the ideal of the desexualized belle and can thus achieve apotheosis. Also, although Marion and her mother have destroyed all evidence to link Gus with the assault, Dr. Cameron is able to identify the marks of rape on Marion's body and "the fire-etched record of the crime" literally burned for all time on the surface of Mrs. Lenoir's retina (C, 313). Alive, both women are the constant care of their neighbors, the Cameron men; dead, their bodies become tangible evidence of black criminality, the necessary sacred text required to validate white supremacist violence.

When the Klansmen capture Gus, in contrast to the undisciplined mob's execution of Dick in *The Leopard's Spots*, these whites formally interrogate their prisoner and investigate the crime in the context of solemn ritual. As in the case of yeoman Camp, the white protectors are associated with the body of the white female victim. But the middle-class Klansmen share a more stylized, less basely physical relationship to Marion's body: Dixon stresses that they are all elaborately robed in white, with phallic spikes on their helmets, and on the breast of their garments is a circle of red enclosing a white cross. According to descriptions of early Klan robes, the white of the uniforms signified "purity for the preservation of the home and for the protection of women and children" while the red emblem stood for "the blood which Klansmen were ready to shed in defense of the helpless."[55] For much of the novel, Marion herself has been robed in white. She wears white when she commits suicide and her death posture is emblematic of the Klan's breast patch. When she is found at the bottom of the cliff, her "fair blonde head" lies "in a crimson circle sharply defined in the white sand" (C, 311). Thus, as an uncompromisingly masculine reincarnation of the dead girl, the robed Klansmen occupy the space of the rape victim, whose bodily violation is strategically concealed to leave only the aura of violated purity.

When Dr. Cameron uses hypnosis to force Gus to relive his assault on Marion, the Klansmen relive the rape in the girl's place, appropriating the space of female victim, as Tom Camp does after Flora's assault, but with a significant difference:

The negro began to live the crime with fearful realism. . . . Gus rose to his feet and started across the cave as if to spring on the shivering figure of the girl, the clansmen with muttered groans, sobs and curses falling back as he advanced. . . . Strong men began to cry like children.

"Stop him! Stop him!" screamed a clansman, springing on the negro and grinding his heel into his big thick neck. A dozen more were on him in a moment, kicking, stamping, cursing, and crying like madmen.

Dr. Cameron leaped forward and beat them off:

"Men! Men! You must not kill him in this condition!"

Some of the white figures had fallen prostrate on the ground, sobbing in a frenzy of uncontrollable emotion. Some were leaning against the walls, their faces buried in their arms.   (*C,* 322–24)

The Klansmen are feminized in the posture of both Marion and the helpless witness Mrs. Lenoir; yet even as they live Marion's violation as their own, their demand to have the assault rehearsed puts them in the category of rapists, because they directly violate Marion's wish for secrecy. In seeking to place themselves in the space of her victimization, the voyeuristic Klansmen enact a second trespass on Marion's imagined body; but in the context of ritual, the merging of black and white identities is denied and subverted. Thus Marion's death, originally an act of ironic self-preservation, is recharged with new ideological meaning as the image of her rape is exhibited repeatedly to awaken white manhood to vengeance, not female protection.

The rape revitalizes the Klansmen with a drive toward violence in much the same way as it does Tom Camp, but again, "[r]itual murder averts a sacrificial crisis of indiscriminate violence. It ushers in the distinction between culture and nature."[56] Following Dr. Cameron's caution for restraint, they undertake a complex series of rituals before finally throwing Gus's dead body onto the front yard of the corrupt mulatto lieutenant governor, Silas Lynch. Gus's lynching takes place offstage, so as not to taint the meaning of Klan's act of vengeance. Thus any relationships between the middle-class lynchers and their victim are masked: they have destroyed his body and appropriated his power; but unlike the mob in *The Leopard's Spots,* the Klansmen have also purified, not polluted themselves with violence.

## The Problem of Black Women
### in *The Sins of the Father*

Both *The Leopard's Spots* and *The Clansman* designate male lust as a black disease, a mark of black bestiality. But as I have suggested earlier, since the black woman had been associated with the slaveholder's sexuality in the antebellum South, her apparent absence in Dixon's representation of postwar

America speaks to denial of the tradition of white-authored miscegenation in a postemancipation context. In *The Clansman* Dixon does present the interracial relationship between Austin Stoneman, the Northern pro-black politician, and Lydia, the sinister mulatto housekeeper; their affair epitomizes the misguided Northern attachment to the ex-slave, and the novel's plot works to alert the Stoneman family (and white readers of the North) to the grave mistake made by the Yankees. In *The Sins of the Father* (1912), Dixon finally makes the problem of white male desire for the black woman his central focus. This novel never achieved the popular success enjoyed by *The Leopard's Spots* or *The Clansman,* perhaps in part because of its dismal prediction of white racial self-destruction.

*The Sins of the Father* follows the fortunes of Daniel Norton, Confederate veteran, Klan leader, editor, politician. And like Dixon's previous novels about race war, *The Sins of the Father* rehearses the familiar struggle to regain control and defeat a corrupt Yankee-installed black government. On the public front, Norton is at the height of his success: he is feared and respected as an editor; he controls the Ku Klux Klan with an iron fist, keeping the rougher elements among the Klansmen in place; in politics, he is marked for success as the great white supremacist hope for the White House: "I'll start a fire that can't be put out until it has swept the state—the South— . . . and then the Nation!" (*S*, 216).[57] But while Norton's public persona represents the national success of white supremacy, his personal life threatens its defeat: Norton must choose between Cleo, the fair-skinned, oversexed quadroon, and his white wife, Jean, the direct descendent of aristocratic plantation stock, and the traditionally pure, desexualized white belle.

As the descendent of slaves and as Jean's halfsister, Cleo embodies an incestuous racial heritage (her father slept with his black half-sister Lucy) that speaks Dixon's fears of a white patriarchy unable to control its own impulses or to delineate its own social boundaries. Dixon obviously intends Cleo to function as a retributive figure in the life of one white family, as a way of pointing to the need for complete racial separation. But as a link between the political contexts of slavery and post-Reconstruction, the sexual domination of the black body once thought to be the sign of the white slaveholder's complete power as master is now revealed to be the very evidence of his weakness, as the triumphs of the past become the liabilities of the present. The white ability to shape and control the national racial destiny, then, might be proved to be completely arbitrary.

Though his work was dedicated to a belief in white superiority and in the possibility of separating the races, in *The Sins of the Father* Dixon is fascinated with imaging white masculinity in a state of complete, self-generated powerlessness. In contrast to the "delicate[,] . . . petted invalid" (*S*, 20) Jean Norton,

Cleo is presented as the seductress, precluding the possibility of rape and at the same time absolving Norton of responsibility for his actions of adultery and miscegenation: "she felt . . . that the mad desires that burned a living fire in every nerve of her young body had scorched the man she had marked her own from the moment she had first laid eyes on his serious, aristocratic face" (*S,* 42). Yet simultaneously with presenting Norton as Cleo's sexual victim, *The Sins of the Father* grapples with the problem of potentially erasing the white hero's own idealized will to resist the invasion of an inferior race. When Norton's family physician upbraids Norton for his transgression ("We spend our time and energy fighting the negro race in front and leave our back doors open for their women and children to enter and master our life" [*S,* 121]), he is in effect attempting to restore a white male agency to Norton that seems to have been relinquished through the tradition of miscegenation.

Predictably Dixon flirts with the idea of white culpability, signified by Norton's failure as husband and race leader, by distancing it through the figure of Jean. As the novel begins to enact a series of avoidances, Jean Norton is portrayed as the overly perfect Southern belle who poses the chief impediment in Norton's battle against sexual desire for the black:

> [Naively, Jean] believed in the innocence of her husband. The fact that the negro race had for two hundred years been stirring the baser passions of her men—that this degradation of the higher race had been bred into the bone and sinew of succeeding generations—had never occurred to her child-like mind. (*S,* 124)

She refuses to "realize that this thing is . . . a living fact which the white woman of the South must face" (*S,* 122). Consequently, her own adherence to Southern ideals of female virtue—the quality that makes her most faithful to the Southern patriarchy—makes her the source of the racial Other's triumph over Norton, and therefore makes her a traitor to her white society. And finally her own self-willed death becomes the ultimate betrayal, because the maternal absence thus created gives Cleo an opportunity to fill the void as housekeeper/mother/wife.

Following in the footsteps of other Dixonian heroines, Jean's real usefulness to her community only comes with her death. Her suicide marks her as the traditional fallen white woman, now cast as a fallen white race, her hearing and sensibility contaminated by her knowledge of her husband's adultery. That Jean is of more value dead than alive is underscored by Norton's erection of "an altar" beneath her portrait, before which "he kneels in the twilight and prays": "The picture and frame seemed a living flame in its dark setting. The portrait was an idealized study of the little mother. The artist had put into his canvas the spirit of the tenderest brooding motherhood" (*S,* 243). In her death Norton achieves an empowering purification: vowing to raise his legitimate son away from the contaminating influences of blackness, he breaks with Cleo and sends their octoroon daughter to live in an orphanage.

Yet Dixon's usual rituals seem superfluous in this context because the problem at hand is not the management of black male and white female bodies, but rather the management of a fatally dangerous white male desire. Despite Norton's best efforts, his son eventually marries a young woman whom Cleo later implies is her daughter by Norton. In the face of this repetition of antebellum white traditions of breaking sexual and familial taboos, father and son attempt a double suicide, a strange plot twist that appears to be Dixon's prediction of white race suicide unless trends are reversed. Yet after dangling this possible fate before his audience, Dixon redeems his heroes in a clumsy ending: Norton is fatally wounded, thereby paying the price for his indiscretion, but Tom Norton is discovered to be only slightly hurt. At this point a guilty Cleo reveals that, after all, Tom's young wife is really a white orphan she had claimed as her own, the child by Daniel Norton having died in infancy. With family and racial purity apparently intact, Tom vows never again to allow a negro to enter the Norton home.

But despite such measures, the security of white families like the Nortons is based on coincidences of racial histories, not on a white ability to control racial knowledge or navigate national destinies. As a quadroon the sexual partner and surrogate parent to white men and children, Cleo symbolizes, for Dixon at least, a threatening white dependence on African Americans, enforced by whites themselves. The end of *The Sins of the Father* enforces an erasure of the white male hero—a fate reserved in Dixon's other novels for African Americans. As a mulatto designed to reference specifically white male sexual excess and not black male sexual transgression, Cleo allows Dixon to imagine, but not distance the possibility of a white destiny of self-destruction. In *The Leopard's Spots* and *The Clansman,* white political power is reaffirmed and exercised through the identification and execution of the black rapist. With its subplot of political agitation for the South, *The Sins of the Father* must confront the possibility that the white supremacist political platform of white domestic defense is infeasible, not because of the presence of African Americans, but because of a tradition of white failure. Dixon saves the day at the end of *The Sins of the Father,* but just barely. Mistakes are righted, and undesirables are expelled; but the real potential, if not the reality, of white male defeat cannot be unvoiced.

We cannot consider Thomas Dixon's fiction as merely a successful attempt to codify and broadcast white supremacist propaganda, without exploring at the same time the ways in which that fiction's war against an American multiracial destiny was uneasy and deeply conflicted. Dixon's novels provide a useful example of how white supremacist discourse hinged on a denial of alternate black and white voices, and a figuration of anxieties through the bodies of racial and sexual others. Precisely because in *The Sins of the Father* the lascivious Cleo becomes finally an undeniable reference for Norton's bodily desire Dixon is forced to kill his hero to cleanse the novel's idealized white world. Thus, because they provided a more palatable fantasy of a white male rescue based on disciplining of unruly bodies, Dixon's *The Leopard's Spots* and *The Clansman* achieved considerably greater popularity.

In the turn-of-the-century context of American white supremacy, Dixon's fiction underscores how the struggle to resolve questions of race and political agency was structured through contemporary debates about masculinity. This discourse of race and masculinity in turn structured the ways in which writers working to counter the effects of white supremacist fiction would articulate their opposition. In their work, black writers such as Charles Chesnutt or Sutton E. Griggs sought to reinvent African American masculinity and validate black male claims to political entitlement. Part of their strategy included a decriminalization of both black male sexuality and black male aggression; they would also have to challenge white supremacist definitions of the victim, in order to prove that lynching itself was a criminal act and that the black rapist was an imaginary threat. At the same time, might the recuperation of black manhood result in an appropriation of the kinds of class and gender discourses exemplified in Dixon's fiction? Writers in opposition to the forces represented by Dixon also drew on the idea of the endangered space of the domestic (in this case black, not white) to underscore white supremacy's threat to an orderly progress of African American life from slavery to freedom, and they especially emphasized the hypocrisy of white male traditions of miscegenation. But what were the nature and the effect of their usage of black women as emblems of a besieged race? And in their refocusing of attention from the white to the black family, what happened to the figure of white womanhood? Since American literary responses to white supremacy included black and white women, how did their particular figurations contribute to the ongoing debates on race and rights occurring in their respective communities?

### CHAPTER TWO

# Mark Twain, Charles Chesnutt, and the Politics of Literary Anti-Racism

Taught that they are oppressed, and with breasts pulsating with hatred of the whites, the younger generation of negro men are roaming over the land, passing back and forth without hindrance, and with no possibility of adequate police protection to the communities in which they are residing.

Senator Ben Tillman

In warning the South that it may place too much reliance upon the cowardice of the negro, I am not advocating violence by the negro, but pointing out the dangerous tendency of his constant persecution. . . . [C]are should be taken against goading him to acts of desperation by continuing to punish him for heinous crimes of which he is not legally convicted.

Frederick Douglass,<br>"Lynch Law in the South"

For thomas dixon and other late-nineteenth- and early-twentieth-century white supremacists, the anxiety generated by the stereotype of the black rapist was tied directly to anxiety over the meaning of citizenship and racial identity in the wake of Emancipation and Reconstruction. As a result, questions of political entitlement were expressed through a rhetoric of white domestic self-protection and the need for white racial unity—a rhetoric that justified the steady erosion of black citizenship supposedly guaranteed by the Fourteenth and Fifteenth Amendments to the Constitution. Particularly painful to African Americans was that increasingly they were omitted from national visions of post-Reconstruction unity, despite their attempts at full participation in American life. In a speech before Congress in 1907, Senator Ben Tillman referenced the idea of "the younger generation of negro men . . . roaming over the land" presumably in search of white female victims; such a characterization of blacks as nomadic savages denied the possibility of imagining African Americans—

especially African American men—as viable contributors to communities black or white, or as themselves members of respectable domestic units.[1]

And this was precisely the problem: the figure of the black rapist and the spectacle of lynching threatened to dominate all public discussion of race and equality, without fostering a corresponding recognition that white supremacist violence was perpetrated against African American lives, bodies, and homes. Even for whites who were horrified by lynching, the notion of either guiltless black manhood or sexually exploited black womanhood was not always conceivable. Theodore Dreiser's 1901 anti-lynching story, "Nigger Jeff," provides one example of the possibilities and limitations of a white envisioning of the black home ravaged by the practice of lynching. The story is told through the eyes of an eager young city reporter covering a small-town lynching: the rapist admits his own guilt, and though the story clearly does not sanction vigilante violence, there is an enforced distance between the viewer and the lynch victim, who in the grip of terror finally resembles the subhuman figure of white supremacist discourse: " '[O]h, my Lawd, boss, don't kill me! I won't do it no mo'. I didn't go to do it. I didn't mean to dis time. I was just drunk, boss.' . . . He was by now a groveling, foaming brute. The last gleam of intelligence was that which notified him of the set eyes of his pursuers" (*N*, 101).[2] After witnessing the execution of the black rapist the reporter decides to visit the black victim's cabin. Though dilapidated, the shack emits "the glow of a home" (*N*, 107), and the reporter is touched to learn that the black rapist Jeff Ingalls was caught by the mob because he returned home to bid his mother goodbye.

Entering the cabin, he is led by Ingalls's sister to a darkened room containing the covered body of the lynched black, but the reporter also senses a nearby presence:

> he seemed to catch the shadow of something, the figure of a woman, perhaps, crouching against the walls, huddled up, dark, almost indistinguishable. . . . He approached slowly, then more swiftly desired to withdraw, for he was in the presence of an old black mammy, doubled up and weeping. . . . Before such grief his intrusion seemed cold and unwarranted. The guiltlessness of the mother—her love—how could one balance that against the other. The sensation of tears came to his eyes. He instantly covered the dead and withdrew. (*N*, 110)

In place of the now dead rapist Dreiser substitutes the vaguely visible, grief-stricken black mother to signify not the terror of blackness, but its tragic entry into a post-Reconstruction world. The erasure of the very body and face of the mother in a room where the sheet-covered rapist predominates, and then her referencing in antebellum terms as the "old black mammy" gestures to the idea of a black family space that has barely been able to articulate itself outside of slavery. This notion is carried through in the body of the rapist's prepubescent sister. In the cabin she is figured less as an individual than as a collection of almost cartoonish images: an "unformed figure and loose gingham dress," overly large hands and feet, "little pigtails of hair done up in white twine, . . . dark skin . . . made apparently more so by contrast with her white teeth and the whites of her eyes" (N, 108). Indeed, Dreiser's catalogue of her grotesque bodily features stands in contrast to his earlier fleeting but more conventional reference to the white rape victim as young and beautiful. Thus the story's ambivalent ending calls for an old-fashioned sentimental empathy for the mother and daughter, while at the same time distancing them from the viewer by stressing their alienness and alienation from the white world.

In response to both the systematic attack on their civil rights and the denial of black domesticity, post-Reconstruction African Americans vigorously promoted the existence of a black patriarchal family structure in which black men and women were redeemed as American citizens and as true women, respectively. Thus, in *A Voice From the South,* black intellectual Anna Julia Cooper declared that "[w]e must point to homes, average homes, homes of the rank and file of horny handed toiling [Negro] men and women of the South (where the masses are) lighted and cheered by the good, the beautiful, and the true,— then and not till then will the whole plateau be lifted into the sunlight."[3] Cooper's model of black working-class respectability was considerably refined by African American novelists who utilized the trope of the cultivated, middle-class mulatto to suggest an ideal of black cultural and class development that countered the stereotype of the regressive black rapist. According to Claudia Tate, the styling of ideal blackness, particularly along the lines of white bourgeois Victorian prescriptions of social virtue, was a crucial feature of turn-of-the-century African American culture, "because appropriation of gentility meant approximating racial equality." According to Tate, "the highly noticeable exercise of conservative Victorian gender roles was a candid sign of the black middle-class' claim on respectable citizenship, just as the appropriation of bourgeois gender conventions in general [was] fundamental to the emancipatory discourse of nineteenth-century African Americans."[4]

More specifically, on the subject of African American manhood itself, the question remained how to rehabilitate black masculinity as moral but also aggressively self-defensive. While on the one hand Booker T. Washington sought to quell white fears with the image of industrious African Americans concerned only with racial harmony, more militant blacks such as the minister-writer Sutton Elbert Griggs opted in his novels for a virile image of black manhood. According to Griggs, "[t]he cringing, fawning, sniffling, cowardly Negro which slavery left, had disappeared, and a new Negro, self-respecting, fearless, and determined in the assertion of his rights was at hand."[5] In light of this idea, the statesman and African American leader Frederick Douglass could well surmise that "the negro will not always rest a passive subject to the violence and bloodshed by which he is now pursued."[6] Black journalist John Edward Bruce was bolder in suggesting that African American men "[m]eet force with force everywhere it is offered," an idea echoed by Ida B. Wells in her 1892 pamphlet *Southern Horrors: Lynch Law in All Its Phases:* "a Winchester rifle should have a place of honor in every black home, and it should be used for that protection which the law refuses to give."[7] However, while many whites sympathized with victims of racist violence, few were willing to advocate such acts; and writers and activists such as Albion W. Tourgée, George Washington Cable, and Ray Stannard Baker attempted to counteract white supremacists by more pacific means.[8]

Yet without losing sight of the crucial role opponents of white supremacy played in the struggle for black rights, we need to interrogate anti-racist responses by African Americans and American whites, not just for their politically laudable attempts to reorient public opinion about the black "character" in general and black masculinity in particular, but also for the ways they draw on common nineteenth-century racialized and gendered discursive patterns shared by white supremacist fiction. As Paula A. Treichler has articulated in another context,

> paradoxically as struggle and counter-struggle seek to define their own limits, they may grow closer together. An innovative structure—or a deviant definition—lives a double life for it may grow out of a struggle with a dominant structure which continues to shape it, even cannibalize it. Counter-discourse does not arise as a pure autonomous radical language embodying the purity of a new politics. Rather, it arises from within the dominant discourse and learns to inhabit it from the inside out.[9]

In this chapter, I focus on how two novels that can easily be read in opposition to white supremacist fiction—namely, Mark Twain's *Pudd'nhead Wilson* (1894) and Charles W. Chesnutt's *The Marrow of Tradition* (1901)—attempt to counteract white supremacist assumptions by problematizing questions of regional and racial unity, the family, and masculine heroism. In so doing, Twain and Chesnutt engage closely with the kinds of strategies, successes, and failures that mark works such as Dixon's *The Leopard's Spots* (1902). My purpose here is not to indict Twain and Chesnutt, but rather to offer case studies of how anti-racist or anti–white supremacist stances are conditioned by and in dialogue with the very discourses they work to challenge. Addressing the topic with which Dixon struggles so unsuccessfully in *The Sins of the Father* (1912), Twain and Chesnutt argue in their respective novels that black/white sexual contact was a custom long upheld by whites themselves and that the real cause of violence along the color line was the white struggle to determine the rights of citizens according to race. But just as Dixon's novels demonstrate unwittingly how radical white supremacist ideology could unravel and contradict itself around the complex workings of gender, class, and domesticity, some of the same problems emerge in the fiction of what modern-day readers would consider to be more progressive writers.

Through the historical tension arising between *Pudd'nhead Wilson*'s antebellum setting and its post-Reconstruction creation and publication, Twain's novel functions as a complicated address to both white supremacist violence of the late 1890s and white nineteenth-century anxieties about racial purity. However, as Michael Rogin among others has suggested, the novel's "force resides not in the author's detached judgment against the world depicted, but in his participation in such a world," precisely because *Pudd'nhead Wilson* walks a fine line in its flirtation with black criminality and its representation of not one but two murderous black figures.[10] One might argue then that Twain's assault on white supremacy fails in its very attempt to effect a counterdiscourse working against white supremacist ideology. But to focus on Twain's "success" or "failure" is to construct the falsely monolithic (in terms of its context, tone, and discursive strategy) category of "anti-racist" fiction. Though *Pudd'nhead Wilson* depicts blacks figuratively and literally killing whites, Twain himself was clearly aware that killing across the color line was often committed by whites; and in a 1901 essay on "The United States of Lyncherdom," he condemned lynching as "this epidemic of bloody insanities."[11]

If we read *Pudd'nhead Wilson*'s critique of white supremacy as what Susan Gillman has termed the turn-of-the-century "American race melodrama," centered primarily on notions of family and "hidden race mixture," we see an anti-racist text that is itself problematically constructed around varying notions of the significance of black emancipation, the continuing public discourse on the nature of race, the justifiability of black anger at social and political injustice, and the (im)possibility of black and white union, all set against the backdrop of larger national fantasies about sectional reunion.[12] As such, the novel's aim to undermine late-nineteenth-century white supremacist ideology on the terms of its own contradictions runs into trouble when Twain is faced with the challenge of redefining the meaning of a racialized American identity outside of the vocabulary already provided by nineteenth-century racism.

The particular brand of racism epitomized in Dixon's fiction flourished in part because it reiterated general white middle-class patriarchal ideals about the gendering of power, the nature of men and women, and the boundaries between public and private—ideals that newly freed blacks appropriated, sometimes subversively, sometimes not, for themselves and their descendents. In contrast, Chesnutt's *The Marrow of Tradition*, while it neither argues for a simple inversion of the white-home-in-danger thesis nor advocates black violence as a method of masculine rejuvenation, does register the possibility of black defensive violence and the expression of black male anger, and it does refigure black women at the center of a domestic ideal. Chesnutt is of course arguing for a recuperation of black women in *The Marrow of Tradition*, but it is worth thinking through how he does and does not refigure some of the representational strategies used by Dixon.

A fictionalized account of the infamous Wilmington, North Carolina, race riot of 1898, *The Marrow of Tradition* examines the tangled skeins of race and family in a Southern town and, on the levels of plot detail and social philosophy, achieves a rewriting of both Twain's earlier novel and Dixon's later ones. Indeed, as an ambitious writer who had begun to attract a national white audience, Chesnutt set himself up as a direct opponent to Dixon in particular: when *The Leopard's Spots* was published a year after *The Marrow of Tradition*, Chesnutt sent copies of his novel to President Roosevelt and to some members of Congress, to demonstrate that his view represented a radically different social and philosophical alternative.[13]

Chesnutt specifically attempts to define a turn-of-the-century South where patriarchal power is structured through class rather than racial identifications, and his novel's mulatto characters become metaphoric expressions of the political and social ethos of this new region. But as in the work of Dixon and Twain, we are left with the question of how women, as objects of desire and icons of domestic sanctity, ultimately figure in the novel's vision of the American racial future.

### On Black Men with Knives: Mark Twain and *Pudd'nhead Wilson*

Though it was published as a novel almost twenty years before Dixon's *The Sins of the Father*, *Pudd'nhead Wilson* tells the very similar story of how a white world that paradoxically sanctions both miscegenation and racial separation is almost destroyed by a scheming mixed-race mother. But while *The Sins of the Father* unravels despite Dixon's desperate attempt to authorize white racial power, Twain takes a perverse delight in the racial disorder of *Pudd'nhead Wilson*.[14] Set in 1830 in the little Missouri town of Dawson's Landing, the story of racial confusion rolls into motion when an octoroon slave named Roxy substitutes her white-skinned infant son for the master's heir, Tom Driscoll. In the pampered environment of wealth and power, black Tom passing for the overindulged white slaveholder grows up cruel, violent, and dissolute, while his "black" slave counterpart Chambers resides in bondage below stairs. When Tom finally learns of his "tainted" blood, he has already matured into a fashionable, dissipated "white" gentleman plagued to desperation by mounting gambling debts. The news of his true identity merely causes his corrupt sensibilities to degenerate further; and in an effort to end his financial woes, he dons a blackface disguise to rob and murder his "uncle" Judge Driscoll. A recently arrived pair of Italian twins is blamed for the murder, but fortunately for them and for the white community of Dawson's Landing, Tom's guilt and the secret switch at birth are finally exposed by David "Pudd'nhead" Wilson, a lawyer and accountant who uses his hobby of fingerprinting to solve the two crimes.

*Pudd'nhead Wilson* was initially serialized in *Century Magazine* in 1893–1894, as part of editor Richard Watson Gilder's ongoing project to establish the magazine as a primary advocate for the peaceful spiritual reunion of North and South. From 1884 to 1887 Gilder masterminded a "War Series," which included combatants' memoirs and handsomely illustrated articles on important Civil War battles, as a way to "clear up cloudy questions with new knowledge and the wisdom of cool reflection: and to soften controversy with that better understanding of each other, which comes to comrades in arms when personal feeling has dissipated."[15] By the 1890s, Gilder was attempting to satisfy Northern readers' enormous appetite for stories about Southern customs and Southern people. Within and without the magazine, from Henry James's *The Bostonians* (serialized in the *Century* in 1885–1886), to Kate Chopin's *At Fault* (1890), to Thomas Nelson Page's *Red Rock* (1898), to Dixon's *The Clansman* (1905), the theme of sectional reunion was often literally staged as an intersectional marriage—a sexualized metaphor for a more acceptable vision of the fruits of Reconstruction, in lieu of any proposed social unity between blacks and whites.

With its story of mulatto substitution enabled in part by the South's tradition of white-authored miscegenation, *Pudd'nhead Wilson* calls into question precisely the nature and the adequacy of this myth of national unity advocated by Northerners and Southerners alike, by exposing and exploring the reality of a different kind of union. Indeed, by their presence, Roxy and Tom are meant to speak to the embarrassingly sexual side of slavery's property relations, which otherwise remained unaddressed in popular white fiction dedicated to the rehabilitation of the South and its Lost Cause. And, because Roxy's is essentially a revenge plot against her master, the novel taps into white fears of black retaliation over the steadfast denial and suppression of black civil rights in the wake of a long history of black/white intimacy. Consequently, since *Pudd'nhead Wilson* frames for a post-Reconstruction audience the antebellum story of Roxy's struggle to empower her child as a white man, the novel forcibly juxtaposes the disenfranchisement of black slaves before the war and the national reenactment of the same with regard to freedmen by the 1890s.

Rather than appealing to the comforting illusion of progress usually entailed by the traditional sectional reunion romance, Twain's novel implies a sense of national regression because of the sectional alliances forged by its eponymous white hero: when the New Englander David Wilson (renamed "Pudd'nhead" by his Southern neighbors) solves both Judge Driscoll's murder and Roxy's plot of substituting the slave for his master, Roxy is disempowered, Tom is enslaved, and the freely indulged practice of miscegenation that created white vulnerability in the first place is left unaddressed. Wilson's actions are not presented as an indication of his belief either in slavery or in black inferiority. Rather, his use of the science of fingerprinting ultimately to "fix" the incredibly complicated lines separating black from white (and therefore slave from free) identifies him as a new kind of American who combines Yankee ingenuity with a Southern ideology of racial control and exclusion. Like many Northerners after the war, Pudd'nhead Wilson is a willing participant in, rather than a dupe of, his Southern neighbors' system of racial governance; and in part this feature of the novel surely accounts for its 1894 book publication title, *The Tragedy of Pudd'nhead Wilson.*

The novel's play on skin color and its farcical indictments of the nostalgia for life before the Civil War suggest not only Twain's questioning of a white notion of social control, but also his critique of white knowledge about racial essence. At the precise moment when late-nineteenth-century antimiscegenation hysteria seemed to characterize the nature of black men by using the metaphor of the black rapist, the mulattos Roxy and Tom emerge from Twain's historical tale to literalize the blood ties between slave and master, black and white, attempting to confound the racial distinctions of blood and nature that whites had always assumed to exist. The chaos initiated by Tom and Roxy calls into question knowledge about the nature of whiteness, since Tom can masquerade for twenty years as a white man of property and standing.

Indeed, the effectiveness of Twain's critique surfaces when he exploits the moments of Tom's double masquerade as a white and a black man, as when Tom plays the "white" gentleman decked out in his Eastern clothes, lording it over the humbler residents of Dawson's Landing. In a move that unwittingly names Tom's racial identity but also lampoons the white heir's class position, the townspeople rebut with "the old deformed negro bell-ringer . . . tricked out in a flamboyant curtain-calico exaggeration of . . . [Tom's] finery, . . . imitating his fancy Eastern graces as well as he could" (*PW,* 85).[16] Without getting into the unanswerable and interminable question of Twain's own intention to argue for "nature" or "nurture," we can at least appreciate the juxtaposition of such moments as Twain's attempt to re-present Tom's frustrated queries about race and power ("Why were niggers *and* whites made? What crime did the uncreated first nigger commit that the curse of birth was decreed for him? And why is this awful difference made between white and black?" [*PW,* 117]) to white audiences at once terrified by the question of "the Negro problem" and overly secure in their belief that social repression was a responsible answer.

Twain also refuses to use white womanhood or rape as moments of mediation between races. Rather, through his emphasis on Roxy's white skin and her sexual accessibility as a slave concubine, Twain evacuates white women from the text and inserts instead a black woman as the desired object of white male lust—a reality far more damning to the arguments of white supremacy. Apparently given dignity as a "white" heroine and mother, the hale and robust Roxy functions to parody white female frailty: she is "up and around the same day" she gives birth, whereas her mistress "Mrs. Percy Driscoll died within the week" (*PW*, 58). The real white women of the novel either die or remain ineffectual to the point of invisibility, whereas Roxy, "majestic [in] form and stature" and with "the rosy glow of vigorous health in the cheeks," brown eyes, and "a heavy suit of fine soft hair" (*PW*, 64), becomes, at least in the initial stages of the novel, the ideal physical woman circulating as a sexual commodity, reproducer of property and caregiver within the aristocratic reaches of Dawson's Landing.

The substitution of an octoroon concubine for the white wife allows Twain to subvert the entwined Southern narratives of sex and rights traditionally used to describe the feared attack on anglo-saxon privilege through the rape of white womanhood, in order to expose the equally traditional but largely unacknowledged exercise of white power through the ownership and manipulation of the black body. As the tongue-in-cheek "white" female bearer of "black" children, Roxy is, as James M. Cox asserts, the final proof of not black, but white male lust: "in rearing the white man's legitimate children and giving birth to his illegitimate ones, Roxana bears what their honor cannot bear; the innocence in which they pride themselves is maintained by thrusting all guilt upon her."[17] At the same time, in the context of the novel's production, the disenfranchisement of Roxy and her offspring because of race points to white rather than black assaults on democracy, since Roxy's child must follow her condition.

Though he is no rapist, even the fickle, murdering, transvestite Tom Driscoll is pressed into service to poke further fun at a post-Reconstruction audience's anxieties over the unspoken terror of a black male/white female embrace implied and denied by Roxy's role as concubine. When Tom stalks Dawson's Landing "wearing a suit of his mother's clothing" (*PW*, 121), his transvestism shrinks the distance between the categories of black male and female, of mulatto and white, so that, when he cross-dresses as a white girl, the collapse of black male/white female bodies functions as a veiled reference to miscegenation.[18]

Enacting a scene of white discomfort, Twain plays this unspoken anxiety to the hilt when a voyeuristic Pudd'nhead Wilson stares into the upper-story window of the Driscoll home, only to see a mysterious white girl prancing around in Tom's bedroom: "It was a young woman—a young woman where properly no young woman belonged; for she was in Judge Driscoll's house, and in the bedroom over the Judge's private study or sitting-room. . . . Who could she be and how came she to be in young Tom Driscoll's room" (*PW*, 98). Wilson is left "fretting, and guessing, and puzzling over it, wondering who the shameless creature might be?" (*PW*, 122). Of course, Twain plays here with notions of the white woman as sexual object as well as sexual actor, implied in Pudd'nhead Wilson's unarticulated assumption that Tom has a white mistress—an assumption further complicated by Tom's hidden identity as a mulatto. Since the reader knows Tom to be black, is this finally Twain's attempt to argue for the absurdity of black men being necessarily a danger to white women, as well as to play mischievously with the suggestion of white female desire for the black (or just white female desire)? And is Tom's "white mistress" also a reference to the already shameless "white" woman who occupied the house earlier in the form of Roxy?

Twain clearly disempowers and makes fun of white supremacist discourses on rape and white womanhood (and by implication the arguments for the enforcement of segregation and black enfranchisement such discourses supported), and he calls into question the distance between "imitation" whites and "imitation" niggers; but what is the resulting judgment of his black characters? *Pudd'nhead Wilson* exposes white hypocrisy around sectional reunion and race, but the novel undermines its own indictments of racial difference by stumbling in the very act of defining the kind of alternatives to corrupt whiteness posed by the black mother and son, Roxy and Tom. Despite his ridicule of the novel's First Families of Virginia, with their archaic recall of the myth of Southern cavaliers in the midst of their hypocritical coupling with black slave women, Twain still maintains *Pudd'nhead Wilson* as a story about the conflict between black and white. Indeed, his use of the mulatto as metaphor implies not a merger of races, but their eternal conflict, here played out in the body of figures such as Tom Driscoll.[19] More accurately, the novel embodies a struggle between black and white families; and it is on the terrain of race and family that *Pudd'n-head Wilson* loses its battle with white supremacy over the structuring of American racial identity, property ownership, and civil rights.

Part of the problem of *Pudd'nhead Wilson* lies in its attack on sentimentality as a legitimating force for his black characters: after evacuating the kind of romantic racist sentimentality Americans were used to in Harriet Beecher Stowe's *Uncle Tom's Cabin*, Twain fails to provide readers with any alternative framing device through which to validate the black characters in the context of the novel's production—that of African American emancipation. With all their absurdity, weaknesses, and social culpability, the white Driscolls evoke sympathy as the dominant and defining notion of family in *Pudd'nhead Wilson*, because theirs is the legitimate traditional patriarchy. On the other hand, Roxy's makeshift family stands for a black domestic space that, whatever its historical realities, had in both antebellum Dawson's Landing and in Twain's 1894 America been denied full articulation as a comparable social unit. Indeed, as an offshoot of the black beast fantasy, "[a]cademic and popular sociology alike proclaimed the black family to be inherently or environmentally corrupt," its " 'failure' . . . a sign of racial degeneration" among African Americans.[20] In contrast to the besieged patriarch Judge Driscoll, Roxy emerges as a figure whose maternal identification is severely qualified by her sexualized representation: the stereotype of black male lust may have been replaced by an acknowledgment of white male desire, but the related stereotype of black female promiscuity is fully sustained. Thus, the very thing that makes Roxy workable as part of Twain's farce also makes her unworkable within the traditionally recognizable categories of legitimate womanhood—and motherhood—in late-nineteenth-century American middle-class culture.

At first Roxy emerges as a heroic slave mother because she is terrified that her child might be sold from her on the whim of her master: "Then she would gather it [the baby] to her heart and pour out her love upon it in a frenzy of kisses, moaning, crying and saying 'Dey sha'n't, oh, dey *sha'n't!* yo' po' mammy will kill you fust' " (*PW,* 69). This thought eventually leads to a plan to kill both herself and the child. Mulatto mothers driven to desperate acts for the sake of their children are of course central features of Stowe's novel (here think of Eliza and Cassy). But when the moment of truth approaches, Roxy becomes distracted with her "death-toilet": "She took off her handkerchief-turban and dressed her glossy wealth of hair 'like white folks'; she added some odds and ends of rather lurid ribbon and a spray of atrocious artificial flowers; finally she threw over her shoulders a fluffy thing called a 'cloud' in that day, which was of a blazing red complexion. Then she was ready for the tomb" (*PW,* 70). Twain's comedic tone here relies on the minstrel image of Roxy as the black buffoon hideously approximating whiteness, a move that deflates the very sentimentality he relies on in his initial modeling of Roxy as the novel's chief heroine and principal maternal figure. Eventually, the result is a lampooning of the black family that transforms Roxy into a figure of monstrous black femininity.

In placing her own child in the heir's cradle, Roxy takes "military advantage of the enemy" (*PW,* 67), and the text undermines its sympathetic representation by rendering her act as a decidedly black attempt at white genocide, since in the novel black emancipation and the assertion of black maternity in freedom is achieved by cutting off completely the Driscoll family line. Because her actions activate a plot of racial passing, white males are made to father "legitimate" mixed-race offspring, the figure of confusion who contaminates white domestic space. Just before the switch, Roxy addresses the white infant: "I hates yo' pappy; he ain't got no heart—for niggers he ain't, anyways. I hates him, en I could kill him!" (*PW,* 69). Her substitution of the black child for the white enables this threat to be carried out fully, so that in effect her unleashing of the mulatto "kills" off the Driscoll line because of its permanent transformation of the real Tom Driscoll into the slave Chambers.[21]

There are no white women to be raped in *Pudd'nhead Wilson,* and Tom, despite his resemblance to "the black beast of racial radicalism," is for all intents and purposes not a rapist.[22] Yet the idea of white domestic vulnerability is still present in the novel: Roxy's actions toward the Driscoll family cause her to achieve the same threat posed by the imaginary black rapist, a figure Roxy seems originally to negate in her function as a referent for white male lust. (And after all, the black rapist works as a white supremacist metaphor for the undesirable black citizen, since what Roxy seeks to gain for her descendants through her attempt to make Tom his master's equal, is freedom, economic opportunity, and the right to vote.) Her substitution of the real Tom Driscoll for the mulatto Chambers destroys the sanctity of the white family by contaminating white bloodlines, so she claims as victim not the white female but the white patriarchy. Percy Driscoll now has a black child forced on him, a child who, because of the crime of black infiltration, will be entitled to the economic and political power of whiteness. Meanwhile, the real Tom, now renamed "Chambers" by Roxy's action, is rendered as impotent as his father, since both are unable to reinstate whiteness, having been made helpless by Roxy's command over the white family.

The sustenance of her black family, then, must result in the destruction of the Driscolls' white privilege. Roxy's reward for switching the babies is not merely the protection of her son but the promise and confirmation that black emancipation will unleash a pattern of black revenge and violence. As the leader of a black family unit competing for power against and within the white home, Roxy engenders a black-run world fueled as much by anger against whites as by concern for black children: thus she is "happy and proud, for this was her son, her nigger son, lording it among the whites and securely avenging their crimes against her race" (*PW*, 82). Indeed, Roxy's protection of her son from slavery seems eventually to be in competition with her desire to act out her own revenge fantasies against her oppressors. Before she finally reveals the truth about his race, Roxy threatens to expose the "white" Tom's gambling debts to his uncle Judge Driscoll, a pronouncement that brings Tom to his knees:

> The heir of two centuries of unatoned insult and outrage looked down on him and seemed to drink in deep draughts of satisfaction. Then she said:
> "Fine nice young white gen'l'man kneelin' down to a nigger-wench! I'se wanted to see dat jes once befo' I'se called. Now, Gabr'el, blow de hawn, I'se ready . . . . Get up!" (*PW*, 109)

Within the terms set by the novel, to celebrate Roxy's heroism as a black slave mother is also to celebrate the demise of white America.

Roxy's status as heroic slave mother also gives way during the moments of the novel's considerable fascination with her penchant for aggression. Traditionally readers have focused on Tom's role as the black murderer in *Pudd'nhead Wilson*, locating within him Twain's ambivalent response to the stereotype of the post-Reconstruction black beast. But Roxy herself threatens to embody the image of black racial regression, often at the very moments of articulating her nobility as a beleaguered slave mother. We see a clear example of this phenomenon when she is sold down the river to an Arkansas planter by her son, to refinance his debt. Although badly treated on the Arkansas plantation, Roxy does not resist until she witnesses the overseer's assault on a black child who has befriended her. Then she attacks with fury: "All de hell-fire dat 'uz ever in my heart flame' up, an I snatch de stick outen his han' en laid him flat. He laid dah moanin' en cussin', en all out of his head" (*PW*, 183).

But in light of future episodes, Roxy's justifiably aggressive reaction heralds the transformation of her original role of despairing black mother when she next escapes to St. Louis to visit her treacherous son—in the disguise of an armed black man. Threatening to destroy the son who has betrayed her, Roxy, in blackface, her hair and female body masked by men's clothes, holds a knife to Tom: "I'se going to jam it into you" (*PW*, 190). This after she had once told Tom " 'Ain't you my chile? En does you know anything dat a mother won't do for her chile? Dey ain't nothing a white mother won't do for her chile' " (*PW*, 174). In their identities as mulattos, Tom and Roxy's masquerades as "white" men and women represent the false distance between black and white; however, their blackface transformation into armed black men, the era's most terrifying vision of race war, threatens the distance between their symbolic representation of race as fiction, and their symbolic representation of race (in their case, blackness) as the definition of separate natures.

In a moment highly ironic even for *Pudd'nhead Wilson*, Roxy accounts for her son's moral failings by observing that "It's the nigger in you" (*PW*, 157). Yet it is the "nigger" in her—cruel, debauched, petty, capable only of the status of "imitation" white, and offering no alternative in Dawson's Landing but chaos— that becomes most clearly defined within the novel. Thus, existing simultaneously with Twain's critique of white-initiated miscegenation is a vision of African American violence and moral degradation that, whatever its source and whatever its "retributive" function, continuously constructs blackness—and specifically, the black family—as a signifier of white death and as a vacuum in the absence of white civilization. That Chambers and the Driscoll family are in effect the white victims of a racial war initiated by Roxy brings into sharp focus Tom's alternate identity as the black monster effecting a vicious, senseless slaughter of his white adversary. Tom has internalized the worst of whiteness: as a slave master he becomes another Simon Legree, since Roxy as well as Chambers become "merely his chattel, . . . his convenience, his dog, his cringing and helpless slave, the humble and unresisting victim of his capricious temper and vicious nature" (*PW*, 81). Thus his role as white slaveholder merges with his role as black man, at once evoking white culpability yet cloaking it with the immediate need for white self-protection.

I opened this discussion of *Pudd'nhead Wilson* by orienting its critique of national fantasies of post–Civil War sectional reunion, and I want to close with a further meditation on how Twain's final surrender to the stereotype of the black as beast inflects his critique of sectional reunion. Despite the defeat of

Roxy and Tom by Pudd'nhead Wilson by the story's end, the novel entertains an alternate notion of postwar reunion as interracial in the figures of the dark and light twins Angelo and Luigi. In Italy, after their father ends up on the losing side of a national conflict, they share poverty and loss, survive slavery, and eventually emerge free to stand together as one identity, a kind of European version of the American South with blacks and whites idealized as brothers rather than enemies after the war. But finally this fantasy of (racial) bonding disintegrates in the face of Twain's inability to resist the more compelling fantasy of black undesirability:

> A native servant slipped into our room in the palace in the night, to kill us and steal the knife on account of the fortune encrusted on its sheath, without a doubt. Luigi [the "dark" twin] had it under his pillow; we were in bed together. . . . Luigi was awake . . . and slipped the knife out of the sheath and was ready and unembarrassed by hampering bed-clothes, for the weather was hot and we hadn't any. Suddenly the native rose at the bedside . . .; but Luigi grabbed his wrist, pulled him downward and drove his own knife into the man's neck. (*PW*, 131)

Luigi's empowerment with the knife is in no way a threat to Angelo, but in fact bonds the pair together. And they fight and expel an ambiguous, exotic black presence to maintain a fundamental fraternal unity. (The signification of blackness as evil is still intact, but purged somehow and externalized from the union of the dark- and fair-skinned twins). Interestingly, the bond between Luigi and Angelo is homoerotically charged and stereotyped as a harmonious contrast to the competition of masculinity that deteriorates into violence in the plot of the Dawson's Landing twins, Tom and Chambers.

A unit of interracial twins has no place in the real South, since Tom himself insults them as freaks, ridiculing them in public as a "human philopena" (*PW*, 135), and later casts Luigi's act of self-protection as "murder," thereby signifying that racial tension, not fraternal harmony, is the only option. When the murder of Judge Driscoll has been committed and the townspeople seem inclined to lynch Angelo and Luigi, Pudd'nhead Wilson's emergence to correct the chaotic results of black violence demonstrates that only African American repression (Tom is sold into slavery) can protect against black disorder. Angelo and Luigi protect themselves by murdering the black servant; Wilson sanctions that murder by fixing the black servant as inherently criminal.

By righting the problem within a court of law with the aid of scientific methods of detection, Pudd'nhead Wilson exposes blacks as pretechnocratic and destructive; after all, Roxy's plot and Tom's murder of Judge Driscoll are solved by the science of fingerprinting, while the criminals use the mere illusion of skin color to hide their misdeeds. They are therefore unfit for freedom. In the end, Tom is sold somewhere down the river—not killed, just reinserted into an unreformed system. Roxy is pardoned and pensioned once Tom, the source of her original power, is gone. Such punishments correct the social distortions created by Roxy's actions, since emasculating slavery will destroy Tom's male identity, and Roxy's new dependency on white male charity returns her to the servile position she occupied at the start of the novel. Perhaps a major source of crisis at the end of *Pudd'nhead Wilson*, then, lies not just in the inadequacy of Pudd'nhead Wilson's coup (he uncovers racial identity and also the hypocrisy of the community's racial double-standards) nor in the fact that the role properly belonging to the racial other has been completely displaced onto whites by vicious black intervention. Rather, in its endless undoing of moral categories, *Pudd'nhead Wilson* disallows any viable vision of blackness to stand in place of the images eventually codified by the forces that Twain set out to ridicule.

What the novel leaves us is the final, ironic image of Chambers, doomed to play out as his own identity the very fantasy of the docile, safely unassimilated Negro that seems never to have existed in Twain's reading of American race history: "The real heir suddenly found himself rich and free, but in a most embarrassing situation. He could neither read nor write, and his speech was the basest dialect of the negro quarter. His gait, his attitude, his gestures, his bearing, his laugh—all were vulgar and uncouth; his manners were the manners of a slave. Money and fine clothes could not mend these defects or cover them up, they only made them the more glaring and the more pathetic" (*PW*, 225).

### ON LOOKING BACK TO THE PRESENT: CHARLES W. CHESNUTT AND *THE MARROW OF TRADITION*

Published in 1901, some seven years after *Pudd'nhead Wilson*, Charles Chesnutt's *The Marrow of Tradition* articulates a plot that also depends on the metaphor of twinning as a means of exploring regional and racial (dis)union. Among other issues, the novel addresses the enabling contexts for black freedom, the powerful influence of the slave past on the domestic worlds of both blacks and whites, white self-destruction via hypocrisy over the family and miscegenation, and violence as a political tool perpetrated by blacks and whites alike. At the same time, Chesnutt argues for a new kind of post–Civil War black/white mutual dependency that must be achieved for Southern survival: not the kind of white paternalism and black subservience advocated by conservative racists, but a more daring acknowledgment of blacks' capacity for improvement and advancement as equal citizens, and of the crucial economic, social, and political role they might play in the advancement of the South.

As the historical focus of the novel, the Wilmington riot offers an apt example of how the economic, racial, and sexual politics of the post-Reconstruction era were intertwined in the struggle for political power. On November 10, 1898, just after Election Day, a thousand angry white supremacists went on a rampage that claimed the lives of eleven of Wilmington's black residents and destroyed much black-owned property. Attracting whites from all social classes, the riot had been organized as a public retaliation for black participation in the political life of the city. Though African Americans made up roughly 56 percent of the city's population, as Richard Yarborough puts it, "the 'Negro Domination' of Wilmington consisted of a Collector of Customs, three aldermen out of ten, two fire companies, one of five members of the Board of Audit and Finance, two lot inspectors, and a number of police officers and magistrates. In other words, as any objective observer could see, blacks scarcely controlled the city's political life."[23] Also, as Yarborough and other scholars have stressed, the riot must be read against the backdrop of a Southern white press's continual sensationalizing of the "problem" of miscegenation and the threat of black rape. Indeed, one of the riot's contributing factors had been the excessive publicity given to a verbal skirmish between Wilmington's Alexander Manly and Georgia's Rebecca Latimer Felton. A white feminist and the wife of a Georgia senator, Felton had claimed that only an increase in lynching ("a thousand times a week if necessary") would ensure the protection of rural white women from black attack; Manly, the leading black journalist of Wilmington, responded that white females might actually be attracted to black men and not desire such protection. This assertion cost him his newspaper and very nearly his life, as his was the first black-owned building razed in Wilmington on the day of the violence.[24] Though not centrally concerned with the Manly–Felton exchange, the plot of *The Marrow of Tradition* does incorporate the story and offers support for the outspoken black journalist.

*The Marrow of Tradition* was written with a view to reforming black social conditions by addressing white racial attitudes. As early as 1880, when he first entered professional life as a young mulatto schoolteacher in his family seat of Fayettesville, North Carolina, Chesnutt had linked an ambition to become a commercially successful writer with a missionary ideal to educate white Americans about the reality of race relations. As a writer, Chesnutt surmised that he would work

> not so much [for] the elevation of the colored people as [for] the elevation of the whites,—for I consider the unjust spirit of caste which is so insidious as to pervade a whole nation . . . a barrier to the moral progress of the American people; and I would be one of the first to head a determined, organized crusade against it. Not a fierce indiscriminate onslaught; not an appeal to force, for this is something that force can but slightly affect; but a moral revolution which must be brought about in a different manner.[25]

In *The Marrow of Tradition* Chesnutt fuses literary sophistication with a moral activism against white racial violence, but the novel's severe indictment of whites could hardly have won him a wide mainstream audience; indeed, one of the targets of *The Marrow of Tradition* is the fiction of Anglo-Saxonism as the epitome of morality and civilization. Unlike *Pudd'nhead Wilson*, however, *The Marrow of Tradition* does not threaten the replacement of one race by the other; rather, in his refashioning of contemporary theories of eugenics, Chesnutt argues that the forces of racial survival point to the possibility of racial union by the early twentieth century.

Chesnutt's analyses of reunion, violence, miscegenation, and the family rest on a very careful bifurcation of the novel into closely aligned political and domestic plots. In the political plot, the riot's organizers—newspaper editor and Southern aristocrat Major Carteret, General Belmont, and the ill-bred, nouveau riche Captain McBane—are pitted against Mr. Delamere, the aging, ineffectual white aristocrat who belongs to a lost generation of honorable and fair-minded white men, and Dr. William Miller, the ambitious, rich, highly talented mulatto who advocates nonviolence. Also counterpoised against the white supremacists is the dark-skinned black laborer Josh Greene, who is tired of ill-treatment and disfranchisement at the hands of whites and does advocate violence, but only as a means of self-defense. Racial animosity dominates the domestic plot as well, since Major Carteret's wife Olivia nurses an intense resentment toward Dr. Miller's wife Janet. Olivia's mulatto half-sister and near twin, Janet is the product of a secret Reconstruction-era marriage between Olivia's widowed father Sam Merkell and his mulatto housekeeper Julia Brown. Her presence in the novel bespeaks the endurance of traditional racial ties bred in the blood and articulated at the core of black/white domestic relations— ties that Carteret and his associates believe they can eradicate through violent intimidation and political disenfranchisement.

According to John Edgar Wideman, in *The Marrow of Tradition* "Chesnutt wishes to render on a broad canvas a panoramic view of Southern society," since "the truth of the South can be encompassed only by a comprehensive overview that includes all classes, both races, and a variety of perspectives— social, economic and political."[26] The crucial element missing from Wideman's list, but overwhelmingly present in *The Marrow of Tradition*, is of course Chesnutt's examination of the role of gender in the structuring and execution of group ambitions. Indeed, Chesnutt's own uses of gender in his representational vocabulary point to his complex engagement with turn-of-the-century white supremacist visions of victim and aggressor, masculine heroism, and the sanctity of womanhood. Perhaps the most striking (and one of the least addressed) feature of *The Marrow of Tradition* is Chesnutt's foregrounding of white supremacy as a set of social beliefs that both objectify white women and demand their necessary participation as social actors in defense of their race. Consequently, for Chesnutt, the white exercise of power is a complex process spread over a broad field of social and political intercourse.

When blacks "intrude" on the white domestic world of the novel, they surface not as an independent threat to white female virtue but in the more indicting context of white desire. Early in the novel, Olivia's aunt Polly Ochiltree recounts her struggle to wrest control of the late Sam Merkell's estate from his mulatto second wife (and former housekeeper) Julia Brown: " 'When your father died, I turned the mother and child [ Julia Brown and Janet] out into the street. The mother died and went to—the place provided for such as she. If I hadn't been just in time, Olivia, they would have turned you out. I saved the property for you and your son! You can thank me for it all!' " (*MT*, 129).[27] Paradoxically Mrs. Ochiltree's story of legitimation is really the narration of a theft, the result of conflicting policies over the posture of masters to former slaves, since the envelope of papers Polly Ochiltree removes from Merkell's room contains the Reconstruction-era marriage certificate proving his legal ties to Julia Brown, as well as a will naming Olivia and Merkell's second, black family as beneficiaries. In a tone contemptuous of Merkell's betrayal of his race (and his rejection of her as a possible mate), Mrs. Ochiltree condemns her brother-in-law's miscegenation and his willingness to put his entire ancestral line and property at risk by an act for which he is "stricken unto death by a hand of a just God, as a punishment for his sins" (*MT*, 134).

In the absence of a responsible white patriarch, Mrs. Ochiltree acts to right the chaos initiated by Merkell, and she describes a scene of retribution against Merkell's black family that, by Ochiltree's own memory and narration, approximates a physical attack on the black woman. When Mrs. Ochiltree finds Julia vainly searching for the will after her husband's death, she accuses her of trying "to strip the house." Describing Julia Brown as " 'a wild beast at bay' " (*MT*, 136) Ochiltree savagely taunts her for her inability to prove her marriage:

> "She was hit so hard that she trembled and sank into a chair. But I had no mercy . . . !
> 'Stand up,' I ordered. 'Do not dare to sit down in my presence. I have you on the hip, my lady, and will teach you your place.'
> She struggled to her feet. . . . I could have killed her, Olivia! She had been my father's slave; if it had been before the war, I would have had her whipped to death." (*MT*, 137–38)

While the "violent" clash between Ochiltree and Brown is plainly figurative, it is the first scene of white aggression in the novel, and it bears out Chesnutt's recasting of white violence as a struggle over property and the power shifts brought on by Emancipation. Mindful of white supremacist sensationalizing of the spectacle of violated white womanhood as proof of the devastating results of black citizenship, Chesnutt follows the argument that indeed the domestic sphere is the real battleground over race and rights; but here it is the white woman Polly Ochiltree who violates Julia's home to achieve black dispossession. At the same time, Chesnutt figures the problem of interracial sexual contact as not the black rape of white women, but the threat of consensual marriage between whites and blacks. In the case of white male desire, marriages are denied; in the case of white female desire, according to Wellington's *Afro-American Banner,* the result is the lynching of black men "for voluntary acts" against which "neither nature nor religion . . . interposed any insurmountable barrier" (*MT,* 85). The *Banner's* protest is of course Chesnutt's invocation of Manly's retort to Felton, and he vindicates Manly by having the white suprema-cist Captain McBane admit the real reason for the offensiveness of such state-ments: "Truth or not, no damn nigger has any right to say it" (*MT,* 86).

The story of Samuel Merkell and Julia Brown's consensual union allows Chesnutt to evacuate from the text the notion of victimized white womanhood, the idea of rape, and (therefore) the stereotype of black male criminality. In-stead, Chesnutt presents the targeting of a feminized *black* family constituted by the legitimate widow Julia Brown Merkell and her infant daughter, a situa-tion that deglamorizes considerably the white supremacist idea of white vio-lence as a heroic enterprise against alleged black savagery. On the other hand, Ochiltree is transformed into a heavily ironic female symbol of Southern white values. Whereas, despite Twain's failures in *Pudd'nhead Wilson,* the figure of Roxy ultimately challenges Twain's audience to reevaluate plantation fiction myths about black contentment during slavery, Polly Ochiltree in *The Marrow of Tradition* challenges the white supremacist representation of white women as a national ideal of womanhood, and indeed implicates white women in a long tradition of interracial violence preceding Emancipation. And as a figure look-ing beyond Reconstruction, Ochiltree embodies her race's journey as a process of moral degradation that begins under the power structure of slavery.[28] By transmitting her story to Olivia, Polly Ochiltree ensures a dual legacy to her niece: illegally gained property and a model of white womanhood fully anti-thetical to the stated goals of middle-class femininity. Not surprisingly, then, when her aunt is brutally robbed and murdered, Olivia—who begins the novel in such a state of nervous and physical delicacy that she barely survives child-birth—rushes into Mrs. Ochiltree's room, coolly stepping around her aunt's body to retrieve the marriage certificate and will originally stolen from Julia Brown.[29]

The ties of blood and tradition that Wellington's white men attempt to sup-press through the riot, continually surface in the domestic drama surrounding the Merkell-Brown family history. In an effort to preserve the wealth and social standing of her family, Olivia eventually destroys the documents. But as she soon realizes, to fly in the face of Julia Brown's legitimate position as a wife is also in part to attack the very legitimacy and value of her own social role:

A marriage certificate, rightfully procured, was scarcely less solemn . . . than the Bible itself. Her own she cherished as the apple of her eye. It was evidence of her wifehood, the seal of her child's legitimacy, her patent of nobility,—the token of her own and her child's claim to social place and consideration.   (*MT,* 263)

As Eric J. Sundquist argues, "Olivia Carteret must ignore the law in order to preserve her untainted legacy from Janet Miller."[30] Specifically she defies the pronouncements of her own father and thereby exemplifies a white struggle to come to terms with the meaning of Emancipation and the question of black and white equality under civil law, rather than any notion of the laws of eugenics and unbridgeable racial difference. *The Marrow of Tradition's* domestic plot thus mirrors the basic issues at stake in the public sphere: pride, property, the fictions of race that criminalize blacks and shield whites from their own moral confusion, and the legitimacy of black claims to citizenship and self-determination.

Olivia's struggle with the social facts behind black/white social relations in the South and with the resulting crisis in legitimization of white authority is matched by her husband's struggle with the contradiction of his charge of black rape as the prime motivation for organizing the riot in Wellington. Just as the outbreak of the real-life Wilmington riot had been preceded by the white press's fomenting of anxiety over miscegenation, Wellington's violence is preceded by similar sensationalizing—and distortion—of the facts around a supposed assault of a white woman. The victim is none other than Polly Ochiltree: like Judge Driscoll in *Pudd'nhead Wilson,* Ochiltree is found dead one morning, with a wound to her head and her money chest broken open. The news spreads quickly; and immediately Sandy, the black servant of the old white cavalier Mr. Delamere, is arrested for the crime, since eyewitnesses report seeing a similarly dressed black man approach and then leave the Ochiltree home at around the time of the murder. By the time word of Ochiltree's murder reaches Carteret's offices, the charge has already been exaggerated to include rape: "He [Sandy] has assaulted and murdered a white woman—an example should be made of him" (*MT,* 181). Not surprisingly, when the murder investigation opens, a lynch mob stands ready to execute Sandy, while Carteret explains the "rape" as one more example of a degenerating black population which cannot survive outside slavery's disciplinary influence: "Left to his own degraded ancestral instincts, Sandy had begun to deteriorate, and a rapid decline had culminated in this robbery and murder,—and who knew what other horror? The criminal was a negro, the victim a white woman;—it was only reasonable to expect the worse" (*MT,* 181–82).

But the killer is actually Tom Delamere, grandson of Mr. Delamere, scion of one of the best white families of the town, suitor to Carteret's younger sister,

and Mrs. Ochiltree's own nephew. Like Tom Driscoll in *Pudd'nhead Wilson,*
Tom Delamere had killed and robbed to pay off gambling debts, and he deliberately commits the murder in blackface to throw the blame on Sandy. Precisely
because the criminal is white Tom Delamere posing in blackface, Chesnutt uses
the metaphor of minstrelsy to emphasize white rather than black perversion.
In *Pudd'nhead Wilson* the mulatto Tom Driscoll's disguise in blackface serves
to remind the reader of his "true" nature as a black man; but Tom Delamere's
blackface points to a complicated indictment of whites on the very terms of
racial difference and disintegration they reserve for blacks. In regard to Tom
Delamere, Chesnutt turns Carteret's rhetoric of evolutionary rise and fall
against whites themselves: "If . . . it took three or four generations to make a
gentleman, and as many more to complete the curve and return to the base
from which it started, Tom Delamere belonged somewhere at the downward
slant, with large possibilities for further decline. . . . Tom was merely the
shadow without the substance, the empty husk without the grain" (*MT,* 95–
96).[31]

The revelation that the killer is actually Tom Delamere deals a particularly
devastating blow to Carteret's elevation of the white race instinct, since his lie
about rape would now make the crime against Mrs. Ochiltree also one of incest. In an attempt at justice, Carteret successfully advocates for the release of
Sandy, but he refuses to announce the real murderer's identity or to retract his
charge of black rape, since "the success of the impending 'revolution,' . . .
depended in large measure upon the maintenance of their race prestige, which
would be injured in the eyes of the world by such a fiasco" (*MT,* 228). Thus,
while Carteret at first set out to prove "that drastic efforts were necessary to
protect the white women of the South against brutal, lascivious and murderous
assaults at the hands of negro men" (MT, 185), he achieves success on dubious
terms that require an unredressed sacrifice of a white woman at the hands of
her own race.

This threatened inward collapse among Wellington's white elite is mirrored
in the chaos displayed by the rest of the city's white population. Even the venerable Mr. Delamere recognizes that, as a restoration of "order," the proposed
lynching of Sandy after Mrs. Ochiltree's assault is in fact merely "a pretext for
turning the whole white population into a mob of primitive savages" who are
hoping to dance "in hellish glee around the mangled body of a man who has
never been tried for a crime" (*MT,* 212). Indeed, though the lynching of Sandy
is averted, the preparation for the execution that might have been points to the
development of increasingly gruesome social rituals in Wellington that bind
whites together across classes and generations: "the railroads would run excur-
sions from neighboring towns to bring spectators to the scene; . . . the burning was to take place early in the evening, so that the children [brought to see
the execution] might not be kept up beyond their usual bedtime" (*MT,* 219).

The desire for bloodletting aroused by Ochiltree's murder is finally satiated during the riot, when what was supposed to be an organized coup by armed white men deteriorates into a general slaughter of blacks performed by the lower classes. Thus the fiction of marauding black murderers is replaced by the reality of marauding white ones. These white citizens of Wellington later come to realize their mistakes ("Elaborate explanations were afterwards given for these murders, which were said, perhaps truthfully, not to have been premeditated, and many regrets were expressed" [*MT,* 290]), but without an awareness of themselves as the race in need of restraint.

This representation of white race instinct as the impulse toward social chaos rather than the social revolution imagined by white supremacists, functions as Chesnutt's larger attempt to sketch Southern whites as heavily compromised by their adherence to race-based appeals to solidarity. If order is to be reestablished, Chesnutt suggests it must arise from a new class of Southerner. Carteret has already identified the need for new alliances, but he wrongly assumes that only those animated by racial interest are feasible. The last remaining representatives of an increasingly impotent class of Southern aristocrats, Carteret and his associate General Belmont have been forced to join forces with the wealthy but ill-bred Captain McBane, a man whose "strength, energy and unscrupulousness" is vital for their organization of the riot (*MT,* 32). Carteret's unease over his links with the crude McBane suggests that "the purity and prestige" (*MT,* 72) of the aristocrat's class-bound status is already put at risk in a postwar world where, according to one of the novel's black characters, McBane "ain't nothin' but po' w'ite trash nohow . . . . 'Pears ter me de bottom rail is gittin' mighty close to de top" (*MT,* 36).

In fact, both Miller and McBane represent a shift in class and power bases in the wake of black emancipation. Carteret's particular hatred for middle-class blacks like Miller rests not just on racial animosity or on the fact of Janet's birth, but on Miller's economic advancement. The son of a frugal black stevedore, the European-educated Miller runs his own hospital and lives in what was once the Carteret family mansion. The son of an overseer, McBane was a member of the early Ku Klux Klan who achieves his social rise by contracting black convict labor after the Civil War. But precisely because he reinstitutes de facto slavery through institutions like the convict lease system, McBane represents a return to antebellum racial values and he must be disqualified as an inheritor of Chesnutt's ideal post-Reconstruction South. Eventually McBane leads his own band of poor whites during the riot and perpetrates the destruction of Miller's hospital—the final example of a region gone mad over racial misalliances.

In contrast to proponents of a race-based model of regional reunion, Chesnutt advocates alliances based on new kinds of class interests. Because of their industry and community values, the black middle-class population of Wellington, led by Miller, represents an alternative route for progress in the South. Indeed, the Millers represent a powerful alternative to the racist McBane, as well as a challenge to white supremacist arguments for racial separation. As mulattos they are visible acknowledgments of the region's traditions of interracial sex under slavery, but they also embody the possibility of an "erasure of the marker of color, the semiotic of skin, historically distinguishing between the civilized and the uncivilized, the godly and the unregenerate." [32]

Though there is a clear racial solidarity among most of the novel's African American characters, modern readers have often been disturbed by the lines of separation based on color: educated black characters—specifically mulattos like Miller and Janet, who signify the mixing of races Chesnutt favored—move upward from their humble origins, while fully black, lower-class characters like Sandy and the old Mammy Jane, the Carteret family retainer, do not. In other words, one group (the mulatto middle class) embodies progress for the race, as reflected in their way of life, while the other (darker-skinned ex-slaves who cannot move out of their old roles) represents the relationships of the past, which will not survive into the twentieth century. When the dust settles, the only possible alliance must be between the white elite (the Carterets) and the light-skinned black elite (the Millers). [33]

The novel's argument for this alternative to white supremacy is finally given impetus when Carteret himself comes to recognize that, while he can incite a riot, his assumed alliance of race with the other white classes in Wellington, does not enable him to control events ("I meant to keep them [the blacks] in their place,—I did not intend wholesale murder and arson" [MT, 305]). Eventually the effect is the threat of mutual destruction for whites and blacks: on the one hand, Miller's child is killed by a stray bullet; on the other, Carteret's infant child is abandoned by his black caretakers as they flee in fear for their lives, and he develops a life-threatening case of croup. The white child's only hope is a tracheotomy, and predictably only Miller is skilled enough to perform the operation. The Carterets object to Miller because of his race and his wife's relationship with the Merkell family, but if they want to save their race through their dangerously ill infant, they have to confront the widespread destructiveness of their prejudice and recognize, as one white friend of Miller's says, "Your race must come up or drag ours down" (MT, 51). As one would expect, the novel ends with Miller's arrival to the Carteret house just in time to save the white child.

But while Chesnutt suggests that the problem of racial harmony in the South can be achieved through black/white middle-class reunion, he also simultaneously challenges his white audience to reconsider the post-Reconstruction black man as the heroic ideal. Aware of the traditional role of violence as a socially acceptable means of solidifying masculine identity, Chesnutt offers two alternative black male responses to the riot, encoding them in class terms: on the one hand, passive endurance in the mode of Booker T. Washington, which Miller advocates; on the other, armed resistance, which is the strategy followed by the working-class, dark-skinned Josh Green. The "underdog" Green's method of violent self-defense addresses the problem of enforcing justice in a world gone mad: "De w'ite folks are killin' de niggers, an' we ain' gwine ter stan' up an' be shot down like dogs. We're gwine ter defen' ou' lives, an' we ain' gwine ter run away f'm no place were we've got a right to be; an' woe be ter de w'ite man w'at lays han's on us!" (*MT,* 281). As a complicated figure whose final adherence to defensive violence is both attractive and repulsive, Josh is brave and heroic— a born leader who is nevertheless foolhardy, since whites have firepower and organization on their side. In the end he does kill McBane, but he and his followers are themselves killed in the riot. Still, as Eric J. Sundquist argues, Josh is sketched along the lines of a black folk hero, which suggests Chesnutt's validation of and admiration for the kind of stance Josh employs.[34]

In contrast to Josh's defensive aggression, the ultimate goal of Miller's pragmatic passive resistance lies in winning time and saving black lives. However, his own repudiation of violence is itself never clear: after turning away from Josh's call to lead a band of blacks in their defense against the mob, Miller is "conscious of a distinct feeling of shame and envy that he, too, did not feel impelled to throw his life away in hopeless struggle" (*MT,* 285). This very phrase is full of ambivalence and confusion, since to engage in Josh's style of resistance would mean Miller could claim his right to manhood. Despite the fact that, for him, "[r]esistance only makes the matter worse" (*MT,* 295), Miller's response to and preoccupation with the issue of black violence itself do not constitute a repudiation of the latter, but rather express a concern for the problem of its representation:

> The qualities which in a white man would win the applause of the world would in a negro be taken as the marks of savagery. So thoroughly diseased was public opinion in matters of race that the negro who died for the common rights of humanity might look for no meed of admiration or glory. At the same time, in the white man's eyes, a negro's courage would be mere desperation; his love of liberty, a mere animal dislike of restraint . . . . Or if forced to admire, they [the whites] would none the less repress. They would applaud his courage while they stretched his neck, or carried off fragments of his mangled body as souvenirs, in much the same manner that savages preserve the scalp. (*MT,* 295–96)

Such a statement differentiates between two forms of violence: on the one hand, the wanton destruction whites engage in under the name of preserving American democracy from the black peril, which points to their own racial regression to the same state of savagery whites claimed throughout American history that "lesser" peoples of color have occupied; and on the other an ennobling, idealized violence in a justified cause. Within the racial climate of the United States, where such distinctions are continually being denied and distorted especially in the case of black men, Chesnutt may be doubting the very usefulness of violence itself.

As Chesnutt says at one point, "[t]here never was, on the continent of America, a successful slave revolt," because whites were too strong. Nevertheless, the slave was continuously watchful of the slaveholder, who was never "quite free from the fear that there might be one" (*MT*, 276). In Josh and Miller, respectively, Chesnutt represents the real possibility of a righteous male violence in the turn-of-the-century struggle for racial power and the repudiation of that violence in favor of racial harmony. Such a dual strategy allows Chesnutt simultaneously to affirm, in the words of Sutton Griggs, the possibility of "far off sounds of awakened negroes coming to ask for liberty, and if refused, to slay or be slain," and also to stage a black male show of magnanimity that figures African American masculinity as the American ideal governed by both virile nobility and progressive pragmatism.[35]

Importantly, Chesnutt's ultimate validation of black masculinity occurs not just in the context of Wellington's black community but in a final scene of confrontation with white womanhood as well, on the occasion of the Carterets' appeal to Miller to save their child. At first when Carteret humbly applies to Miller for his aid, the justifiably angry mulatto doctor refuses to help: "There lies *my* only child, laid low by a stray bullet in this riot which you and your paper fomented; struck down as much by your hand as though you had held the weapon with which his life was taken! . . . I cannot go with you. There is a just God in heaven!—as you have sown, so may you reap!" (*MT*, 320). Miller's reaction is understandable, but his refusal to save a life in effect continues the violence of the race riot. Only when Olivia herself goes to the Miller house and makes an appeal to Janet's empathy as a mother and possibly as a sister does the tide turn in their favor.

As Olivia attempts to gain entrance to the Miller house, having come "like a wild thing" (*MT*, 322) to plead for her child's life, her meeting with Miller becomes a dramatic rewriting of Carteret's (and later Dixon's) worst nightmare. When she arrives at the door, Miller sees "[a] lady . . . so near the image of his own wife, . . . that for a moment he was well-nigh startled" (*MT*, 323): "She wore a loose wrapper, which clothed her like the drapery of a statue. Her long dark hair, the counterpart of his wife's, had fallen down, and hung disheveled about her shoulders. There was blood upon her knuckles, where she had beaten with them upon the door" (*MT*, 323). Olivia—the supposed symbol of racial purity—is indistinguishable from black, in effect "negroized" because of white- rather than black-authored miscegenation. Her female vulnerability and her resemblance to Janet weaken Miller's resistance, and he lets her enter. Once inside the door, she clings to Miller: "with a sudden revulsion of feeling, she had thrown herself at his feet,—at the feet of a negro, this proud woman,—and was clasping his knees wildly" (*MT*, 324). The erotic suggestions of Olivia's posture of abjection in this scene must have made at least some of Chesnutt's white readers cringe, and at this point one cannot help but be reminded of Alexander Manly's suggestion that white women of a refined class often seek out black men of their own accord. Of course for Olivia and Miller, there is no hint of a sexual attraction, yet the scene's construction mimics an imagined scene of either interracial rape or, if both sides are willing, interracial sex. Instead Chesnutt alters the ideological meaning of the moment to insist on white social acceptance of blacks, specifically black masculinity, undermining the image of the African American male as it would have traditionally been used. At the same time, Chesnutt's presentation of Olivia in such a posture with such a plea constructs whites as the victims of their own disastrous schemes, even as his presentation empowers the black man of science, fairness, and restraint to be the ultimate savior of Wellington's ruling class. (In a sense Miller is a new black version of Pudd'nhead Wilson, too, since his success de-centers the white male authority that seeks to separate races: the black male intellectual is now offered the opportunity to articulate an even stronger tie between the town's blacks and whites.)

But according to Chesnutt, the task of reconciliation must also lie with whites themselves, and he articulates this desire by having white womanhood—until now a negative example of white moral action—symbolize this desired move to racial unity. Not only does Olivia prostrate herself before Miller, but in a desperate attempt to get him to save her son, she willingly reconciles with Janet, claiming kin and shared blood: "Listen, sister! . . . You *are* my lawful sister. My father was married to your mother. You are entitled to his name and half his estate" (*MT*, 327). This acknowledgment of kinship by a white woman undercuts the theoretical underpinnings of white supremacy in the political plot, returns whites (especially white women) to the path of morality, and saves the race as a whole. All this is achieved by having the white woman, the figure who must always be hidden away from the black presence, doing the very thing (consorting with and acknowledging the equality of and connection to blacks) that had been pronounced immoral and unthinkable by white racists. Thus the possibility of Olivia's "submission" to a black man is tantalizingly suggested, then undercut and replaced by her submission before the figure of Janet. In melodramatic fashion, Janet stands like a female god dispensing justice by the body of her dead child, pouring out a torrent of abuse and well-deserved condemnation on the white sister who earlier tried to cheat her out of an inheritance: "I throw you back your father's name, your father's wealth, your sisterly recognition. . . . But that you may know that a woman may be foully wronged, and yet may have a heart to feel, even for one who has injured her, you have your child's life, if my husband can save it" (*MT*, 329).

Clearly, by the end of *The Marrow of Tradition*, Janet Miller embodies the true ideal of womanhood, and her confrontation with Olivia reverses the initial degradation suffered by her mother at the hand of Polly Ochiltree. A largely silent figure throughout the novel, Janet is a class-bound figure of patience and sisterly love, in contrast to the white, aristocratic Olivia's violent animosity. As the more virtuous sister, despite her racial and class origins, Julia sends her husband to help Carteret, even though her child has died as a result of Carteret's racist agitation. Julia's action completes the novel's moral shift from white to black middle-class values of reconciliation and community service. The feminization of whiteness, both in the body of Olivia and in the body of her child, and their utter dependence on Miller's skill reinstate black masculinity with a nobility that cannot be captured by violent black resistance.

Janet's speech to her sister is a curious melding of an almost masculine nationalistic declaration of black independence with a feminine rhetoric of sentimentalism: her speech echoes the vehement anger and call for justice echoed in both Miller and Josh's philosophies, but her feelings are tempered by the life-affirming feminine mercy of the new embodiment of true womanhood, the black middle-class woman. Thus Janet's speech affirms and acknowledges the ever-present theme of black male anger in the novel; at the same time, such male anger is tempered by a complementary black female outpouring that breaks the earlier silence of Julia Brown in the face of Polly Ochiltree's abuses, but stops short of punishing with an eye for an eye. Instead, Janet provides the moral direction for her husband, sending him off to save the Carteret child. At the end of *The Marrow of Tradition*, Janet embodies a new middle-class black philosophy of resistance that validates black men (Miller) who endorse nonviolence, within a framework of moral opposition to white corruption.

Despite Chesnutt's initial hopes for the effects of his novel, *The Marrow of Tradition* itself proved too controversial in its indictment of white racism. When the hitherto supportive William Dean Howells reviewed the novel in 1901, he declared rather mournfully that "[t]he book is, in fact, bitter, bitter. There is no reason in history why it should not be so, if wrong is to be repaid with hate, and yet it would be better if it was not so bitter." Ironically, in 1902, both *The Marrow of Tradition* and Dixon's *The Leopard's Spots* were reviewed in the *Independent*, and considered "equally bad," with Chesnutt and Dixon being attacked for their use of "history as a war cry to the prejudices of their own people," though perhaps Chesnutt gets the worst of it, when the reviewer calls him "a negro . . . with the bloodthirsty imagination of an outraged man."[36]

Both *Pudd'nhead Wilson* and *The Marrow of Tradition* offer radical and complex indictments of post-Reconstruction white supremacy, using the very terms that radical racists erected for their arguments. In their respective novels, Twain and Chesnutt challenge the fantasy of white male heroism produced in the context of the black rapist: for both writers, the descendents of the First Families of the South have to confront the increasingly national hysteria over black rape as primarily the result of a projected anxiety over their own long-established practice of miscegenation, a context that makes a mockery of any attempt to articulate white racial reunion.

The problem to which *Pudd'nhead Wilson* can only gesture, however, is that of the role and place of African Americans outside slavery: by his use of the revengeful mulattos Roxy and Tom, Twain repudiates the model of the black rapist as the final expression of aberrant black citizenship; but he does little to theorize the nature of alternative black articulations beyond the threat of a veritable explosion of black anger in the face of disenfranchisement. Relying on the realist novel instead of the more limited dimensions of farce, Chesnutt goes a step beyond Twain in resurrecting black domesticity to achieve a recuperation of black men and women within the acceptable terms of a Victorian middle-class differentiation of gender. The result is an attempt to capture the dimension of black anger that so overwhelms the characterizations of *Pudd'nhead Wilson*, while at the same time suggesting that anger might fuel a progressive racial revolution rather than precipitate a race war.

And yet to simply read *The Marrow of Tradition* as an improved version of *Pudd'nhead Wilson* is to miss the ironic dilemma of Chesnutt's own inescapable adherence to the values of a male heroism built upon a certain pattern of female silencing. While Miller and Josh both suffer at the hands of white supremacists, by the end of the novel they achieve a heroic status. They stand in contrast to the silent, passive Julia Brown, the victim of Sam Merkell's cowardice and Polly Ochiltree's cruelty, who is destined to die in obscurity, and in whom Chesnutt at best only vaguely suggests the special kind of suffering under white supremacy that black women might experience. One might argue that Julia is refigured in her daughter Janet Miller, but Janet, who is also generally silent until the end of *The Marrow of Tradition*, ultimately symbolizes a black communal articulation of both anger and mercy, rather than a specifically black female story of recuperation. To put it another way, Janet is made to embody the emotions of a black patriarchal community; but through her embodiment, the specific ways in which responses to racial violence might be gendered are never fully addressed.

Then there is Polly Ochiltree, whose ultimate service to her race—and to Chesnutt—comes when she is either defeminized or her corpse brutalized. Like the white women in Dixon's fiction, Polly is worth more dead than alive. In white supremacist fiction, the figure of the assaulted white woman functions as a metaphor for the imagined political rape of the white home and the white nation; in this fiction, the figure of the white victim also suggests a containment of white female desire (white women who are not careful of their companions get raped) and a transformation of the unstable white female body into a distanced expression of white vulnerability, around which white men can unite and be recuperated through an avenging violence against blacks.

Chesnutt uses the murder of Polly by her nephew Tom Delamere to expose the false rationalizations behind lynching and mob violence in retaliation for alleged black rape. However, he achieves this critique through the enactment of the literal murder and figurative rape of white women in the novel. This suggests that, like white supremacist novelist Thomas Dixon, Chesnutt still has to use the metaphor of violated white womanhood to talk about masculine action. The metaphor is sustained throughout the novel, as from Polly Ochiltree we move to the prostrate Olivia, at once the mother of her race and the potentially seductive white woman, still the space of male resurrection and still in need of rescue by someone—if not a white man then certainly a black one.

In white supremacist ideology, the white female is merely transformed into essentially a figurative space where white men can slay the black beast to protect their racial integrity. Why, within Chesnutt's exposé of white supremacy, is there no revision of this construction of the white woman? In white supremacist thinking black women are invisible and their experience of lynching and rape completely denied. Why, within Chesnutt's revised representation of the new South, are black women still only barely visible as virtuous figureheads? By the end of The Marrow of Tradition, women never rise above the surface of what is essentially a narrative closely determined by a masculine, interracial struggle over political rights: black and white men, though they squarely oppose each other, employ the same gendered vocabulary to dramatize their cause, a vocabulary that is ultimately based on a denial of black and white female subjectivity. Chesnutt is clearly no white supremacist; yet his construction of the role of the feminine within the turn-of-the-century war over black rights closely approximates the very racist ideology he desperately wants to demolish. Even Chesnutt's ultimate redemption of blackness, like the redemption of whiteness purveyed by white supremacists before and after him, occurs at the expense of women, the one group essential to but too often silenced in the war between black and white men.

# Black Women and White Terrorism: Ida B. Wells, David Bryant Fulton, Pauline E. Hopkins, and the Politics of Representation

Throughout their entire period of bondage colored women were debauched by their masters. From the day they were liberated to the
present time, prepossessing young colored girls have been considered
the rightful prey of white gentlemen in the South, and they have
been protected neither by public sentiment nor by law. In the South,
the negro's home is not considered sacred by the superior race.
White men are neither punished for invading it, nor lynched for vio-
lating colored women and girls.

Mary Church Terrell,
"Lynching from a Negro's Point of View"

Oklahoma, 1914. Marie Scott of Wagoner County, a seventeen-year-
old Negro girl, was lynched by a mob of white men because her
brother killed one of two white men who had assaulted her. She was
alone in the house when the men entered, but her screams brought
her brother to the rescue. In the fight that ensued one of the white
men was killed. The next day the mob came to lynch her brother,
but as he had escaped, lynched the girl instead.

*The Crisis*

W HEN THOMAS DIXON, JR., and Mark Twain published their own
novelistic "red records" of the post-Reconstruction years, they could not have
been farther apart ideologically; yet to differing extents their fiction reflected
popular white male fears of emasculation, dispossession, and disenfranchisement. As the object of these fears, the black male body under the "discipline"
of lynching became a familiar image in the American turn-of-the-century
imagination through novels, photographs, and newspaper descriptions, all of
which dramatically referenced a public spectacle that white supremacists took
as a sign of a racial threat subdued, but that anti-lynching activists regarded as
proof of white supremacy's wanton bloodletting.

The victims of white violence, however, were often black women and children, and the "institutionalized rape of black women" especially functioned as "an instrument of political terror, alongside lynching in the South."[1] At the same time, the fetishization of the black male body as the object of a white mob's fury divorced the notion of blackness from any association with domesticity. Indeed, the possibility of a white recognition of black female victimization through sexual assault was deferred and denied because many white Americans claimed they could not "imagine such a creature as a virtuous Negro woman."[2] Such a claim was possible because the stereotype of promiscuous black womanhood masked fundamental conflicts about race, sexual desire, gender, and power, allowing an enforcement of difference between images of disciplined white civilization and chaotic, savage blackness.

In *The Marrow of Tradition* (1901), Charles Chesnutt aimed to reinvent blackness, creating positive stereotypes that would effect a complete recuperation of black masculinity and a public acknowledgment of black female respectability. Only then would blacks be able to prove the existence of a morally strong African American community whose progressivism, solid middle-class values, and belief in full democracy designated blacks as true Americans worthy of protection. In the novel this refiguration was achieved in part by Chesnutt's reframing of black women in the context of the home—the altar of sensibility and domesticity—as a means of encouraging national moral outrage at the disruptive and deadly effects of white supremacist violence.[3] Chesnutt avoided the actual rape of black women entirely by presenting Julia Brown as the victim of her white master-husband's moral cowardice, not his lust.

Since Chesnutt chooses not to talk directly about rape as a facet of white supremacist violence, his novel offers a starting point for considering larger questions about the representation of black women and white aggression. For one thing, how might one interrupt the traditional white American silence surrounding violent attacks on black women, especially when such attacks took the form of rape? And what role might black women themselves have had in attempting to break this silence? At the World's Congress of Representative Women held during the 1893 Columbia Exposition in Chicago, black educator Anna Julia Cooper spoke daringly of the "yet unwritten history" of black women, emphasizing the "painful, patient, and silent toil of mothers to gain a fee simple title to the bodies of their daughters, the despairing fight, as of an entrapped tigress, to keep hallowed their own persons."[4] Her speech underscored a fact long recognized by early African American female activists: that the black woman's struggle for ownership of her body was closely tied to the historical struggle to maintain a voice within an American public arena.[5]

One remedy was essentially to invent a new set of readings for the black female body. Women such as Cooper, Fannie Barrier Williams, Mary Church Terrell, and Josephine St. Pierre Ruffin promoted the "type of colored woman who represents the farthest reach of progress amongst us"—namely, the morally pure, refined, educated black woman of middle-class status.[6] Hoping to effect a dismantling of the popular image of black femininity as immoral, these women worked directly against lynching and for woman's suffrage; they also worked to introduce the "standards of genteel Victorian domesticity into the cabins of Georgia and Alabama peasant women."[7] These activities were designed to advance the race in general and black women in particular, by using the image of uplifted black femininity as a symbol of the black race's impulse toward industry, middle-class morality, and civilizing domesticity.[8]

Turn-of-the-century black feminists did not advocate a wholehearted embrace of the received conventions of white true womanhood. Rather, like their counterparts earlier in the century, they worked to adapt, supplement, and culturally rewrite these conventions to accommodate black women of all colors, economic stations, and personal histories, who had traditionally been excluded from respectability. Thus turn-of-the-century black women's novels such as Frances E. W. Harper's *Iola Leroy, or Shadows Uplifted* (1892) exemplified this shift in self-presentation toward the triumph of black female strength of character. These novels signified a departure from antebellum abolitionist literature, which had used "slave women primarily as examples of the extremes of the depravity to which slaveholders descended and of the degradation to which black men, through their inability to protect and to provide, were forced."[9]

At the same time, this search for an appropriate public persona normalized certain strategies of address within late-nineteenth-century black feminist discourse. As they emerged on the national stage as reformers and teachers, African American women formulated a verbal style characterized by a creative brand of genteel domestic feminism that for the most part avoided bellicose or injudicious speech—a move demonstrating their capacity for delicacy. The strategy did not, however, compromise their ability to voice protest against American racism: when Fannie Barrier Williams spoke at the 1893 World's Congress of Representative Women, her seemingly innocuous report on "The Intellectual Progress of the Colored Women of the United States Since the Emancipation Proclamation" attacked the widespread belief in Negro degeneration, the stereotype of the black rapist, and the lack of public concern for the rape of black women.

Arguing fervently that "our women have the same spirit and mettle that characterize the best of American women," Williams stressed African American women's "recuperative power . . . to regain their moral instincts" despite the degrading slave past of their ancestors and the exclusionary vision of virtuous womanhood as a white category. On the subject of rape, instead of using graphic language or harsh critiques, her strategy of address relied on innuendo. According to Williams:

> Out of this social purification and moral uplift have come a chivalric
> sentiment and regard from the young men of the race that give to the
> young women a new sense of protection. I do not wish to disturb the
> serenity of this conference by suggesting why this protection is needed
> and the kind of men against whom it is needed.[10]

Thus, as Paula Giddings suggests, "[b]y implying that White men were the real
culprits, Williams attacked not only the myth of Black promiscuity, but the
notion that women themselves were wholly responsible for their own victimization." [11]

Still, Williams's less-than-direct referencing of the tangled skeins of sex, race,
and history binding black and white bodies during slavery and up to that moment is evidence of the restrictions on womanly decorum that determined her
strategy of public address. As Lynn A. Higgins and Brenda R. Silver have argued, "the act of rereading rape involves more than listening to [or breaking]
silences; it requires restoring rape to the literal, to the body: restoring, that is,
the violence—the physical, sexual violation." [12] African American writers would
not hesitate to represent graphically the violence of lynching as used against
black men especially, as proof of the danger of white supremacy; notwithstand-
ing Fannie Barrier Williams's determination to bring up the delicate issue, the
representation of the rape of black women could not be discussed in similar
terms.[13]

If, however, we look at the work of Ida B. Wells, David Bryant Fulton, and
Pauline Elizabeth Hopkins, we begin to see that in some black writing on rape
there was a self-conscious refiguration of domestic discourse that began from
the point of rape's unspeakability—rather than the violated black female body
itself—as a means of initiating an alternative dialogue. Wells, Fulton, and Hopkins focused on a host of issues surrounding white violence: the fact that only
white women are figured as victims of rape; the narrow representation of mob
violence as solely the lynching of black men; the contested representation of
black women themselves; the internal contradictions faced by black communities in their own attempts to confront lynching and rape. Journalists by trade
and training, Fulton and Hopkins addressed rape and black women in their
respective novels, *Hanover; or The Persecution of the Lowly: A Story of the Wilmington Massacre* and *Contending Forces: A Romance Illustrative of Negro Life
North and South,* both published in 1900. In *Hanover* and *Contending Forces,*
Fulton and Hopkins follow African American literary convention by using the
domestic novel as the site for the discussion of black female experience, though
their contextualization of that experience against the backdrop of white supremacist violence pushes the genre to its limits. Despite an early ambition to
be a fiction writer, Wells chose to devote herself full-time to journalism and
protest writing, producing a stream of fiery editorials, articles, and pamphlets

on lynching, rape, and the mythologies supporting white supremacy. Ironically, because she chose militant journalism, a man's medium for her female political commentary, Wells's very right to speak as a woman in public, was continually challenged.

### WELLS AND THE POLITICS OF SUBSTITUTION

For Ida B. Wells the decision to become an anti-lynching activist was motivated by her own high sense of virtue and morality. In an 1888 article on "The Model Woman," Wells describes the model African American woman as one who "hoards and guards . . . her virtue and good name," one who "scorns each temptation to sin and guilt," and one who "strives to encourage [black men] in . . . all things honest, noble and manly." [14] While such rhetoric seems to situate Wells squarely within the idealized boundaries of nineteenth-century feminine behavior, her definition of the place and purpose of virtuous black womanhood—and indeed the manner of "encouragement" it was her duty to render—poses somewhat of a problem. Indeed, the very conduct of Wells's life seems to fly in the face of any kind of conventional genteel feminism. In 1884 Wells refused to bow to Jim Crow laws and leave a first-class railroad car for which she had bought a ticket, putting up a spirited physical defense by biting the hand of a white train official who attempted to drag her bodily from the train. After this episode she sued the railroad company, initially winning compensatory damages before the ruling was overturned by a higher court. Later, as the editor and co-owner of the black Memphis *Free Speech*, Wells made a fact-finding trip to the Oklahoma territory and then openly defied white business interests by encouraging Southern blacks to migrate west to escape racial violence. And when discussing the unequal sentencing practices used against blacks who stole proportionally less than white criminals, Wells urged black thieves to "steal big." [15]

Though she argued for the moral capacity of black women, Wells was no pacifist. After the 1892 lynching of her friend the black Memphis grocer Thomas Moss and his two business associates Calvin McDowell and Henry Stewart, Wells bought a pistol. Reflecting on that moment later in her autobiography, Wells declared "that one had better die fighting against injustice than . . . die like a dog or a rat in a trap. I had already determined to sell my life as dearly as possible if attacked. I felt if I could take one lyncher with me, this would even up the score a little bit" (*C*, 62).[16] Indeed, in her 1892 pamphlet *Southern Horrors: Lynch Law in All Its Phases* she advised that "a Winchester rifle should have a place of honor in every black home, and it should be used for that protection which the law refuses to give" (*SH*, 42).[17] Plain-speaking to the point of bluntness, Wells felt it her solemn duty to report the facts behind lynching, and she provided her audiences with graphic descriptions as a means of impressing upon whites and blacks alike that white racial violence had reached crisis proportions. Between 1893 and 1895, Wells made three speaking tours—two in Britain and one in the United States—as part of an effort to alert national and international audiences to the danger lynching posed not only to blacks, but also to whites themselves: from her point of view, the wholesale, systematic slaughter of African Americans demonstrated that American history was a record of white degeneration, not civilized democratic progress.[18]

Her most sophisticated work came in *Southern Horrors* and in two other pamphlets, *A Red Record: Tabulated Statistics and Alleged Causes of Lynchings in the United States, 1892–1893–1894* (1895), and *Mob Rule in New Orleans: Robert Charles and His Fight to the Death* (1900). These texts provided a complex political analysis of how lynching functioned as a means of social, economic, and political oppression, allowing whites to "get rid of Negroes who were acquiring wealth and property and thus keep the race terrorized and 'keep the nigger down' " (*C*, 64).[19] Drawing on white press accounts of actual lynchings, the pamphlets were often extremely graphic in their descriptions, a feature that no doubt further called into question Wells's claims to gentility as a black woman writing. Wells never hesitated over rules of decorum, however, and whenever possible she focused on the public's lack of regard for stories about black women victimized by rape; she was especially adamant about calling into question accounts of helpless white victims circulated by both the white press and law enforcement officials. According to Wells, black male lynching victims were often "poor blind Afro-American Sampsons who suffer[ed] themselves to be betrayed by white Delilahs" (*SH*, 14).

Such statements enforced Wells's particular isolation on the public stage and often fueled detractors who sought to tarnish her image of respectability. Accused of everything from "race hatred" to "exaggeration of . . . mind" (*C*, 204), she was labeled a "Negro adventuress" (*C*, 187) by the white press and discussed "in language more vulgar and obscene than anything the *Police Gazette* ever contained" (*C*, 181). At one point white journalists deliberately circulated false stories about her sexual liaisons with male associates at the *Free Speech*. Her critics included black men as well: on arrival in New York in August 1894 from England, Wells reports that "I was waited on by a delegation of the men of my own race who asked me to put the soft pedal on charges against white women and their relations with black men" (*C*, 220). After her presentation to an African Methodist Episcopal (A.M.E.) church ministers meeting in Philadelphia in the same year, one clergyman objected to the group's support of Wells "on the ground that they ought to be careful about endorsing young women of whom they knew nothing—that the A.M.E. church had representative women who ought to be put before the public and whom they could endorse unhesitatingly" (*C*, 222). Essentially a rebuke of Wells's character, the minister's comment suggested that she did not qualify as a black woman adequately equipped to "represent" her race, because she had crossed the bounds of decency.

Clearly Wells had dramatically redefined virtuous black womanhood in order to claim access to all topics without regard to community judgment, even when that judgment threatened to defeminize her. In 1892 after she joined T. Thomas Fortune's militant *New York Age*, the conservative black *Indianapolis Freeman* criticized the aggressive tone of their work, caricaturing Fortune and Wells as barking dogs, the caption "Fortune and his 'Echo' " running with the cartoon. Such demeaning characterizations indicated that her male counterparts expected that, as a journalist who insisted on addressing unwomanly topics, Wells "must take a man's fare." Though he expressed his opinion of Wells in a more complimentary light, Fortune himself could not help associating her peculiar black female activism with masculine behavior, declaring that if Wells "was a man she would be a humming independent in politics. She has plenty of nerve; she is as smart as a steel trap, and she has no sympathy with humbug."[20] Yet it was precisely in her refusal to give in to such attempts to defeminize her nature that Wells maintained her modesty and virtue as a true woman: "With me, it is not myself nor my reputation, but the life of my people which is at stake" (*C,* 209). By repeatedly expressing such sentiments even as she continued her militant writings, Wells sought to use the incongruity of her position to erect a unique political platform for black feminist social activism.[21]

In her first pamphlet, *Southern Horrors,* this strategy was to prove especially effective, as she made visible the connections between racism, sexuality, and violence and the underlying difficulties in reporting on black female victimization. The pamphlet grew out of a widely reprinted *New York Age* article Wells had written in June 1892. Originally entitled "Exiled," it told the story of her dramatic confrontation with two white Memphis newspapers. It was in a May 1892 *Free Speech* editorial, while she was still a journalist in Memphis, that Wells had first charged that the cry of rape used to justify the lynching of black men was false, since white women were often willing sexual partners. When white citizens of Memphis publicly threatened her life, ran her coeditor out of town, and then permanently shut down the paper, Wells (who had been away when the offending editorial circulated) decided to seek refuge in New York. In the following months of exile, Wells rehearsed this story again not only in her article for the *New York Age,* but also in her public speech to a group of black women who rallied for her support. With money collected by these women supporters, Wells was able to broadcast her story once more, in the form of the pamphlet *Southern Horrors.*[22]

Heralding Wells's entrance into what would be a national and finally international anti-lynching campaign, *Southern Horrors* is a complex document that functions not only as an early political statement against lynching, but also as Wells's attempt to reaffirm her virtue at the very moment at which the tabooed

subject of her speech (the sexual economy behind lynching) threatens to dis-
qualify her from respectability. In a move suggesting that black male leaders
did indeed sanction her activism, Wells opens *Southern Horrors* with a letter of
praise from the venerable Frederick Douglass; at the same time, she affirms
her support from anonymous yet equally committed black women activists by
dedicating the work to "the Afro-American women of New York and Brooklyn"
who provided her with the funds to publish the pamphlet in the first place.
Wells records in the preface a feminine reluctance to dip "my hands in the
corruption here exposed," justifying her unladylike discourse by her desire to
attack not only lynching itself, but also "the prejudice it fosters and the stain it
places against the good name of a weak race" (*SH*, 14–15). The suggested link
here between the need to defend the reputation of the "weak race" and that
race's "weaker sex," is made explicit by the pamphlet's repeated emphasis that
a discussion of the lynching of black men must include a reexamination of
restrictive American ideology about female virtue and injustice to black womanhood.

The main body of the pamphlet begins with a recounting of the hostile
exchanges between the black *Free Speech* and the white Memphis newspapers
over the issue of the black rapist. Without identifying herself as the author of
the original black newspaper commentary, Wells quotes immediately from the
offending portion of the *Free Speech* editorial:

> Nobody in this section of the country believes the old thread bare lie that
> Negro men rape white women. If Southern white men are not careful,
> they will over-reach themselves and public sentiment will have a reaction;
> a conclusion will then be reached which will be very damaging to the
> moral reputation of their women.    (*SH*, 17)[23]

According to her account, the white editors of Memphis urged an immediate
response:

> Patience under such circumstances is not a virtue. If the negroes them-
> selves do not apply the remedy without delay it will be the duty of those
> whom *he* has attacked to tie the wretch who utters these calumnies to a
> stake at the intersection of Main and Madison Sts., brand *him* in the
> forehead with a hot iron and perform upon *him* a surgical operation with
> a pair of tailor's shears.    (*SH*, 18—emphasis added)

Importantly, the crime for which this lynching is proposed is not that of rape
itself, but the very act of immoral speech. Only after some pages does Wells
claim the editorial as her own work; thus, the pamphlet's narrative is designed
not to elicit sympathy for Wells herself, but rather to provoke audience distaste
for white supremacist supposed truth-telling. This demonstration of female
modesty foregrounds Wells's dilemma in seeking to establish herself as an un-

willing spokes*woman* in the face of a male monopoly of the public discourse on racial violence, precisely because the white press cannot conceive of her either as a woman writing in protest or as a woman in need of respect and protection.[24]

Wells's quotation of the white Memphis editorial deserves special attention, since it represents perhaps the most extreme public attempt to defeminize her, by specifically transforming her into the predatory black fe/male. The white paper reads Wells's editorial as a figurative rape of white womanhood and as such their assumption that she must be a black man erases her identity as a woman writing; thus, her woman's voice is made to register as aberrant black male desire because it challenges racial mythologies. The white demand for her public castration and lynching is even more ironic since Wells's dangerously uncontrollable potency arises not from male sexual organs, but from her own moral outrage as a black woman at such acts of white brutality. (And it is worth noting that her repeated narration of the story of the two editorials—as an article in the *New York Age,* as a speech to the gathering of black women, and finally in pamphlet form—would have worked to mock and indict white supremacist rhetoric itself, proving that white supremacy subsisted on fabrications that turned black female journalists into dangerous black male criminals.)

In its unwitting merger of Wells's female body with that of the black beast, the white editorial essentially demonstrates how white supremacist ideology is supported in part by the imposition of a convenient, figurative invisibility on the black woman as either resisting participant or victim. But the juxtaposition of Wells's black female voice, as the present narrator in *Southern Horrors,* with the white male voice of the white editorial challenges this invisibility; at the same time, it argues into public consciousness the black female body itself as a primary site of white aggression, because the retelling of the events around the destruction of the paper forces the reader to contemplate what the mob answering the white press's call would have done, had it found Wells at the *Free Speech* headquarters.[25] While Wells implies that her purpose is not self-vindication, the account of her clash with the white Memphis papers dramatizes the comparable physical dangers faced by black women and men, since Wells might have been raped as well as lynched by the mob. She might thus have joined the ranks of the martyred, thereby becoming invigorated as a symbol of those wrongly persecuted.[26]

The rest of the pamphlet addresses the suppressed histories of literal rather than figurative black male and female victims. Reiterating her editorial, Wells launches into description after description of false "rape" stories that surface when white women are discovered to be willing sexual partners with black men. The effect of nearly a dozen stories of white female indiscretion with black men debunks the notion of natural white feminine purity and centralizes black rape as a myth white women who engage in miscegenation might use to shield themselves from the wrath of their own communities. Importantly, Wells details black male/white female mutual seduction, drawing at times from published white testimony. Says one white woman, a Mrs. Underwood:

> "He [the black man with whom she had sexual intercourse] had a strange fascination for me, and I invited him to call. . . . He called, bringing chestnuts and candy for the children. By this means we got them to leave us alone in the room. Then I sat on his lap. He made a proposal to me and I readily consented. . . . He visited me several times after that and each time I was indiscreet. I did not care after the first time. In fact I could not have resisted, and had no desire to resist." (*SH*, 20–21)

Such testimony from the mouth of white womanhood exposes the desire for miscegenation as finally white not black, calling into question "natural" racial antipathies that white supremacists claimed made rape the only possible explanation for sexual contact between black men and white women.

Part of the shock value of Mrs. Underwood's testimony comes from the transformation, in her own words, from dutiful mother to adulterous woman, in a domestic setting that includes her children in close proximity. The sanctity of privatized white domesticity is thus violated by whites themselves, not by predatory blacks, a reality masked by the obsession with the black rapist. Also, with a white, not black female voice referencing sexual misconduct, the return to the female body—the site of sexual transgression—is approached by a white narrator, through the tabooed discussion of white female lust. Stories such as Mrs. Underwood's therefore provide important contexts for the pamphlet's later accounts of silenced black women, some of them children, who have been raped and/or lynched by white men who are allowed to go free. Also, Mrs. Underwood's account of white deceit protected by white privacy places in sharper relief tales of black women sexually assaulted in public, on open roads, in drugstores, and on the job as domestic servants. It is important to note, too, that Mrs. Underwood's is a fairly detailed, verbatim testimony that enters the realm of the unspeakable because it describes a willing seduction and the cultivation of white female sexual desire for a black man.

Wells, on the other hand, can draw on no similarly published reports of the fate of black women, because of the white public's lack of interest in their welfare, so she must render their stories in her own words. Nevertheless, Wells curtails considerably her account of black female victims so as not to offer up for public display the details of black female victims' bodily suffering.[27] As a negotiation of indecorous accounts that threaten her claims to virtue and thus credibility, Wells seeks to publish the facts of *Southern Horror* in order to effect a rewriting of the public record on race, women, and rape, without doing damage to the image of black women in general; by the same token, in her narrative strategies, Wells also seeks to protect herself from indictment as an unwomanly speaker.

As a comprehensive analysis of racial violence, *Southern Horrors* does focus on the lynching of black men and especially on the false accusations leveled at blacks for everything from rape to arson to burglary. However, the last mention of lynching is the story of the "legal" hanging in Columbia, South Carolina, of "poor little thirteen year old Mildred Brown" who had allegedly poisoned a white infant (*SH*, 44). Hers is not the first female execution: earlier Wells mentions in passing the burning and lynching of three other women, as part of her refutation of the thesis that lynching is a punishment for black rape. But this final interruption of the expected vision of a black male lynch victim, this substitution of a lynched black girl, brings us back full circle to the pamphlet's opening story of Wells's own near-lynching, and the white press's transformation of her into the black beast—indeed, the reduction of all black victims to this one obliterating stereotype. The final image of a child's lynching recontextualizes the black body as feminine, and its mutilation as a state-sanctioned violation of domesticity and femininity. Wells's point here is not to describe an emasculated black male body, but rather to evoke sympathy for an endangered black familial space. Thus, the seeming incongruity of the lynched woman (an image incongruous at least in the rhetoric of white supremacy) dramatizes two primary issues embedded in *Southern Horrors:* that the rape of black women is rendered invisible in the obsession with the white rape victim/the lynched black rapist; and that Wells's own virtuous dedication to the truth is obscured by debates about personal conduct.

It is fitting then that Wells ends *Southern Horrors* with a characteristic blend of modesty and a call to arms. Here she seeks no special recognition, but represents her aggressive journalism as a force working in tandem with black male vigilance and public action:

> The country would have been aroused and South Carolina disgraced forever for such a crime [the lynching of Mildred Brown]. The Afro-American himself did not know as he should have known as his journals should be in a position to have him know and act.
>
> Nothing is more definitely settled than he must act for himself. I have shown how he may employ the boycott, emigration and the press, and I feel that by a combination of all these agencies can be effectually stamped out lynch law, that last relic of barbarism and slavery. "The gods help those who help themselves." (*SH*, 45)

Here Wells's address to African American manhood bolsters black patriarchal authority under attack by white supremacists; thus black male agency becomes the solution to safeguard the black family and American civilization. As the source of truth and moral action, Wells then takes her place as the female inspiration for justice.

Karlyn Kohrs Campbell has argued that, as the text of Wells's first major public speech, *Southern Horrors* evinces "no stylistic markers indicating attempts by a woman speaker to appear 'womanly' in what is perceived as a male role—that of rhetor."[28] Yet Wells recalls in her autobiography that she delivered the lecture version of *Southern Horrors* in tears. Ever sensitive to charges of dishonesty, Wells felt compelled to state in her autobiography that, as one who had never before given a public address, she "had no knowledge of stage business" (*C*, 80); her weeping, she argued, sprang from the fact that "every detail of that horrible lynching affair was imprinted on my memory":

> As I described the cause of the trouble at home and my mind went back to the scenes of the struggle, to the thought of the friends who were scattered throughout the country, a feeling of loneliness and homesickness for the days and the friends that were gone came over me and I felt the tears coming. (*C*, 79)

With this description of herself as simply a medium for truth, with the key words *home* and *friends* referencing a black domestic world trespassed, Wells's supplementary self-portrait as exiled, unprotected and forced to bear alone and unwillingly the memory of having witnessed white brutalities, demands the same sympathy we might accord to the black female victims she describes. Not surprisingly, at the end of her presentation, Wells received word from the meeting's organizers that her weeping "made an impression on the audience favorable to the cause and to me" (*C*, 80). Thus, as Wells's strategy in *Southern Horrors* proves, framing was everything.

As an effective speaker and pamphleteer, Wells demonstrates on the level of historical reality the problem of confronting the multiple intended and unintended discourses that spring up around any discussion of black women and racial violence. In texts such as *Southern Horrors*, Wells forced the collision of stereotypes about black and white women in order to construct, at the point of fragmentation, the traces of an alternative discourse on racial violence and women. In their responses to the same problem, David Bryant Fulton and Pauline Hopkins employed the structure of the novel to arrive at a more satisfactory and more idealized resolution, and Hopkins especially could somewhat mitigate with regard to herself Wells's problem of authorizing the female speaker.[29] To achieve resolution, however, both Fulton and Hopkins would have to address the same problems encountered by Wells: the fact of having to speak first through the mass of references enforcing both the centrality of the black male body as the site of white violence and the traditional debasement of the black female body as a point of mediation for turn-of-the-century white American perceptions of racial violence; the consequence of black community politics and the promotion of black "true womanhood"; and the problem of effecting a return to the female body and its violation, without extending that violation through an enforcement of prurient spectatorship.

### HANOVER AND THE IDEALIZATION OF BLACK FEMALE HEROISM

Dedicated to Ida B. Wells, David Bryant Fulton's 1900 novel *Hanover; or The Persecution of the Lowly: A Story of the Wilmington Massacre* works toward the militant woman journalist's goal of reclaiming the story of black female experiences within public debates over the lynching of black men. As such this novelistic account of the 1898 Wilmington riot has been called "one of the most thoroughly 'feminist' novels by an Afro-American male."[30] Not surprisingly, Fulton's feminism draws heavily on late-nineteenth-century middle-class notions of female activism, so his women heroes are mostly wives and mothers.

A native of Wilmington, North Carolina, Fulton moved to New York in 1888, pursuing a variety of jobs as a Pullman porter and as an employee for both a music publishing house and Sears, Roebuck. In his alternate career as a writer he published extensively under the pen name "Jack Thorne." Though he wrote on a host of issues, Fulton consistently echoed Wells's political messages against lynching and the rape of black women in numerous essays, short stories, editorials, and pamphlets: "No Negro woman of the South, no Negro child . . . has as yet been enabled to successfully indict a man of the dominant race who seeks by law and custom to hedge in one woman and destroy another." He was especially vocal about the lack of solidarity between black and white women, claiming that "instead of keeping up the cry of 'wolf,'" the white woman should "extend a helping hand to the black woman, the prey of the men of both races in the South."[31] In both *Hanover* and *A Plea for Social Justice for the Black Woman* (1912), he urged black communities to "begin the work of properly safe-guarding the mothers of our children" from white rape and from the temptations of prostitution.[32] His efforts earned him the respect of black women themselves, and in 1923 he was invited to read his "Mother of Mine; Ode to the Negro Woman" at the annual meeting of the New York Colored Women's Clubs.[33]

Like Charles W. Chesnutt's *The Marrow of Tradition*, Fulton's novel challenges the white argument that the Wilmington riot of 1898 was an attempt to protect white women; and like Chesnutt's novel, *Hanover* problematizes black male choices between passive resistance and defensive violence; but like *Southern Horrors*, Fulton's novel explores tensions attendant on the representation of black female experience of white violence. Also, as suggested by its titular echo of Harriet Beecher Stowe's *Uncle Tom's Cabin; or Life Among the Lowly* (1852),

*Hanover* addresses white women, this time not simply as domestic reformers working to save African Americans, but as participants in a white supremacist ideology that oppresses all American women, regardless of race.

*Hanover*'s rhetoric on race and femininity is embedded in a seemingly chaotic juxtaposition of journalistic and novelistic styles, which together produce "a somewhat diffuse group of stories centered on a historical event."[34] The novel's prologue consists of headlines and an article about the riot, presumably both part of an Associated Press report. Clearly an attempt by the white press to represent the riot as a legitimate police action to control "obnoxious" whites and Negro "ringleaders, who were inciting their race to violence," the report stresses that "good government was to prevail in Wilmington from this time, and would commence immediately" (*H*, 3–4). Such reports signify the received narrative all Americans absorb about racial violence—namely, that of black men being terrorized (or punished, depending on the sympathies of the reader) by white mobs. This "factual" account is contradicted by Fulton's own "Introductory Note," which vehemently condemns "an attack upon the character and integrity of the Negroes of Wilmington, in order to justify the massacre of Nov. 10th" (*H*, 10), and thereby establishes his text's agenda as a disruption of traditional mainstream reporting.

The struggle to control the public record is thematized in Fulton's retelling of the infamous dispute between the editor of the black Wilmington *Record*, Alexander Manly, and Georgia's Rebecca Felton, over the reality of rape in America. Some three months before the Wilmington riot, in a speech at an agricultural society meeting in Tybee, Georgia, Mrs. Felton had advocated lynching "a thousand times a week if necessary" to protect isolated white women in rural areas of the South from lustful black men. Echoing Ida B. Wells, Manly responded in an editorial that often what was called black rape was actually the revelation of voluntary sexual relations between black men and white women, and he especially attacked white male hypocrisy over miscegenation.[35]

*Hanover*'s first chapter opens with Manly rejecting a timid acquaintance's suggestion that he retract his editorial. Instead of backing down, he heightens his attack on Felton (Mrs. Fell in the novel) by describing her "clamoring and whining like a she wolf for more human sacrifices, and an increased flow of human blood" (*H*, 11). Manly's attention is especially drawn to the problem of white rape ignored by Felton/Fell: " 'White girls in isolated districts exposed to lustful Negro brutes.' Colored girls in isolated districts exposed to lustful white brutes; what's the difference? Does the Negro's ruined home amount to n[a]ught?" (*H*, 13). And it is precisely as a narrative about "ruined homes" that *Hanover* gains its power: racist Southern aristocrats and their poor white accomplices use Manly's editorial as a pretext for the riot; thus Felton, in the act of protecting "home," falls under the reign of white supremacy, finally offering a perverted model of the kind of domestic feminism exemplified in Stowe's novel. The stage is then set for an alternative model of female action to materialize.

Instead of utilizing a solid plot-driven narrative, *Hanover* moves episodically through a series of character portraits, featuring various "types" of white supremacists in the town, their family members, and members of the town's black community. Fulton's signal strategy here is to construct a mosaic of town life in which female characters are made to stand out, especially those who articulate their own domestic "riot" against the hypocrisy of white supremacy: the wife of a poor white would-be rioter who urges her husband not to join the attack; the high-minded wife of a white aristocrat who leaves her husband after discovering his adultery. But what distinguishes *Hanover* from *Uncle Tom's Cabin* is Fulton's more consistent emphasis on black women: their thoughts, their actions, the context of their social construction in America, their sexual exploitation, and especially the militancy of their own brand of "domestic" feminism.[36]

Juxtaposed against "factual" reports of white-on-black violence is the history of mulatto prostitute Molly Pierrepont, the product of a master's rape of his slave daughter after emancipation. Despite her access to education and the love of an honorable black man, Molly chooses a "life of ease with shame," rather than enduring "honor with poverty" (*H*, 36, 35). That Molly is the mistress of one of the white mob's ringleaders, Ben Hartright, is significant. Here Fulton provides the flip side of Manly's critique—that white men who lynch to prevent racial admixture would "risk the fires of hell to be in [a black woman's] . . . company, intensely as he pretends to hate her" (*H*, 35). White men's adultery, argues Fulton, breeds fear and guilt that are in turn unleashed against blacks: "it is not the reckless dare deviltry of the Negro that terrorizes the South, but the conscience of the white man whose wrong treatment of a defenseless people fills him with fear and intensifies his hatred" (*H*, 35).

A woman in whose body the destructive forces of incest, white rape, and lust cross, her long hair streaming, her arms enclosed with bands of gold to signify a new kind of enslavement, Molly compares herself to Stowe's Cassy, a quadroon whose trust in white lovers leads to her downfall. She awakens fully to the meaning of her own position after Hartright casually reveals to her the plans to slaughter Wilmington's blacks: "I am a Nigger and will be dealt with as such" (*H*, 38). Yet while Cassy ultimately achieves redemption through a return to motherhood, Molly transcends her situation by enacting her own salvation through an affirmation of racial allegiance to African Americans.[37] Abandoning the role of race traitor, Molly emerges as a new Delilah about to undermine the cause of a white lover:

> . . . it['] s Delilah's duty to warn her people of the dangers that await them. Men whose lives are threatened must be warned; women who are

in danger of being ignominiously dealt with must be put upon their guard; must know that these defenders of virtue, these Southern gentlemen who are thirsting for blood of a slanderer . . . of white women are hypocrites, who strain out a gnat and swallow a camel.   (*H*, 38)

Following the revolutionary feminism of Fannie Barrier Williams and others, Fulton thus dramatizes black female potential for selfless heroic action, making Molly redeemable as a virtuous woman regardless of her past life and her origins. And instead of linking her with a white female mentor (a move Stowe makes in *Uncle Tom's Cabin,* for example, by linking the quadroon Eliza with the white mistress Mrs. Shelby), Fulton aligns Molly immediately with the novel's progressive middle-class black women. Their Union Aid Society is already strategizing about how to cope with the coming violence, and when Molly informs them of Hartright's plans they in turn fully support her move from prostitution to a life of community service.

In his account of the riot, Fulton devotes space to violence done to men as well as women, but in particular his description of black women's suffering at the hands of rioters provides the novel with its most riveting passages. At the start of the violence, Molly rushes out to warn black male workers in the local cotton press, only to find herself confronted by a road block. After initially mistaking her for a white woman, the rioters quickly put into action the plan they have in mind for all the African American women they meet:

> "You've got ter be searched, ole gal," said one of the men, with a mocking smile of triumph in his face, ["]an' you jes' es well let these boys go through them duds er your'n an' have done with it. Come now, hands up!" and they all glared like hungry wolves at the woman. . . .   (*H*, 81–82)

Molly's response is the kind of black female militancy reminiscent of Stowe's Cassy, but especially of Ida B. Wells:

> Molly drew herself up to her full height. "Cowards!" she shrieked. "Not satisfied at the cutting off of every means of defense from the black men of Wilmington, that you may shoot them down with impunity, you are low enough to take advantage of their helplessness to insult weak women. But here I stand!" she cried, stepping backwards, and drawing a gleaming revolver from beneath her cloak. "Search me! but it must be done when the body is lifeless; I'll be a target for the whole of you before I'm searched; so let the battle begin."   (*H*, 82)

In Molly's face-off with the mob, Fulton renders the idea of sexual assault as the intended occurrence, but instead of proceeding to the spectacle of rape, he affirms Molly's subjectivity as an empowered woman. Her unexpected posture earns her the grudging respect of the rioters, and they declare "not er hair un her hed mus' be tech'd!" (*H*, 82).

Reminiscent of Wells's seemingly defeminizing transformations, Molly's description of herself as a weak woman tempers the shock of her metamorphosis into a gun-toting demonic female. Indeed, her charge that the rioters capitalize on the helplessness of black men under siege emphasizes first that the ideal of chivalry is ultimately a sign of black, not white male codes of conduct, and second that white supremacist violence targets traditional middle-class domestic settings in the black community. Such an assault on African American life demands Molly's self-authorization as an aggressive figure; however, once she warns the black men, she relinquishes her stance and falls into a dead faint from the strain of events. Only after the fainting scene does Fulton display her "prostrate form . . . lifted up, and borne to a place of safety" (*H*, 83) by the grateful black men whose lives she has just saved, offering her up not as a victim of rape but as the victorious symbol of wayward black womanhood restored by its own moral and physical heroism to a protective black community.

Though the rioters may not have intended to kill Molly, her experience suggests that the bodies of black women are subject to dangers no less serious than those experienced by black men. Here Fulton makes available to black women as well as to black men the kind of appropriation of violence called for in Wells's *Southern Horrors;* consequently, *Hanover* moves beyond the nonviolent resistance advocated by the domestic feminism of *Uncle Tom's Cabin,* as Molly's new creed of aggressive female heroism is echoed at other moments in the novel. All through the town, groups of "colored citizens, mostly women," armed with "broomsticks, stove-pokers, hoes, axes and other rude implements of war," defend their homes and their persons, declaring (in a rough paraphrase of Wells) that " 'Dey says dey gointer kill niggers, but we's gwine ter tek er few er dem long wid us' " (*H*, 87, 88). Moments such as these are memorialized in the novel as less visible female experiences that were never recorded in standard accounts of the riot; and the force of these incidents is to assert that, because these women survive, their bravery must be acknowledged along with that of their African American men.

Yet *Hanover's* celebration of black women as both physically and morally heroic does not revolve simply around their ability to handle weapons. Another story of attempted white rape in the novel pits unarmed Lizzie Smith against yet another hostile white mob. Having watched "a woman struggling to free herself from the grasp of several men who were, in turn, slapping her face and otherwise abusing her," Smith challenges the mob by using her physical defiance as a tool of intimidation. When the rioters call for her to be strip-searched, Smith tears off her clothes to prove "I am jes' like yo' sisters an' mammies" (*H*, 95). Smith continues until she is completely nude: "Oh no, . . .

I'm goin' ter git naked: yer got ter see that I'm er woman" (H, 95). In the end her actions prompt even white women looking on to protest such treatment, so that her cry "I'm er woman" is validated by female witnesses and the shame-faced white rioters are forced to retreat in helplessness. Surrounded by whites, Smith's powerful claims to womanhood in such a forum unites her with the white femininity Rebecca Felton falsely claims to be under assault. Yet Smith's demand for equality is achieved at the very site of supposed difference: hers is the black female body criminalized from the past moment of slavery up to the present moment of post-Reconstruction 1898; but like Molly Pierrepont's body, Smith's is transformed into an emblem of white defeat.

The scene of Smith's defiance not only echoes that of Ida B. Wells, but it is also reminiscent of two moments in the life of an earlier black woman heroine, Sojourner Truth: her famous 1851 Akron, Ohio, speech "Ar'n't I a Woman" before the Woman Rights Convention, where she challenged American rhetoric on womanhood to validate black female experience; and her disrobing before pro-slavery hecklers in Kansas in 1858, in answer to those who claimed she was really a man in disguise, an abolitionist fraud.[38] Truth's narrative had been republished in the post-Reconstruction era, and this seemingly intentional par-allel between Lizzie Smith and the black abolitionist beset by Southern oppo-nents returns the reader's attention to historically unaddressed moments of white sexual harassment, reframing the exposed black female body and re-scripting its fate. Thus a pattern of exploitation is defeated by a more powerful tradition of black women reforming American gender mythologies and voicing political critique.

In the cases of Molly Pierrepont and Lizzie Smith, *Hanover* offers a triumph-ant reimaging of the clash between black women and white supremacy; but the novel also registers moments of suffering writ large on a communal, famil-ial black female population—a tragic contradiction of white supremacist argu-ments that the riot was aimed only at unruly black men. Consistent with his desire to have *Hanover* serve as an alternative document to counteract the "of-ficial" white reports of the riot, Fulton inserts into his narrative a letter presum-ably written by a black survivor who has taken refuge in New Bedford, Massa-chusetts. In her first-person account, Mrs. Adelaide Peterson describes the mob's "wanton disregard for womanhood" as "the most atrocious and unpar-donable act" of the riot (*H*, 95). Peterson praises both Molly Pierrepont ("She stood like a goddess" [*H*, 93]) and Lizzie Smith, but she spends most of her letter recounting forgotten details of the riot, such as the case of terrified groups of black children who take refuge in their school, one child literally dying of fright. During the riot, Peterson had accompanied a black minister with food and clothing for those who fled into the nearby woods, and in retro-spect she describes the scene of suffering in terms of its impact on black women and their families: many are driven mad by the events of the riots, while others—including a woman who had given birth during the night—die from exposure. Peterson's account of such tragedies, as well as the larger narrative's description of how these black women finally return to Wilmington only to find their homes occupied by white squatters, reveal more fully the consequences of such acts of violence where, in addition to loss of life, the very domestic fabric of a community is destroyed.

To underscore that *Hanover* is finally about the experiences of women within the context of a black/white male struggle, Fulton returns at the end of his novel to the ideal of white female activism advocated by Stowe in *Uncle Tom's Cabin*. As a means of urging white female action against white supremacy, he stages a discussion in which the town's white women come to terms with their own complicity in and confinement by white supremacist ideology. As a measure of the theoretical and political distance between themselves and the novel's black women, many of *Hanover*'s white female characters are still reluctant to decry the hypocrisy of the alleged black rape, even after the evidence of the Wilmington riot, until one woman argues earnestly for a recognition of the shared fates of black and white women. Paying homage to both Wells and Manly, Fulton has the white women themselves argue that "lynchings and burnings . . . in the South are intended as warnings to white women" who have inherited the "taint of lust in the blood" from their slave-owning fathers or who might be attempting to "acknowledge that in the Negro man are the elements of genuine manhood." Thus anti-miscegenation laws are proof that "the men do not trust us as implicitly as they pretend" (*H*, 117). Finally, the white women acknowledge that the resurrection of black women must be at the heart of any enterprise to end racial violence. As one woman declares,

> just so long as the safeguards around Negro women are so weak, so long as the laws upon the statute books of Southern States brand her as a harlot, pure or impure, and keep her outside the pale of pity and consideration, just so long will our representatives have to resort to murder and intimidation to get to Congress. The strength of any race rests in the purity of its women, and when the womanhood is degraded, the life blood of a race is sapped.  (*H*, 116)

Such a discussion of the linked elements of sexuality and race surpasses the analyses offered by the white women of *Uncle Tom's Cabin* and indeed by many white suffragists at the turn of the century. From Fulton's perspective, in the present climate of racial violence, if there is a potential for the same kind of feminist reforming zeal that helped end slavery, it must lie in a bolder recognition of the gender politics behind lynching.

Though less well known than Chesnutt's *Marrow of Tradition*, Fulton's *Hanover* provides an important example of how black writers were attempting to recontextualize rape as racial violence, and how they sought to alter the tone and nature of national debates about such violence to include a consideration of gender politics. Thus Fulton's *Hanover* imagines a black community united around such a recognition, operating from a newly forged set of values from which to judge and support an entire population of black women under siege.

Still, in Fulton's dramatic representation of the gendered context of the Wilmington riot of 1898, one is struck by how much *Hanover* works both to reclaim black women as public icons of black communal suffering and to idealize black community solidarity and resistance. Despite her background, by the end of the novel Molly Pierrepont has been taken offstage, to be apotheosized in Peterson's letter as the symbol of newly redeemed black womanhood. Her example suggests that black women recuperate themselves through public service rather than through the fulfillment of individualistic desire.[39] Thus Fulton's novel follows in lockstep a late nineteenth-century African American literary tradition of portraying black women "without exception" as "static, disembodied, larger than life characters . . . invariably exemplary, characterized by their self-sacrifice and by their tireless labor for the collective good."[40] Though her own novel follows a similar pattern of characterization, Pauline Hopkins's *Contending Forces* offers alternative readings of the symbolic black heroine and of the homogeneity of black community in the post-Reconstruction context of rape and lynching.

## BLACK COMMUNITY POLITICS AND THE PROBLEM OF RAPE IN *CONTENDING FORCES*

Having languished for years under the judgment that it was just another stiff black novel of domestic manners peopled with light-skinned characters, Hopkins's *Contending Forces* has reemerged as an important African American text exploring the politics of race, gender, and especially racial violence.[41] Politically Hopkins remains difficult to characterize, precisely because both her writing and her personal history display a tension between conservatism and radicalism. As literary editor of the Boston-based *Colored American Magazine* from 1903 to 1904, she seems to have developed, like Ida B. Wells, a reputation for a certain aggressiveness that was presumably not attractive in a turn-of-the-century woman. In a 1912 article in the *Crisis,* W. E. B. Du Bois looked back on Hopkins as "not conciliatory enough" for the tastes of the *Colored American Magazine*'s increasingly conservative management.[42] Reflecting on the magazine's brief life, poet William Stanley Braithwaite, the book editor who worked under Hopkins, complained in a 1947 article of her "temperamental" nature and her apparent lack of modesty concerning the value of her own fiction.[43] It may well have been for these "faults" that Hopkins was quietly fired in 1904 after the *Colored American Magazine* was acquired by allies of Booker T. Washington.[44]

Hopkins's early commentaries on women and politics in the magazine's "Women's Department" give more clues to the complexity of her opinions. In one memorable issue she praises "the ramification of woman in all directions where she has seen the slightest chance for business or intellectual progression" but suggests in the next moment that black women would find fulfillment "if they elect to live for others." She also suggests on the one hand that women not be given the vote because the political system run by men was one of moral depravity, but on the other that one reason against women's suffrage is the untrustworthiness of white women: "we ought to hesitate before we affiliate too happily in any project that will give them [white women] greater power than they now possess to crush the weak and helpless."[45] Thus Hopkins seems to view black female social and political empowerment as a complicated process of negotiating the contradictions and demands on the middle-class American New Woman on the one hand, and racism within the women's suffrage movement at the end of the nineteenth century on the other.

In *Contending Forces,* Hopkins's discussion of rape is deeply contextualized by a sustained examination of complex internal black domestic and communal politics. Indeed, in the novel the body of the raped black woman is displaced by the social body of the African American female community—a community nevertheless overshadowed not just by rape as both a historical tragedy and a contemporary reality, but also by the effects of South to North black migration, class conflict, and regional and racial prejudice. As signaled by its full title, *Contending Forces: A Romance Illustrative of Negro Life North and South,* the novel explores black successes as well as shortcomings in the wake of a turn-of-the-century moment of intense, sometimes destructive social transitions. Through the voice of one of her characters, Hopkins argues that

> conservatism, lack of brotherly affiliation, lack of energy for the right and the power of the almighty dollar which deadens men's hearts to the sufferings of their brothers, and makes them feel that if only *they* can rise to the top of the ladder may God help the hindmost man, are the forces which are ruining the Negro in this country. It is killing him off by thousands, destroying his self-respect, and degrading him to the level of the brute. *These are the contending forces that are dooming this race to despair!* (*CF,* 256)[46]

In *Hanover* Fulton pays attention to self-destructive forces within black communities by offering a brief portrait of Calvin Sauls, a black pimp who willingly sells his vote to the highest bidder. Hopkins's novel also has its black villains and morally unreproachable heroes, but her text reveals a more subtle figuration of a black community in active transition, where members are constantly negotiating the paths between personal interest and public good, between male and female spheres, between white middle-class values and black appropriation and modification of these, and between slavery's past and the novel's contemporary present on the eve of the twentieth century.

As a way of engaging issues of history and region, Hopkins connects antebellum and postbellum black America, North and South, by structuring her novel's plot around two accounts of rape. Set in the 1830s, the first involves the assault on Grace Montfort, in tandem with the lynching of her husband Charles, a wealthy English planter who moves his family from Bermuda to North Carolina to avoid losing his slaves under the British Emancipation Act. The narrative hints at the possibility that "a strain of African blood" (*CF*, 23) runs through Montfort's veins, and whites are convinced Grace's creamy complexion has a negroid tint. Soon a white "committee on public safety" (*CF*, 53) led by the lustful Anson Pollock arrives at the Montfort residence with the excuse that Charles is "a West Ingy half-white nigger" who plans to offer his slaves gradual emancipation (*CF*, 61).

When the mob commits murder and theft, Montfort is killed off-stage, so the narrative shifts almost exclusively to Grace's experience as two committee members who had previously been insulted by Montfort proceed to whip her. As Hazel Carby has persuasively argued, the beating Grace receives functions as a displaced representation of rape:

> She was bound to the whipping post as the victim to the stake, and lashed with rawhides alternately by the two strong, savage men. . . . O God! was there none to rescue her! The air whistled as the snaky leather thong curled and writhed in its rapid, vengeful descent. A shriek from the victim—a spurt of blood that spattered the torturer—a long, raw gash across a tender white back. . . . Again and again was the outrage repeated. Fainting fit followed fainting fit. The blood stood in a pool about her feet. (*CF*, 68–69)[47]

After her ordeal, Grace is shackled to her black maid Lucy and claimed by Pollock as his concubine. Grace finally escapes further brutalization by committing suicide, forcing Pollock "to take Lucy in the place he had designed for Mrs. Montfort" (*CF*, 71).

Hopkins's decision to begin the novel with such graphic detail has the same shocking effect as the lynching of Mildred Brown in *Southern Horrors* or Molly's confrontation of the mob in *Hanover*: it disrupts what might normally have been an account of black male torture. In addition, the rape of Grace functions as a complex metaphor that links together past and present patterns of victimization, without sacrificing historical specificities. Thus, as an uncanny referencing of the world of 1900, Hopkins locates the assault within the complex terms of a gratuitous white violence that seeks to reestablish white male supremacy through the subordination of its "opposite" blackness. Grace is not raped as a consequence of white male lust or within the context of a slaveholder's need to capitalize on her reproductive power. Rather, the suspicion and fear of Montfort's blackness comes precisely at a moment when the small North Carolina town has just had to punish the racial disloyalty of a young white man who tried to escape to Canada with his black paramour. The Montforts loss of control over the designation of their racial identities is a displacement of white communal anxiety over a tradition of miscegenation. Here Hopkins might well have been thinking of the 1896 *Plessy v. Ferguson* case, in which the nearly white Homer Plessy unsuccessfully challenged the constitutionality of state-mandated Jim Crow laws.[48] Thus, the pre–Civil War tragedy of the Montfort family is simply a harbinger of things to come for all blacks after 1865.

The event of Grace's "rape" also allows Hopkins to expose the lie of Southern chivalry, since its stated goal of protecting white womanhood was used so widely in the post-Reconstruction era to justify atrocities such as the Wilmington race riot. Hopkins in fact never confirms the rumor that the Montforts are a family of mulattos: if we concede that Grace is white, then the woman to be protected by lynch law falls victim to the white protector, the outwardly "suave, genial gentleman" Pollock. At the same time "[r]umor said his ill treatment and infidelity had driven [his wife] . . . to suicide; it had even been whispered that he had not hesitated to whip her by proxy through his overseer, Bill Sampson, in the same way he did his slaves" (*CF,* 51, 50). Grace then is identified as much with white as with black womanhood, so that Pollock's system of white supremacy brutalizes women on both sides of the color line and testifies to the fiction of the privileges of white ladyhood. And whether we see Grace as a victimized white woman or as a victimized quadroon, "[t]he antebellum discourse" of the opening sections of the novel "binds [her] . . . to the conventional fate of the sexually violated heroine—death."[49]

Grace's suicide, which precipitates the final destruction of the Montfort family by forcing her orphaned children into slavery, must be countered not just by a new narrative of black female survival, but indeed by an empowering ideology of womanhood. This idea is partially introduced with the character of Lucy, Grace's black half-sister. Serving as Pollock's concubine after Grace's death, Lucy does survive, finally to bear witness at the end of the novel to the restoration of the Montforts. The merger of Grace and her double Lucy is signified by the novel's third victim of rape, the Louisiana-born Sappho Clark, whom Hopkins sets up as an alternative post-Reconstruction model for black femininity.[50]

After *Contending Forces*'s unorthodox opening of rape and suicide, the story moves quickly into a domestic mode as the narrative shifts to the lives of the widow Ma Smith and her two children, Will and Dora, descendants of Grace's son Jesse, who had fled to Boston to escape Pollock. In contrast to Grace's experience of the South, the Smiths exist in a spiritually fulfilling Northern black community that is highly respectful of black womanhood:

>   Dora lighted the lamps, drew the curtains, and looked about the cozy
> kitchen with a satisfaction which might well be pardoned, for even in
> palatial homes a more inviting nest could not be found. The table was
> carefully spread with a nicely ironed cloth of spotless white, red-bordered
> napkins lay at each plate, a good quality of plated silverware mingled with
> the plain, inexpensive white ware in which the meal was to be served. Ma
> Smith, in her neat calico dress and long white apron, busied herself in
> making the tea and coffee and seeing that the delicate muffins were
> browned to just the right turn, while Dora busied herself in putting the
> finishing touches to a house dress for her mother.  (CF, 88–89)

Here the traumatic vision of violated black womanhood is supplanted by the
minutiae of domestic life: kitchen implements, table settings, linen, artifacts
that mark black female economic and social progress after slavery. The Smith
home functions as a boarding house, but Hopkins's focus on domestic ritual
rather than on moneymaking demonstrates how far black women have been
able to achieve a certain retirement from public circulation, even as they are
fully engaged in promoting new kinds of subjectivity. The complacency of this
scene would thus seem to signify the defeat of the chaotic forces of racism that,
at least in the first half of the novel, destroy the Montfort home.[51]

Into this haven Hopkins introduces Sappho, a Southern-born quadroon
whose experiences reintroduce the history of rape that seems so effectively
erased from the world of the Smith women. Originally named Mabelle
Beaubean, the quadroon was sexually assaulted in New Orleans by her white
uncle and was then forced into prostitution.[52] Refusing to be stigmatized by
sexual exploitation or by the fact that, as a rape victim, she gives birth to an
illegitimate child, Mabelle leaves her son in the care of a relative, changes her
name, and establishes herself in Boston as the stenographer Sappho, secretly
sending money for the upkeep of her child.

One way of coming to terms with Sappho's signification as a quadroon is
to consider her in light of Hazel Carby's useful formulation about the figure
of the mulatto in late nineteenth-century black fiction: in early black novels
"the mulatto . . . enabled an exploration of the social relations between the
races, relations that were increasingly proscribed by Jim Crow laws, and it enabled an expression of the sexual relations between the races, since the mulatto
was a product not only of proscribed consensual relations but of white sexual
domination."[53] In the antebellum section of Contending Forces, Grace's rape
signifies white terror over miscegenation and white lust that was historically
distanced in the fantasy of sexualized blackness. On the other hand, since she
is meant to remind us of Grace, Sappho functions as a symbolic figure facilitat-
ing our entry into the African American community represented in the novel,
specifically with respect to an evolving post-Reconstruction black female

subjectivity and the private and political consequences of white sexual aggression.

Named for the female Greek poet of the seventeenth century B.C., Sappho is necessarily a complex allegorical figure referencing not only interracial social/ sexual relations, but also the contested representation of the very notion of black womanhood for African Americans themselves. Critics have argued that in the late nineteenth century the Greek Sappho (particularly the image of Sappho that Hopkins and other Americans would have encountered) was a figure constructed as much from biographical facts as from the fertile imagination of generations of western scholars and artists. Numerous stories had circulated about her, including the suggestions that she took as sexual partners her female students on the island of Lesbos, and that she committed suicide because of her unrequited love for the young ferryman Phaon. In the context of late-nineteenth-century "fictions of Sappho" (to use Joan DeJean's phrase), Sappho was increasingly constructed in 1890s medical discourse as variously the epitome of the criminalized lesbian and, by some male artists, as a sexual hedonist with a darkened face "burned under the sun of passion"—an important construction for writers like Hopkins, given Sappho Clark's racial identity.[54]

Importantly, the move to condemn the Greek Sappho as a sexual deviant was challenged by turn-of-the-century white feminist writers who were inspired by the myths of Sappho's sexual freedom and artistic talent.[55] As Elizabeth Ammons effectively argues, Hopkins probably invokes Sappho as a model of the silenced woman artist, but her rendering of a "black" Sappho who is also the victim of white rape juxtaposes the stereotype of criminalized black female desire alongside the stereotype of silenced black female victimhood—all this at a moment in the late nineteenth century when the description of both that desire and that story of victimhood would have marked black women as doubly tabooed seductresses and damaged women.[56] Like the Greek Sappho, the heroine of *Contending Forces* is caught in a web of competing public constructions. The subject of continual public appropriation as a black woman and a quadroon, Sappho's tragedy is rape and the denial of motherhood; but hers is also the struggle for black female sexual and social agency, as well as for self-invention within an African American community.

Critics have never tired of attacking the Boston-born middle-class Hopkins for her use of lower-class black characters to provide comic relief.[57] But while there is some truth to this criticism, it is important to note that the light-skinned Sappho's journey toward self-definition is anticipated by two of the Smiths's dark-skinned female boarders, Mrs. Ophelia Davis and Mrs. Sarah Ann White. Illiterate, dialect-speaking, working-class ex-slaves, Davis and White represent a generation of women linking Sappho with Grace and Lucy. As women who have survived slavery, they have no regrets about "immoral" acts committed for the sake of survival:

"Yas'm, when my ol' mistis left her great big house an' all that good stuff—silver an' things—a-layin' thar fer enyone to pick up thet had sense 'nough to know a good thing an' git it ahead of enybody else, I jes' said to myself: ''Phelia, chile, now's yer time!' Yas'm, I feathered my nes', I jes' did. Sarah Ann, you 'member that time, honey, an' how skeered we was fer fear some o' them Union sojers would ketch us. You stuffed yerself with greenbacks, but, honey, I took clo's, too." (*CF*, 105)

Though they are stereotypically fun-loving and unruly black characters, their rewriting of traditional codes of morality to combat their own victimization evinces the kind of rationalizations proffered by Linda Brent in *Incidents in the Life of a Slave Girl* (1861) and by Frederick Douglass in *Narrative of the Life of Frederick Douglass* (1845).

Davis and Allen congregate in the Smiths's parlor so as to "come in contact with brighter intellects than their own" (*CF*, 104), but both women are enterprising enough to move from domestic service into their own business as laundresses, revealing themselves to be as ambitious and as successful in their own endeavors to transcend their histories as their more genteel, lighter-skinned landlady. Thus, in the context of the Smith household, which is really a working-class setting inhabited by men and women working toward middle-class respectability, Hopkins presents Davis and Allen (and by implication, Sappho) as broadly sketched representatives of turn-of-the-century black womanhood in economic and social transition, rather than as cases in point for a repudiation of certain kinds of black women on the basis of color or class aspirations.[58]

Sappho's presence among such women as Mrs. Davis and Mrs. Allen serves to caution the reader against making assumptions about color, the lack of education, or lower-class status as means of validating a simplistic vision of female "progress."[59] Rather, Davis and Allen's own self-transformations contrast with Sappho's inability to assert a stable identity for herself. As Mabelle Beaubean in Louisiana, Sappho moves from virginal child to black prostitute at the whim of the white patriarchal will: " 'It is my belief' " says her lecherous white uncle, " 'that they [black women] were a direct creation by God to be the pleasant companions of men of my race' " (*CF*, 261). But despite her escape North, Sappho is still variously constructed by the novel's upwardly mobile blacks according to each individual's desired fantasy: to John Pollock Langley (the unwitting descendent of Anson Pollock by Lucy), Sappho is the New Orleans *"fille de joi"* fit only for sexual slavery; to her neighbors, she is a remarkable specimen produced under "seductive skies" ("that's somethin' God made, honey; thar ain't nothin' like thet growed outside o' Loosyannie" [*CF*, 338, 114, 107]). She even becomes an object of desire for the friendless Dora Smith, who has "from the first, a perfect trust in the beautiful girl" (CF 98), an ironic comment given Sappho's double life.

Presumably what her sojourn in the comforting woman-centered world of the Smiths is designed to achieve is a return to self-ownership. However, Sappho's interaction with other women allows Hopkins both to pay tribute to the effectiveness of an African American female community and at the same time to critique false black female models engendered by that community. At a sewing circle gathering that combines domestic practice with political discussion, Hopkins introduces the black feminist leader Mrs. Willis, "one of many possibilities which the future will develop from among the colored women of New England" (*CF*, 144). Though Willis offers words of wisdom to those gathered, Hopkins describes her as a selfish opportunist who uses the "advancement of the colored woman" as the platform that will "float her upon its tide into the prosperity she desired" (*CF*, 147).

In keeping with her successful campaign, Mrs. Willis outlines a manifesto that theoretically empowers sexually "degraded" black women by encouraging them to redefine a new vision of virtue:

> "Never mind our poverty, ignorance, and the slights and injuries which we bear at the hands of a higher race. . . . [L]et us cultivate . . . beauty of the soul and mind, which being transmitted to our children by the law of heredity, shall improve the race by eliminating *immorality* from our midst and raising *morality* and virtue to their true place." (*CF*, 153)

Willis's philosophy addresses the negative self-images inspired by racism, stresses the importance of responsible motherhood (a lesson Sappho has yet to learn), and reconstructs black women as moral champions of their race. However, on the verge of revealing her secret to Willis, Sappho experiences "a wave of repulsion toward this woman and her effusiveness, so forced and insincere" (*CF*, 155). With merely a rigid commitment to appearances at the expense of emotional healing for fallen women, Mrs. Willis goes on to counsel continual deception for the woman who shields her past: "I think in her case she did her duty [in hiding her secret]" (*CF*, 156), she tells Sappho with perfect confidence.[60]

Sappho's retreat "as from an abyss" (*CF*, 155) suggests the complex conditions surrounding the alliances among all African American women in *Contending Forces* (in contrast to the easy, idealized contacts they make in *Hanover*), within the context of an evolving black social world of black migrants and northern-born African Americans, even among those who have devoted themselves to the uplift of their sex.[61] While the sewing circle is clearly a successful arena for women's political discussion (Mrs. Willis's lecture does articulate valuable principles), Sappho's retreat emphasizes the difficulties of "break-ing silence" about rape even in the comfort of a black domestic setting.

The subtextual search for an arena in which to address African American women's experience of white rape surfaces dramatically in the middle of the novel, during a Colored American League meeting. In the meeting, although Hopkins stresses black male awareness of the sexual assault of black women as the hidden side of the white supremacist stereotype of the black beast, she warns against the danger of having black female suffering function merely as a backdrop to the political and physical emasculation of black men. The center-piece of the meeting is a cathartic outburst by Luke Sawyer, who, after describ-ing his own suffering at the hands of white supremacists, agitates for immediate action against lynching. Unaware of Sappho's presence, Sawyer also recounts the tragedy of mulatto girl raped by her white uncle. As a male victim, Sawyer finds a structured yet supportive public environment within which to express anger and reconstruct himself as a militant. But his outrage is occasioned not so much by the girl's suffering (she presumably dies in a convent after giving birth) as by the frustration of her male protectors:

> "If I had had the man there then that committed the crime . . . I would have taken him by the throat and shaken him (he hissed the words through clinched teeth), shaken him as a dog would a rat until he was *dead!* Dead! DEAD!"   (*CF*, 260)

The female victim of Luke Sawyer's story is, of course, Sappho herself; and, at the conclusion of his presentation, she falls into a dead swoon in the middle of room.

The long tradition of black female public outcry against rape notwithstand-ing, Hopkins's revelation of a woman's story through a male narrative in the presence of other men, who are unaware of whom or what they refer to, under-scores the problematic transmission of histories such as Sappho's. Luke Sawyer and others see such histories as crucial to the understanding of how white supremacist terror victimizes all black people; however, when Will Smith takes up the discussion and focuses primarily on the black need for enfranchisement as a weapon against white supremacy, the rape of black women is in danger of being reduced to a symbol of black men's oppression, since the attack on their women demonstrates African American male emasculation at the hands of white supremacists. Hopkins's point here is not to attack a necessary black masculine discourse around lynching, but to problematize the ways in which lynching can so easily begin to supersede discussions of rape, even in the most receptive of settings.

Claudia Tate has suggested that scenes of the sewing circle and Colored American League meeting inscribe a division between public (male) and private (female) discursive spaces, and she argues that "Hopkins's use of the trope of manhood . . . seems an expression of the collective political ambition of black people—male and female—as citizens rather than a trope specifically referring to the patriarchal aspirations of enfranchised men." Yet, while *manhood* may function as a reference for the communal whole, the politics of gender difference and discourse are not erased by such an idealized styling. Tate admits as much when she asserts that Luke Sawyer in fact "represents the father's law of patriarchal judgment . . . [which] concludes that she [Sappho] is better off dead than alive." To quote Ann duCille "[p]atriarchy is for Sappho not exclusively white, as it seems to be for so many other female characters in nineteenth-century novels, but profoundly male." [62]

Mabelle may have attempted to empower herself with a new identity as Sappho, but the rehearsal of her bodily torture and her figurative "second death" signified by the fainting fit point to a still unsatisfactory lack of agency—a suggestion once more that Grace's fate continues to haunt her descendants. And while Will and Sawyer are dedicated to the protection of both black men and black women, Hopkins looks squarely at the tragedy that some black men are not so inclined: when John Pollock Langley guesses Sappho's real identity and tries to blackmail her into becoming his mistress, the precipitation of yet another "death"—made doubly tragic because it would have occurred at the hands of one of her own people—underscores Hopkins's warning about the "contending forces" against which African American communities must continually do battle. [63]

While such troubling moments sound a cautionary note on the black gender politics of *Contending Forces,* the novel's formulaic plot resolves tensions through a recommitment to female domestic principles and black male/female domestic union. Thus Sappho flees Boston to avoid Langley and retrieves her son and "the joys of motherhood" (*CF,* 345). Having achieved her redemption, at the end of the novel she is united with Langley's alter ego Will Smith, and the story ends with their marriage and the restoration of the original Montfort estate, leaving Sappho and Will to live happily, sharing "a love sanctified and purified by suffering" (*CF,* 398).

Such an ending offers a complex rewriting of possibilities, without necessarily undermining the kind of communal critique in which Hopkins has engaged. In an "uplift" novel like *Contending Forces,* black female sexual desire is structured through a discourse of marriage as a partnership toward the progress of the race, but Sappho Clark's flirtation with and eventual marriage to Will Smith by the end of the novel is sexualized by the heroine's connection to the legendary woman poet Sappho, who is noted for, among other things, her determination to fulfill personal desire. I would agree here with Ann duCille that, despite the novel's final sanitization of sex through matrimony, "sexual desire is not *displaced* by social purpose but *encoded* in it—regulated, submerged, and insinuated into the much safer realm of political zeal and the valorized venue of holy wedlock."[64]

The end result of Hopkins's *Contending Forces,* then, is not merely a recuperation of the black female body, which is the goal of both the texts of Wells and Fulton discussed earlier, but in addition an attempt to articulate black female subjectivity where virtue and communal activism work in tandem with and not as replacements for black female sexual desire.

As texts that extend turn-of-the-century debates over lynching, rape, and race, *Southern Horrors, Hanover,* and *Contending Forces* use the narration of black female experiences of white racial violence to problematize more general issues of black female self-construction and black communal conflict. A work such as *Southern Horrors* dramatizes the very different politics of reception that came into play once black women sought to address white supremacist violence as explicitly as men did. The challenges facing Ida B. Wells were those of appropriate medium, tone, and forum, but also the challenge of context: as the invisible figure behind the stereotype of the black rapist, or as the victim of white rape, the silent black woman functioned as an enabling figure for either black or white male recuperative visions. When Wells sought publicly to proclaim her subjectivity, the result was a disruption of traditional patterns of reading and writing, dramatized in the moments of expanded signification in *Southern Horrors.* In *Hanover,* David Bryant Fulton's dual focus on black female suffering and black female resistance as a central metaphor for African American experiences of racial massacres such as the 1898 Wilmington riot, also engaged prescribed narratives on race, violence, and gender. Indeed the novel's attempt to forge a new language to portray black women as simultaneously militant and vulnerable, by combining a journalistic mode with the mode of the domestic novel, indicates Fulton's recognition of the bankruptcy of traditional American discourses on racial violence. Yet despite the boundary-transgressing nature of their narrative stances and narrative strategies, neither Wells nor Fulton sought to transcend completely the limitations of community and culture: in Wells's narrative, white female desire is invariably rendered as the flip-side of black female victimhood; for Fulton, Molly must move from the role of black prostitute, circumscribed both by her sexual desire and her desirability, to the role of community savior, within which personal desire is an expression of community ambitions for social and political well-being.

While Pauline Hopkins's *Contending Forces* might seem to be the most conservative and conventional examination of the uses and abuses of black femininity in the context of turn-of-the-century racial violence, the central stories of Grace and Sappho's rapes rupture any complacency over the novel as simply a study of black middle-class manners. *Contending Forces,* like *Southern Horrors* and *Hanover,* is a text concerned primarily with challenging white race and gender ideology; but Hopkins's novel extends that critique into an interrogation of black middle-class constructions of African American womanhood as well. Thus *Contending Forces* echoes (and on other levels seeks to resolve) the frustrated search for articulation of a multidimensional black female subjectivity. Specifically, despite its envelopment of black female sexuality within a turn-of-the-century African American rhetoric of community uplift, Hopkins's novel poses a challenge to the erasure of sexual desire from the model of the redeemed black woman. Thus, whereas Wells's pamphlet problematizes the staging of the black female voice, and Fulton's novel enacts a recovery of black female body as the site of heroism and not shame, Hopkins's own black fiction of Sappho becomes the final gestural return to that body's complete recuperation.

CHAPTER FOUR

*Rethinking White Female Silences:*
*Kate Chopin's Local Color Fiction*
*and the Politics of White Supremacy*

Harris & Page of course wrote from a different standpoint;—that of
the white *gentleman* as I write from the standpoint of a white lady.
                                                        Grace King

IN ANY DISCUSSION of late-nineteenth-century American and African American literary discourses on white supremacist violence, George Washington Cable, Thomas Dixon, Thomas Nelson Page, Ida B. Wells, Charles Chesnutt, Sutton E. Griggs, David Bryant Fulton, and even Pauline Hopkins must
undoubtedly be included as prominent figures. Yet this standard list suggests
that lynching and mob rule were of concern only to black and white male
writers and to black women activists. Much work remains to be done in uncovering how white women participated in debates about white supremacist violence, whether as literary figures or as social reformers. The tradition of white
female activism perfected during the antislavery movement culminated by the
end of the century in women's efforts to secure temperance reform, to improve
the social conditions of the poor, to "Americanize" immigrants, and especially
to extend women's rights to include the vote, access to birth control, and higher
education. Such widespread activity would surely have set the stage for white
female commentary on white supremacist violence.[1]

Not surprisingly, white women ran the gamut of opinions for and against
lynching. By the 1890s, one of the most notorious supporters of the idea of the
black rapist was Rebecca Latimer Felton, wife of a Georgia minister-politician,
an avid suffragist, a supporter of the temperance movement, and later the first
woman to serve as a United States senator. Speaking in 1897 at the annual
meeting of the State Agricultural Society of Georgia on ways to improve farm
life, Felton urged rural whites to look to the protection of their women:

I warned those representative men . . . of the terrible effects that were
already seen in the corruption of the negro vote, their venality, the use of
whiskey, the debasement of the ignorant and incitement of evil passion in

108

the vicious. . . . A crime nearly unknown before and during the war had become an almost daily occurrence and mob law had also become omnipotent.

It was at the same meeting that she made her infamous plea to white men to "lynch a thousand times a week if necessary," provoking the ire of black and white men opposed to lynching, including the black editor Alexander Manly from Wilmington, North Carolina, and Andrew Sledd, a white Southerner and a professor at Emory.[2] Felton's views were popular enough, however, for her to launch a lecture tour aimed at protesting what she saw as white male inaction in the face of black rape.

Because of her sympathy for Southern white supremacists, Frances Willard of the Women's Christian Temperance Union found herself embroiled with Ida B. Wells in a battle over her public reputation as a moral reformer. The furor arose over an 1890 newspaper interview given by Willard in which she described "great dark faced mobs whose rallying cry is better whiskey and more of it." Willard claimed that "[t]he safety of women, of childhood, of the home is menaced in a thousand localities at this moment, so that men dare not go beyond the sight of their own roof-tree."[3] During her first visit to England on an anti-lynching lecture tour, Wells publicly attacked Willard for this stand, a move that prompted the British temperance leader Lady Henry Somerset to publish a new interview with Willard to serve as a vindication. In the interview Willard stood by her belief that Southern families were menaced by blacks, a fact she had heard from "the best people I know in the South"; still, to mollify critics like Wells, she added at the same time that "no crime however heinous can by any possibility excuse the commission of any act of cruelty or the taking of any human life without due course of law."[4] Willard's WCTU eventually passed an anti-lynching resolution in 1893; and despite Wells's protests that Willard's earlier public utterances were tantamount to a support of white violence, the temperance reformer was staunchly defended by William Lloyd Garrison, Frederick Douglass, and Julia Ward Howe.

Compared to Willard, Chicago social worker and NAACP member Jane Addams was much less equivocal in her attack on lynching, publishing in the January 1901 issue of the *Independent* an indictment of mob rule called "Respect for Law." However, as Bettina Aptheker has pointed out, Addams did not reject the image of the black beast; rather, she saw lynching as an act that degraded white participants and enforced a disregard for legitimate institutions of law. Addams admitted that there was indeed "a peculiar class of crime [i.e. rape] committed by one race against another," but she argued "[t]hat the bestial in man, that which leads him to pillage and rape, can never be controlled by public cruelty and dramatic punishment, which too often cover fury and revenge." Addams went on to suggest that

[b]rutality begets brutality; and proceeding on the theory that the negro is undeveloped, and therefore must be treated in this primitive fashion, is to forget that the immature pay little attention to statements, but quickly imitate what they see. The under-developed are never helped by such methods as these, for they learn only by imitation. The child who is managed by a system of bullying and terrorizing is almost sure to be the vicious and stupid child.[5]

Like Willard, Addams was horrified by mob rule; but she also gave credence to the white supremacist notion that "under-developed" black men were driven to rape white women, and that as moral beings blacks were severely handicapped. And again it was Ida B. Wells who responded to what she saw as serious moral lapses in white feminist argumentation on lynching, replying several months later to Addams's comments with her article "Lynching and the Excuse for It," also published in the *Independent*. While more respectful of Addams than she was of Willard, Wells nevertheless pointed out firmly that the belief in black rape was "the same baseless assumption which influences ninety-nine out of every one hundred persons who discuss this question" and urged that "misrepresentation should have no place in the discussion of this all important question, [and] that the figures of the lynching record should be allowed to plead, trumpet tongued, in defense of the slandered dead."[6]

Activists like Wells would fight for decades more to encourage many white women reformers to rethink their stance on white supremacy. The situation was made more difficult by the fact that, in their postbellum campaign, white women suffragists embraced a strategy of "expediency" under which they accommodated white supremacy in order to sign on Southern states behind the campaign for the woman's vote. In 1867, early in the post–Civil War campaign for suffrage, Elizabeth Cady Stanton argued that

[w]ith the black man, we have no new element in government, but with the education and elevation of women, we have a power that is to develop the Saxon race into a higher and nobler life and thus, by the law of attraction, to lift all races to a more even platform than can ever be reached in the political isolation of the sexes.[7]

In terms of a white female organization dedicated to fighting white supremacist violence, Wells and others had to wait until 1930 for the founding of the Association of Southern Women for the Prevention of Lynching organized by Jesse Daniel Ames, herself a white suffragist. Ames's organization "represented an acceptance of accountability for a racist mythology that white women had not created but that they nevertheless served." Unlike earlier suffragists who had argued that "the Negro Problem" and the political and social advancement of women were completely separate issues, Ames saw lynching "not only as an obstacle to regional development and an injustice to blacks, but also an insult to white women."[8] Ames and her organization sought to work with black women against lynching; such interracial cooperation made her recognize more clearly that the practice of lynching was itself supported by stereotypes of black female promiscuity—a fantasy that shielded white men who raped black women.

The record left by Felton, Willard, Addams, and Ames suggests that white women reformers who were interested in improving race relations came late to a sophisticated analysis of white supremacist violence, which is why, for example, overtly anti-lynching works of fiction by white women writers seem so few and far between before 1920.[9] Thus, decades after the efforts of Wells and other black women, the May 1923 issue of *Century Magazine* contains the short story "Nemesis" by Virginia novelist Mary Johnston on the aftereffects of a lynching on a small Southern town. In the story Johnston acknowledges that lynching is less about black guilt (the story's lynchers never actually ascertain whether their victim is guilty) than it is about white male desire for revenge. A number of the lynch mob's leaders are in fact adopted sons of the South, hailing from New England, the Midwest, and the West, revealing Johnston's belief that the responsibility for white supremacist violence was national and not just Southern. The story ends when the ghost of the dead rape victim returns to admonish her husband for his role in the lynching: "John, don't ever say that you-all did that for me! If you're asking me—no! no! no! What good could it do you-all or me or him or anybody? It didn't please and it didn't serve—not anything—not anybody!"[10] Silenced first by the rape attack and then by the imposition of male narratives about black criminality, the woman rejects the crime of murder committed in her name as an act that serves no purpose for the protection of the white home and hearth. Curiously, though, Johnston only implies that the black man lynched is not guilty of rape.

Without disregarding the nature of white female political discourse on lynching and rape, it is equally important to identify how these topics surfaced in late-nineteenth-century white women's fiction, beyond the kind of direct commentary provided by Felton, Addams, Ames, or Johnston. In the field of black women's writing, for instance, only recently have critics paid any attention to how Pauline E. Hopkins explicitly addresses racial violence in *Contending Forces* (1900), a novel ostensibly designed to address issues of race, femininity, and domesticity. Instead of dismissing Hopkins's work as a novel of black manners marred by a "wild portrayal of injustice, cruelty, and brutality," scholars now recognize *Contending Forces*'s explicit contrast of the promise of black domestic life in America with the crisis of lynching and rape as Hopkins's challenge to readers to recognize that the social and political survival of blacks into the twentieth century depended on the defeat of white supremacy.[11]

Given the fact that turn-of-the-century white women writers—already negotiating traditional notions about what passed as suitable subject matter for the female author—were further constricted by the conservative tastes of publishers and public alike, can we also read white women's writing in the 1890s as similarly engaged with lynching and white supremacy through a certain kind of genteel discourse of fiction?[12]

This chapter sets forth a "rereading" of the recently canonized turn-of-the-century white woman writer Kate Chopin, as an attempt to expand the assumed record of American women's responses to lynching beyond the official utterances of the women who actually spoke out on the issue. Reclaimed by twentieth-century feminist scholars because of her iconoclastic representation of female sexual rebellion in *The Awakening* (1899), Chopin has always been portrayed as sympathetic to the New Woman movement at the turn of the century. On the subject of Chopin and white supremacy, critics uniformly turn to her 1893 short story "Désirée's Baby" to demonstrate her critique of nineteenth-century double standards of race and sexual conduct that governed the lives of white men and women. Still, though some attention has been paid to the ethnic contexts of her Southern fiction, little has been done to examine fully how the themes of female sexual liberation can be read specifically in the context of the racial politics of female containment inherent in the ideology of lynching. Similarly, more consideration is needed of how her local color fiction addressed not just miscegenation and black concubinage, but also the problems of regional recovery after the Civil War and Reconstruction, of white male aggression, and of white fantasies of black sexuality.[13] Unfortunately, the traditional simplification by white feminist critics and others of the term *woman writer* renders economic, racial, ethnic, and regional distinctions subordinate to gender, masking the unavoidable convergence of all five categories and severely limiting fuller critical discussion of Chopin and other white female writers within American literature.

As Anne Goodwyn Jones has suggested, even when we assume that "Chopin's concerns more centrally had to do with what she saw as the almost immutable and far from regionally limited relationship between woman and man, the symbols she chose to invest her subject with imaginative power come from her [S]outhern experience."[14] Thus, many of Chopin's short stories, as well as her first novel, *At Fault* (1890), evince a strong preoccupation with white adjustment in the wake of black emancipation, with the problem of internal ethnic and class divisions, and with the shift from rural to urban, from Southern to Northern bases of power.[15]

Chopin's fictional representation of the Reconstruction and post-Reconstruction social scenes are not designed to promote pro-black political activism, as in the case of some of the fiction by William Dean Howells or George Washington Cable. Hers are "thoroughly orthodox" late-nineteenth-century white attitudes toward African Americans; and in much of her work, images of "black suffering, slavery and oppression are all linguistically and thematically appropriated for white women."[16] However, her fiction's representation of white society as heterogeneous and at times violently divided bears some comparison to the conflicted responses to the stereotype of white unity that appear in Mark Twain's *Pudd'nhead Wilson* (1894) and later in the novels of Thomas Dixon. Also, since so many of Kate Chopin's stories are about white men as well as white women, the issue of white supremacy and its attendant violence surfaces as a subject not through the unambiguous lens of racial war, but subtly, within an often all-white context that has been carefully and imperceptibly "shaped and transformed by the presence of the marginalized."[17]

### KATE CHOPIN AS WHITE SOUTHERNER

The "Southern experience" on which Chopin drew heavily to shape her white characters has the potential to complicate considerably how we read her representation of whiteness, and specifically of white masculinity. Unlike Thomas Dixon, Chopin was not reared in the shadow of the Ku Klux Klan, but both her childhood in St. Louis before the Civil War and her marriage to a racially loyal white Southerner tied her on the one hand to the memory of slavery, and on the other to the violence of white supremacy itself.

Chopin was born Catherine O'Flaherty in 1851 in St. Louis, Missouri. Her Irish father, a prosperous self-made merchant, died in a train accident when she was five. After her father's death, Kate O'Flaherty was raised exclusively by the independent women of her mother's family, presided over by Victoire Verdon Charleville, a descendent of the early creole settlers to the city. At the time of Chopin's childhood, St. Louis was technically Northern, but "having been settled by French [slaveholding] colonists from New Orleans" the city did possess a Southern as well as a frontier quality. Though many of its citizens did not own slaves, St. Louis had become a slave trading center, slave auctions taking place "[o]ccasionally . . . on the steps of the [city] Courthouse"; on the eve of the Civil War, the O'Flaherty household included six slaves.[18] Staunchly Confederate in sympathy, with slaveholding relatives living in Louisiana and a son fighting for the Southern cause, the O'Flahertys were disliked by the pro-Union faction in St. Louis and at one point in 1863 a Union flag was draped on their front porch. In what might be considered the only overtly political act of her life, thirteen-year-old Kate O'Flaherty angrily ripped the flag off her home; she narrowly escaped arrest by the pro-Union authorities of the city, but her act earned her the nickname of St Louis's "Littlest Rebel."[19] The family survived the war, suffering some vandalism of their home, but also enduring the death their son George while he served in the Confederate army. And of course they were destined to lose their slaves, including one Louise, who was presumably Chopin's cherished black "mammy."[20]

Kate O'Flaherty's connection to the South was reaffirmed by her marriage to Louisiana-born Oscar Chopin in 1870. After a courtship and a wedding ceremony in St. Louis, and then a European honeymoon that coincided with the Franco-Prussian War, the Chopins returned to the United States late in the year to settle in New Orleans, where Oscar worked as a cotton factor. By 1879 he was experiencing financial difficulties, and he moved his large family (five sons) north to Cloutierville, a small village in Natchitoches Parish where he had purchased some land to augment the remains of his family estate. After bearing her sixth and last child in Cloutierville, Kate Chopin remained there with her husband until his death in 1882.

Oscar Chopin had never been successful as a businessman, and the newly widowed Kate had to resolve her husband's enormous debt in the midst of caring for six children. Undaunted by this challenge, she put the estate in order and in 1884 decided to move back to St. Louis to be with her mother. Thus it was in St. Louis, in the comfort of first and familiar surroundings, that Chopin drew on almost twelve years of life in Louisiana, publishing two novels and approximately a hundred stories about black and white women and men, and the complexities of sexuality, marriage, and maternity. She corresponded frequently with her in-laws in Cloutierville and kept up with the running of the Chopin estate, which was now rented out. She never returned to Louisiana for any extended period, and she died in St. Louis in 1904.

In terms of race relations, Louisiana had a unique history in the South. New Orleans, Chopin's home during the early years of her marriage, offered residents a rich mélange of French, African, Anglo, and Spanish cultures. While other Southern states during slavery enacted segregation and anti-miscegenation laws, in Louisiana blacks and whites mixed freely in the Catholic Church, in the street, and at quadroon balls that still occurred after the Civil War; indeed there were even a few interracial marriages, despite the ban against such contact.[21]

Before the war, free blacks "owned real and personal property (including slaves), contracted legal marriages, testified against whites in courts of law, learned trades and professions, and participated in music and the arts."[22] Interestingly, free men of color had never been closely allied with black slaves. After emancipation, however, the fates of both the free *gens de couleur* and the ex-slaves were linked in the struggle for civil rights. According to John Blassingame, the ex-slave, as "the property the white man went to war to preserve, was the ubiquitous reminder of his folly, guilt, humiliation, and defeat. . . . Most whites were bewildered, angered, and humiliated by the change" in the status quo.[23] Thus, despite the seemingly liberal racial atmosphere of antebellum Louisiana, after the war the stage was set for violence as whites moved to regain control.

The worlds of New Orleans, Cloutierville, and the Cane River valley in which Kate Chopin set her local color stories had their own violent racial past, which undoubtedly become part of the fabric of both her Southern identity and her Southern writing. Indeed, as Helen Taylor asserts, "[s]he could hardly have been oblivious to the many class and race tensions in the area, or to the considerable shifts in economic and social power and influence" that marked the tumultuous years after the Civil War.[24] Before the war, her father-in-law, the French-born Dr. Jean Baptiste Chopin, had been a wealthy cotton planter with 94 slaves and more than 4,000 acres of land. Prior to the advent of Dr. Chopin, the land had been owned by Robert McAlpin, said to have been the model for Harriet Beecher Stowe's cruel slaveholder Simon Legree in *Uncle Tom's Cabin*. Comparison and confusion in the minds of local residents between the two was inevitable, since Dr. Chopin was notoriously cruel to both his slaves and his white wife.[25]

As a child Oscar Chopin had been unwilling to brutalize his father's slaves, but as an adult coming of age after the Civil War he was clearly a devoted white supremacist, since in 1874 he enlisted in the Crescent City White League. The White Leaguers, whose members numbered among New Orleans's white elite, sought to oust the state's Republican administration, which was hated for favoring blacks. In the summer of 1874, the armed paramilitary White Leaguers —including Oscar Chopin—stormed City Hall to force the mayor's resignation, and a struggle with the city police ensued. Yet another company of white supremacists moved on the State House, expelling the Republican state government until federal troops reinstated it a week later. Despite nationwide indignation at the League's actions, the federal government did not prosecute the rebels. The "Battle of Liberty Place," as it was latter dubbed by New Orleans whites, resulted in the deaths of twenty people and the wounding of a hundred others.[26]

Oscar Chopin's affiliation with the White League would not have seemed out of place in the racially polarized context of Reconstruction. During this period, Louisiana creoles from all classes—especially in New Orleans—swelled the ranks of the state's many local white supremacist organizations such as the Innocents and the Ku Klux Klan. In 1868 almost half the white male population in many parishes of Louisiana belonged to the Knights of the White Camellia (KWC), an organization founded by the French creole Alcibiade DeBlanc that was pledged toward "the MAINTENANCE OF THE SUPREMACY OF THE WHITE RACE in this Republic."[27] The northern part of the state increasingly became a Klan stronghold; and in 1873, whites murdered 103 blacks in the town of Colfax.[28] Such violence continued through to the end of the century. In 1891 eleven Italian immigrants were lynched by a New Orleans mob after a court failed to convict them for the murder of a police officer. Lynching continued, and in 1898 blacks were disenfranchised with the inclusion of the "grandfather" clause in the state constitution. One of the most infamous race riots in American history occurred in 1900 in New Orleans—the same city Kate Chopin loved to roam during the 1870s, fascinated by the exotic presence of black culture.[29]

The riot began with an altercation between black resident Robert Charles and the city police, and it finally exploded into a bloody white rampage against the city's black population that lasted for four days.[30]

Site of the Chopin family's ancestral home, Natchitoches Parish had a history consistent with the rest of the state, which meant that its black residents (60 percent of the parish's population) were consistently targeted by white supremacists. Cloutierville resident Phanor Breazeale left a "Statement on Reconstruction Natchitoches" that chronicled his and other white supremacists' criminal activities against blacks in the parish from 1872 to 1878, the year before Kate and Oscar Chopin moved north to the town.[31] Dispassionately and in chilling detail Breazeale describes white Democratic election fraud, the purpose of which was to counteract black Republican votes, and his own eager participation in the ambush and lynching of blacks.[32] In one anecdote Breazeale regrets only that, in attempting to lynch a black political activist, his comrades inadvertently murdered a harmless black sexton of the Episcopal church. Despite such "mistakes," Breazeale views his actions and those of other white terrorists with pride, carefully recounting his substantial role in the intimidation and harassment of an elected black official and his family. Ironically, Breazeale makes it clear in his narrative that the motives of such white "patriots" were purely to exercise political control and intimidation, not to protect white women, noting that though "the negro population on the west bank of Red River of ward 3 was enormously in the majority . . . they were good quiet citizens and obeyed the ladies looking after the crops for their absent husbands."[33] Breazeale eventually married Oscar Chopin's sister, and in later years he served as a friend and confidant to Kate Chopin, entertaining her with tales of his Reconstruction-era activities. According to some, Breazeale told Chopin the story that later became *The Awakening*. And, according to Emily Toth, Breazeale might have served as a model for the many attractive but ungovernable white male characters in Chopin's fiction.[34]

The turmoil of politically and racially violent Louisiana in Kate Chopin's lifetime surfaces obliquely in her fiction, mediated through localized representations of domestic disputes and rural community clashes among whites with differing class, regional, and ethnic affiliations (upper-class French creoles still living on the land, urban residents of New Orleans, lower-class cajuns, "American" whites).

### CLASS, RACE, ETHNICITY, AND MALE AGGRESSION IN CHOPIN'S FICTION

In her discussion of pre–Civil War Afro-creole culture in New Orleans, historian Gwendolyn Midlo Hall asserts that the "Afro-creole culture of New Orleans has had a significant impact not only on blacks of Louisiana and Afro-

American culture in the United States but on American culture in general."[35] Both the cultural and political conditions of black life had a continuing impact on white racial consciousness, and Chopin's literary imagination was undoubtedly shaped by her exposure to the political and cultural turmoil of the Reconstruction and post-Reconstruction eras. Thus her short stories often deploy a problematic, unresolved investigation of the limits of white action against the backdrop of increasingly prescriptive social roles for both blacks and whites.

As active characters, blacks are not central to Chopin's exploration of white Southern identities; however, the use of blackness, slavery, and Reconstruction as cultural and historical referents to locate and describe white social experience is crucial in her fiction. Chopin constructs blackness generally (although not exclusively) as benign, separate, and exotic rather than as monstrous. Most characterizations draw on the old standards of local color and plantation fiction: blacks like Old Uncle Oswald in "The Bênitous' Slave" and the servants in "Old Aunt Peggy," "Tante Cat'rinette" and "Nég Créol" are quaint "darky" throwbacks to serene plantation days.

*[margin handwritten note: ✗ portrayal of blacks as benign rather than monstrous]*

When she is critical of Southern culture, as in "Désirée's Baby" and "La Belle Zoraïde," Chopin uses the stereotype of black sexual freedom as a metaphor to criticize hypocrisy over miscegenation and white refusal to come to terms with sexual passion. Chopin does not, however, advocate the abolition of Jim Crow. When the issue of integration surfaces, it is usually seen as an obnoxious act performed half-seriously by local whites who want to harass their own kind, as her novel *At Fault* and the story "In and Out of Old Natchitoches" demonstrate. Blacks in her fiction welcome separation, and mulatto characters in "A Little Free Mulatto" and "In and Out of Old Natchitoches" find peace and happiness in the little black enclave L'Isle des Mulâtres.[36]

When blacks and whites do meet, as long as social distinctions are upheld, they confront each other easily and without tensions, as in "Ozème's Holiday." While the cajun farmer Ozème vacations around the Cane River valley, he stops to nurse black Aunt Tildy's sick nephew and harvest her cotton before the rain. Working side by side in the field with Aunt Tildy, Ozème remarks jokingly: "I am watchin' you, ol' woman; you don' fool me. You got to work that han' o' yo's spryer than you doin', or I'll take the rawhide. You done fo'got w'at the rawhide tas'e like, I reckon" (*CW*, 386).[37] Aunt Tildy is highly amused at this "reminder" of the old days, as the white man "Mista Ozème," who might have beaten her with impunity during slavery, does not mind helping her out of a bind after the Civil War.

Chopin's portraits of blacks are generally one-dimensional, but her representation of the internal world of white Southerners is always marked by an acute sensitivity to the heterogeneity of origins and experiences in terms of class, ethnicity, and generation. In contrast to the cajun farmer Ozème, members of the French creole planter class who bear allegiance to the Old South are almost overwhelmed by the historical turn of events. Such is the case in Chopin's story "Ma'ame Pélagie" where the main character, a former plantation belle, cannot exist outside of the memories of her family's past. For men of Ma'ame Pélagie's class, the difficulty of negotiating change expresses itself in community violence and self-destructive behavior, both of which from Chopin's point of view are counterproductive to the success of the postwar South.[38] The primary example of her complex attitude toward class and white male aggression appears in the saga of the Santien family whose fate Chopin outlines in several stories, including *At Fault*, "In Sabine" (1893), "In and Out of Old Natchitoches" (1893), and "A No-Account Creole" (1894)—works in which the contradictions around class and white male aggression generate their own particular discourse on whiteness.

Like the Chopins and their Cloutierville neighbors the Sampites, the fictional Santiens were wealthy creole planters before the war: "In the days of Lucien Santien and his hundred slaves, [the plantation] . . . had been very splendid in the wealth of its thousand acres. But the war did its work, of course. Then [his son] Jules Santien was not the man to mend such damage as the war had left" (*CW*, 82). The "damage" inflicted by the Civil War comes visibly in the loss of slaves, and the Santiens find themselves unable to manage under the economically altered conditions of the South. After the death of Jules, Madame Santien returns to her family in France, while her sons Hector, Placide, and Grégoire tend to what remains of the family estate, but to no avail.[39] According to Grégoire, "Hec, he took charge the firs' year an' run it in debt. Placide an' me did'n' have no betta luck the naxt year. Then the creditors come up from New Orleans an' took holt. That' the time I packed my duds an' lef' " (*CW*, 751). Eventually Hector chooses to live among the lowlife of New Orleans, and Placide earns the nickname of "a no-account creole" because of his lack of ambition and desultory attitude toward work. Only young Grégoire attempts to integrate himself within a postwar community when he goes to help out on the thriving plantation Place-du-Bois, owned by his young, recently widowed aunt Thérèse Lafirme.

The Santien brothers reference what Joseph G. Tregle calls the "myth" of the creole, a race that

> produced "the aristocracy of the region" through most of the nineteenth century, maintaining family circles renowned for haughty exclusivity as well as cultural refinement and worldly sophistication, the whole invigorated and sustained by fierce conceit of ancestry and a 'chivalry' which gave its inheritors certainty of their superiority over lesser breeds of men.[40]

Quick-tempered, arrogant, but made immensely attractive and sympathetic in Chopin's stories, the Santiens are romanticized in standard plantation fiction style as reminders of a more adventuresome, more passionate past. Thus, in "A

No-Account Creole," Grégoire's older brother Placide inhabits a bucolic world in a crumbling plantation house on his ruined, mortgaged land, content to spend his days doing odd jobs or wandering around the Red River. Though Chopin had originally conceived her story around the life and loves of a woman, Euphrasie Manton, the plot centers squarely on Placide's struggle with destiny and (dis)empowerment in his role as Euphrasie's discarded creole lover.[41] Indeed, Placide holds the story hostage when, gun in hand, he sets out to murder the yankified Offdean for taking possession of his family's land as well as of his childhood sweetheart. Bloodshed is narrowly averted when, as an ultimate demonstration that no one but a creole knows "how to love" (*CW*, 101), Placide decides to make the ultimate sacrifice and free Euphrasie from all romantic obligation.

Chopin's story would function simply as a romantic tribute to male heterosexual passion and the capacity for noble self-sacrifice, were it not for the fact that she places Placide's initial impulse toward murder within antebellum traditions of Southern honor and a legacy of white violence produced and nurtured by the South's defining history of slavery. Meanwhile, both Euphrasie and Offdean are products of an increasingly urban world, where to a great extent the social status of whites is fluid. Importantly, Placide's link to the antebellum past is enforced by the only moment of black narrative in the story. One of Santien's ex-slaves, La Chatte, recalls a chilling incident during her enslavement when a youthful Placide, intolerant of having his desires disregarded, forced La Chatte at gunpoint to drop her other chores and fix him a meal of coquignoles and coffee. During her entire time in the kitchen, until the meal's preparation was complete, Placide held the gun to her head. At the end of her story, La Chatte hints at even more such incidents with the patriarch Jules Santien. As a poverty-stricken black laundress on the decayed Santien estate, La Chatte calls to mind a disenfranchised black population whose collective memory speaks to the historical brutality of life under slavery, as well as to the dual hope and disappointment fostered by Reconstruction and the years beyond. Though each character references a separate group fear of disenfranchisement in both the story's present and its implied future, Placide's tragedy as a failed white man is made to displace that of La Chatte.

The anxiety over white failure engages with but is not analogous to the "failure" of blacks to move from slavery to freedom. Rather, the historical and political isolation suffered by white characters such as Placide both recalls and denies the isolation imposed on American blacks at the historical moment of the story's publication in 1894. Placide is celebrated on white ethnic terms as a romantic creole lover, but his final disqualification as an overly passionate suitor and an irresponsible landowner echoes both the sexual criminalization of black men as beasts/rapists under the regime of late-nineteenth-century white supremacy and their disenfranchisement as post–Civil War citizens. Thus, inasmuch as Placide's violence toward Offdean is not "racial" violence, it is racialized within the context of his past life as a slaveholder's son and of his present life as a white man who operates on his own codes of chivalrous conduct in an economically dynamic, biracial, multiethnic South. Placide's story also references that of countless black men in the South in that both he and his creed must be evacuated to make room for a presumably more acceptable type of lover and landowner in the New South. Thus, though Chopin's sympathetic focus in the story seems to leave room only for Placide, so that blackness can not function as more than a shadowy subtext for the narrative, her articulation of a white man's history in terms that might have been used to describe the fortunes of African American men underscores her dependence on racial discourses about blacks and whites as mutually constitutive, with or without the presence of black characters in her fiction.

This pattern of representation that demands a simultaneous referencing of black and white also marks Chopin's narrative strategy in *At Fault*. The novel's main focus is the romantic relationship between Thérèse Lafirme and David Hosmer, a St. Louis businessman who runs a timber mill on Thérèse's land. In this context Chopin seems to put aside the explosive issues of black suffrage, the Klan, and mob violence, focusing instead on the white domestic haven maintained by Thérèse, the enlightened female despot of Place-du-Bois.

*At Fault* adheres to the standard plot of the North/South reunion romance between Thérèse and Hosmer to signify the promise of Henry Grady's New South: the unity between Southern agricultural power and Northern commercial and business interests. The subplot of racial discontent and violence, however, belongs to two other significant characters: on the one hand Grégoire, who struggles to adapt to the world created by Thérèse and Hosmer; and on the other the destructive, pretechnocratic, mixed-blood character Joçint. Their struggle is figured in the context of a New South coming to terms with the railroad, industrial development by the Northern business establishment represented by Hosmer, and the sudden shift of a black population from slavery to wage labor.

The tension between antebellum white ideals and the postemancipation threat of "color" comes when Grégoire surprises Joçint in the act of burning down Hosmer's mill: instead of relying on more legitimate methods of punishment, the creole fatally shoots the arsonist. While Chopin unmistakably suggests that Grégoire's murderous impulse is horrifying, her narrative allows no sympathy for the victim. Rude, animalistic, and "extremely treacherous" (*CW*, 757) as a direct consequence of his Indian blood, the dark-skinned Joçint represents a version of the black beast stereotype of pro-lynching fiction.[42]

Donald Ringe has suggested that Chopin creates parallel figures in Grégoire and Joçint, figures whose "inner natures simply will not permit" assimilation into the postwar South.[43] However, as a creole Grégoire is allowed a certain heroic measure. As the unruly worker turned saboteur who refuses to adhere to the new order, Joçint and not Grégoire stands as the obstacle to national progress, and as such becomes the primary embodiment of evil in the novel's Southern white community—a fact that demands his extermination.[44] Consequently, as an act of salvation for the New South, Grégoire's murder of Joçint "is seen as less threatening and forgiven more easily by the whole community."[45] His act of racial aggression creates exactly the same effects that real-life acts of white terrorism such as the lynching, Klan rides, and race riots of the type engaged in by Chopin's husband and Phanor Breazeale were supposed to achieve: the black workers who have been pilfering from the Lafirme plantation regard the show of white power with awe and are suitably respectful of traditional racial hierarchies. Thus Chopin's failure to offer a complete condemnation of Grégoire suggests that, though she may not approve of white violence, she respects its usefulness.

While Chopin's characterization of Joçint is consistent with some aspects of white supremacist ideology, she disrupts at least some of the traditional racial assumptions around the black beast in order to re-vision gender and race politics among the white characters. For one thing, the subplot repudiates the specific notion of the black as rapist, since Joçint is never a sexual threat to Thérèse. While the bloodshed in *At Fault* mirrors that of the real-life lynching of blacks, Chopin here implies in part that violence occurs, as even Thomas Dixon himself later acknowledged, "when the Negro ceases to work under the direction of the Southern white man."[46] Thus the conflict between Joçint and his white employers is figured primarily as a clash of racially determined goals over the use of land and labor, rather than as the rape and possession of the white female body. This presentation fractures the rhetoric of white supremacy that fused the objectified and disempowered white female body with the white nation. As a white woman who does not rely on the "necessary" protection of white men, Thérèse's self-sufficiency and independence (as well as her willingness to cultivate her love for the married Hosmer) mark her as the kind of dangerous woman the black beast stereotype was meant to corral.

The reformulation of Thérèse's role in the white South's social and political future articulates a new rhetoric of race, gender, and power that is further exemplified in the contrasts between Grégoire and Thérèse as managers of the land and its black labor force. As an example of the new order of white female management, Thérèse Lafirme handles her intractable black workers with a disciplined yet kindly hand, replacing the male violence of slavery days with her Southern knowledge of the "darky" character.[47] Though the novel begins after the Civil War and affords us little information about her life as a wife and slave mistress, Thérèse Lafirme's ability to weather successfully the era's changing economic and social conditions speaks to Chopin's revision of the myth of the Southern belle. Specifically Chopin replaces this myth with the idea of the

Southern woman as the white man's equal in leadership and business acumen. The roots of such a revision had taken hold during the Civil War, when white plantation mistresses had been required to manage the slaves and land following the departure of their men to join the Confederate army. With her character Thérèse, Chopin argues for a trend identified by her contemporary Wilbur Fisk Tillett in which "a woman is respected and honored in the South for earning her own living, and would lose respect if, as an able-bodied woman, she settled herself as a burden on a brother, or even on a father."[48]

Significantly, At Fault demonstrates that Chopin is willing to challenge the politics of white supremacy only enough to liberate her white heroines, while embracing at the same time its structuring of race relations to consolidate Thérèse's power. Rather than embodying a besieged nation, Chopin's heroine thus becomes a feminized literalization of Grady's New South community spirit, a community that, when dealing with racial inferiors, relies not on "the cowardly menace of mask or shot-gun, but [on] the peaceful majesty of intelligence and responsibility, massed and unified for the protection of its homes and the preservation of its liberty."[49] Chopin's use of Grégoire confirms even Grady's admission that "under this fair seeming there is disorder and violence," but Chopin also uses Thérèse to signify an alternate reality that respects traditional racial codes and racial balances of power without losing sight of the Southern white need for black labor.[50] As Grady himself suggests in his manifesto The New South, Thérèse Lafirme's world "is simply the old South under new conditions."[51]

Grégoire clearly functions as a means of demarcating the space for the existence of a kind of Southern "New Woman," but he also exists to help refigure significantly the meaning of white violence. For one thing, his role as an anachronism of the antebellum South displaces contemporary white anxiety over lynching as a barbarous practice. Grégoire's aggression is depicted as tragic rather than as merely destructive, and he is doubly romanticized as a gentleman and a passionate suitor.

As she does with Placide, Chopin specifically accounts for Grégoire's predilection for violent racial control by linking his behavior to antebellum male models of white behavior: he is fascinated by the memory of McFarlane, the first owner of Place-du-Bois, whose exercise of complete control over the lives of his slaves made him "[t]he meanest w'ite man thet ever lived"; he "can't res' in his grave fur the niggas he's killed" (CW, 751).[52] Thus Grégoire's violence has no roots in the present political or domestic world of Place-du-Bois, and the racial and economic management of the South engineered by Thérèse and Hosmer is vindicated from its own historical submersion within a world of racial turmoil. Their system is based on a subjugation of black labor, but their dominance is masked behind the figure of Grégoire; white racial violence is accounted for as simply a declining problem of creole arrogance out-of-bounds, not a long-standing white antipathy to black economic and political rivalry that might extend into the twentieth century. So, the story implies, violence will disappear upon Grégoire's removal, rather than requiring a reform of black and white power relations.

While few scholars can conceive of naming Chopin, Thomas Nelson Page, and Thomas Dixon in the same breath, it is worth considering that Chopin shares these male writers' uneasiness with white violence. In his trilogy on the Ku Klux Klan, Dixon abhors the chaos of mob aggression, opting instead for the ritualized murder committed by his Klansmen, which he renders as almost a religious experience in its power to rejuvenate white masculinity. Page's *Red Rock: A Chronicle of Reconstruction* (1898) does feature anti-black violence after Reconstruction; but by the novel's end, blacks under white supervision are pressed into service on the frontier as Indian fighters for the U.S. Army, thereby transforming racial aggression into a necessary tool for territorial expansion. Indeed, Page is most like Chopin in his short story collection *In Ole Virginia* (1887), where white violence is romanticized as a pre–Civil War occurrence not against blacks but within the context of Civil War battles and duels. He confronts interracial violence in the ghost story "No Haid Pawn," but within an appropriately distancing context: his white hero, lost on a hunting trip, takes shelter in a haunted antebellum plantation and contemplates the deeds of the estate's long-dead West Indian (rather than American) slave owner, who was guilty of the vilest of deeds. Such a rescripting of the face of the South for a national audience would have minimized any white anxiety over the fifty to eighty blacks lynched yearly in the 1880s, and especially over anti-black riots that occurred in Carrollton, Mississippi, and Danville, Virginia, Page's home state.[53]

In keeping with the need to distance her vision of the postwar South from the reality of lynching and to secure racial boundaries, Chopin uses Grégoire's behavior to repudiate violence as a practice that might put whites in the position of imitating (and thus embodying) the moral deficiency of the racial Other. (And here Chopin seems to echo the rhetoric of Jane Addams discussed earlier.) As an "enlightened" intersectional coalition of white characters, Thérèse, David, and his sister Melicent Hosmer are disturbed by the fact that Grégoire does not "understand [why] . . . he should receive any thing but praise for having rid the community of so offensive and dangerous a personage as Joçint," and collectively they register an emotional shock at his complete "blind[ness] to the moral aspect of his deed" (*CW,* 824). The Northern characters exhibit a more extreme response. Indeed, Hosmer's inward abhorrence of the murder situates Grégoire in the same role of destructive animal inhabited by Joçint:

> Heredity and pathology had to be considered in relation with the slayer's character. . . . [Hosmer] was conscious of an inward repulsion which this action of Grégoire's awakened in him,—much the same as a feeling of disgust for an animal whose instinct drives it to the doing of violent deeds,—yet he made no difference in his manner towards him. (*CW*, 824)

In an outward show of racial solidarity with Thérèse's nephew, Hosmer is silent in front of black workers; but his private characterization of Grégoire draws again on the rhetoric of heredity and eugenics, and it registers a growing fear that violence achieves only the destruction of white morality.

As a potential mate for Grégoire, Melicent Hosmer responds to the young man with a kind of social segregation that mirrors general white hysteria over physical contact with black men. Immediately she makes plans to leave Place-du-Bois and berates Thérèse for tolerating Grégoire's presence after the murder:

> "I don't understand you at all, Mrs. Lafirme. Think what he's done; murdered a defenseless man! How can you have him near you—seated at your table? I don't know what nerves you have in your bodies, you and David. . . . Never! If he were dying I wouldn't go near him." (*CW*, 828)

Melicent is criticized throughout the novel for her distaste at being around black servants and her harsh judgment of Southerners, yet her disciplined enforcement of proper separation between races and types stands in contrast to Grégoire's later undisciplined attempts at integration. Angered by Melicent and Thérèse's condemnation of Joçint's murder, Grégoire becomes a parody of the Northern integrationist when at gunpoint he forces his fellow townsmen to drink with blacks.[54] This chaotic, last-ditch attempt to reaffirm his power as an aristocrat only results in disruption of the community's moral and racial harmony, since whites, angered at this social imposition, begin to threaten the innocent black men Grégoire has ordered into the bar.[55] As the black workers remark, "Grégoir gwine be Grégoir tell he die" (*CW*, 833), so the only option is to expel him from Place-du-Bois.

Still, it is significant that, although Grégoire must be exiled, by the end of the novel he is reincarnated as a heroic ideal. When toward the end of the narrative Thérèse recieves word that Grégoire has been killed in a Texas barroom brawl, all is forgiven as she and her workers grieve for him and revere his memory. This group includes even the black ferryman Nathan, "who had been one day felled to earth by a crowbar in Grégoire's hand, [and] had come himself to look at that deed as not altogether blamable in light of the provocation that had called it forth" (*CW*, 853). This ending makes sense given that Chopin, like her Northern contemporary Frances Willard, does not criticize Grégoire's racial attitude but rather his methods of racial control. Joçint is reprehensible because, as an Indian and a black, he is driven to impulsive destruction. Grégoire is reprehensible because his acts begin to imitate the violence, moral vacuity, and anti-progressivism of nonwhites. In their emotional restraint, their benevolent paternalism to blacks, their civilized acknowledgment of social rules, and their stand for modernization, Hosmer and Thérèse together represent for Chopin an alternative route for white development in the context of North/South social and economic alliances.

Chopin mythologizes aggression and white identity formation in the context of black slavery through the examples of Grégoire and Placide. Yet even as they are condemned for their violent outbursts and lack of self-discipline, theirs is "the only social class that Kate Chopin is really familiar with in this stratified society," and with which, through characters like Thérèse Lafirme, she finally identifies.[56] In *At Fault* Chopin deconstructs white supremacy's myth of the black rapist in order to free her white women characters from restrictive political roles, yet the fact that she does not completely condemn Grégoire's instinct for race protection suggests that she embraces the sense of entitlement offered by the validation of whiteness.

Such validation is exemplified in her short story "In Sabine" where Chopin—in tandem with many of her contemporaries—turns from the planter class to lower-class whites for a portrait of real white evil. The main character in "In Sabine" is again Grégoire Santien, whom Chopin uses this time not to demarcate white shortcomings but to make clear the class-bound dimensions of idealized whiteness. "In Sabine" also functions as a commentary on ethnic division among whites themselves, specifically Americans and creoles in the context of increased anxiety over racial purity after emancipation.

In search of shelter near the Texas–Louisiana border in Sabine Parish, Grégoire encounters Bud Aiken, the "disreputable so-called 'Texan' " (*CW*, 326) who habitually abuses his cajun wife 'Tite Reine. In the context of his rejection by Thérèse and Melicent, Grégoire is mindful of the need to control his behavior in the presence of women and so chooses not to kill Aiken; instead Grégoire merely distracts him with a long poker game and liberal supplies of alcohol. Exhausted from hours of carousing, Aiken falls into a deep, drunken sleep, allowing Grégoire to put 'Tite Reine on a horse headed back to her family in adjacent Natchitoches Parish.

While Grégoire represents for Chopin the aristocratic white man made rigid by his adherence to past values, Bud Aiken signifies by both his alien class and his ethnic origins an even clearer notion of evil, a construction that affords Grégoire a certain absolution in the aftermath of Joçint's murder. As the enemy of the kind of refinement symbolized by Thérèse's new feminine South, Aiken treats Reine like a black slave, sending her "out into the field to pick cotton with old Uncle Mortimer" (*CW*, 331), the neighboring black sharecropper. Such

an attempt to appropriate the lifestyle of a wealthy antebellum planter marks
Aiken as a social upstart, while his enslavement of 'Tite Reine constitutes a
corruption of the kinds of social relations epitomized at Place-du-Bois.

Reine's denigration in Aiken's household is rendered complete when, as she
stares at Grégoire from the shock of seeing a familiar face from home, Aiken
insults her racially: " 'Well, is that all you got to say to my frien' Mr. Sanchun?
That's the way with them Cajuns, . . . ain't got sense enough to know a white
man when they see one' " (CW, 327). Chopin's depiction of Aiken's denigration
of 'Tite Reine's ethnic identity and his literal enslavement of a white woman
evoke the familiar nineteenth-century feminist representation of marriage as
enslavement, and the paralleling of helpless femininity with disenfranchised
blackness.[57] Indeed, Reine suspects that Aiken really wants her not as a wife
but as a slave concubine:

> "sometime' he plague me mos' crazy; he tell me 't ent no preacher, it 's a
> Texas drummer w'at marry him an' me; an' w'en I don' know w'at way
> to turn no mo', he say no, it's a Meth'dis' archbishop, an' keep on laughin'
> 'bout me, an' I don' know w'at the truth!"    (CW, 330)

Anna Shannon Elfenbein suggests that Reine's tale of white abuse is tantamount to a "denial [on Chopin's part] of the chivalrous claims of white men
and their rationalization of lynch law as a means of dealing with the brute
'nigger,'" demonstrating that "Chopin clearly anticipates the dawning racial
awareness of white women" who would later agitate against lynching.[58] This
idea seems confirmed by the actions of the story's only black character. As
Reine tells the story, Bud " 'would 'a' choke' me to death one day w'en he was
drunk, if [black] Unc' Mort'mer had n' make 'im lef go—with his axe ov' his
head' " (CW, 329–30). This scene of a black raising an axe against a white
man might ordinarily result in a lynching. Yet Chopin revises the usual white
construction of black violence to make it chivalric—not to point to blacks'
capacity for heroism but rather to illustrate their imagined faithfulness to good
whites (a fallback here on plantation fiction stereotypes). Mortimer is presented
as asexual, a move that further draws on the plantation fiction stereotype of
black men in order to underscore Aiken's capacity for lawless, abusive sexual
desire. And since 'Tite Reine is abused by one white man only to be delivered
by another in the form of Grégoire, her story functions less to revise the myth
of the black beast for the benefit of African Americans, than to demarcate social
and ethnic categories of whiteness.

Following the Louisiana Purchase in 1803, creole and American ethnic tensions had run high in Louisiana, a fact replicated in Chopin's designation of
Aiken as the alien villain. According to historian Joseph Tregle, however, such
tensions were severely altered after the Civil War because black emancipation
brought (at least for a time) de jure black equality: "In the midst of this convul-

sion, the creole was caught up not simply in a general Southern explosion of antiblack fanaticism, but as well in a peculiar complication which once again set him apart." As Tregle suggests,

> [w]hereas once the danger confronting them had been humiliating loss of Gallic identity to a devouring Anglo-Saxon homogenization, now it was the infinitely more horrible possibility of being consigned to debased status in the "inferior" race, identified as half-brother to the black, a sort of mixed breed stripped of blood pride as well as of any claim to social or political preferment. . . . In such a manner was the cardinal tenet of the now familiar myth born: for those so threatened, henceforth to be creole was to be white.[59]

Traditionally cajuns were "rigorously excluded [from the creole world] having arrived in the colony not straight from the Continent but by way of Canada"; yet in spite of 'Tite Reine's class origins, because Chopin decries the sexual enslavement and "negroization" of her heroine, she proves Reine's value as a white woman and thus argues the case for her salvation.[60] Thus, the urgency to rescue the cajun 'Tite Reine is also the urgency to rescue the identity of nontraditional American ethnicities chafing under restrictive definitions of whiteness, without altering the racial designation of blackness as undesirable.

Ironically, in achieving its rescue of white womanhood from white men, "In Sabine" disturbs the white supremacist fantasy of a natural white masculine solidarity always activated when white women are in danger. Thomas Dixon articulates this fantasy in *The Leopard's Spots* (1902) when he describes community reaction to the alleged black rapist: "In a moment the white race . . . [would be] fused into a homogeneous mass of love, sympathy, hate and revenge. The rich and the poor, the learned and the ignorant, the banker and the blacksmith, the great and the small, they . . . [would all be] one now."[61]

As Joyce Coyne Dyer and Robert Emmett Monroe suggest, Aiken may "represent the savage state that civilization must destroy, conquer and replace," and Grégoire's own submerged desires for 'Tite Reine tie him to Aiken, even as Aiken's class and ethnic differences serve to distance Grégoire from that desire.[62] With the "white" rapist directly represented as a mirror image of the white hero, Grégoire and Aiken exist as bifurcations of the same white male psyche, suggesting Chopin's implicit recognition that both the (white) male impulse to rescue and the (black) male impulse to rape are dual fictions arising out of conflicted white supremacist attitudes toward white women.

Dyer and Monroe also cite Grégoire's connection to Aiken in his sexual attraction to 'Tite Reine, as he recalls "her trim rounded figure; her piquant face with its saucy black coquettish eyes" (*CW*, 326).[63] But what establish Grégoire as Aiken's social and ethnic superior, what affirm his racial and moral purity, are both his designation of 'Tite Reine as white (and therefore deserving of his respect for her) and his refusal to act on his sexual desire. Consequently Grégoire becomes the perfect model of the romantic white lover:

> Grégoire loved women. He liked their nearness, their atmosphere; the tones of their voices and the things they said; their ways of moving and turning about; the brushing of their garments when they passed him by pleased him. He was fleeing now from the pain that a woman had inflicted upon him. . . . The sight of 'Tite Reine's distress now moved him painfully. (CW, 329)

The potential critique of "In Sabine" might have been devastating: instead of the homosocial black/white male struggle over the white female body, Chopin shifts to an all-white male context that refocuses male anxiety over sexuality and power within the terms of a purely white community. But since Reine's final savior is in fact the white Grégoire and not the black Mortimer, Chopin both references and then forecloses a more extended (and dangerous) political discussion of race, masculinity, and desire.

### WHITE WOMEN AND METAPHORS OF BLACK (FE)MALE SEXUALITY

In *At Fault*, "A No-Account Creole," and "In Sabine," Chopin references post-Reconstruction fantasies of the black beast and the white female/nation as victim without relinquishing her impulse toward white racial solidarity. In "A Lady of Bayou St. John" (1893) and its companion story "La Belle Zoraïde" (1894), Chopin sustains her commentary on the restrictive linkage between white female bodies and the South, moving to a critique of ideologies of white sexual suppression through an evocation of desire for the black body. Not surprisingly, this evocation is heavily regulated through her use of the mulatto, the ubiquitous figure throughout Western discourse representing interracial sex. What results is a teasing play on miscegenation that excites and therefore challenges white sexual self-repression, without seriously threatening her contemporary white audience's abhorrence for integration.[64]

Chopin's preoccupation with the taboo of female sexual desire, and her critique of double standards on the subject of male sexuality, is of course made abundantly clear in her stories on Southern women during slavery, in the era of Reconstruction, and beyond. Her characterizations in *The Awakening* and "Désirée's Baby" are obvious examples. Though set during slavery, "Désirée's Baby" critiques white hypocrisy over miscegenation for an audience mindful of racial tensions in the 1890s, and not just of the memories of slavery and the Civil War.[65] However, "A Lady of Bayou St. John" and its companion story "La Belle Zoraïde" advance a criticism of particular white female stereotypes that were directly sustained by and utilized for promoting the myth of the black rapist, and that by implication justified the widespread use of racial violence allegedly to protect whites from blacks.

Set during the Civil War, "A Lady of Bayou St. John" focuses on the appropriately named Madame Delisle, a Southern belle effectively isolated and immobilized on her husband's plantation. Cared for by her black mammy Manna-Loulou, Madame Delisle embodies the stereotype of a male-authored Southern femininity that denies female adulthood and independence to white women. Madame Delisle's inaction is contextualized by the traditional sources of power in the South (the upper-class white patriarchy signified by the plantation), an idealized blackness in submission (the vague reference to her only companions, the slaves), and also the far-off violence of the Civil War, which eventually precipitates a shift in Southern social roles.

But since the story focuses on a world on the verge of transition, an assault on traditional plantation life, traditional forms of white power, and (therefore) traditional forms of white female containment, is indeed the promised end. This end comes not in the form of social "rape" by an emancipated black population, but rather in Madame Delisle's near-seduction via love letters by her white neighbor Sépincourt. Yet, though life with Sépincourt promises more richness and sexual possibility than were hers in her previous existence, Madame Delisle finally fails at the critical moment. Learning of Gustave Delisle's death she rejects Sépincourt and constructs an altar out of her dead husband's portrait: "Can you not see that now my heart, my soul, my thought—my very life, must belong to another?" (*CW*, 301).

Her self-sacrifice reinitiates her into servitude to Southern patriarchy, signifying that, while the Civil War will free Manna-Loulou and the rest of the Delisle slaves, white women's adherence to old constructions will perpetuate their restriction into the post–Civil War era. In Madame Delisle's embrace of this traditional role, she literally becomes the Old South of plantation fiction lore, a living memorial to a past ideal of white manhood:

> "My husband has never been so living to me as he is now. . . . I hear his familiar voice, his footsteps upon the galleries. We walk once more together beneath the magnolias; and at night in dreams I feel that he is there, there, near me. How could it be different! Ah! I have memories, memories to crowd and fill my life, if I live a hundred years!" (*CW*, 301)

Consequently this embodiment of the South through the figure of the belle signifies the death of white femininity, not its protection. White supremacist identification of the white woman with the essence of Southern values and sectional identity is in effect a form of annihilation.

"La Belle Zoraïde" has traditionally been read as Chopin's commentary on what Madame Delisle has lost, since she implicitly contrasts her white heroine with the passionate main character of one of Manna-Loulou's bedtime stories. Like Madame Delisle, the octoroon slave Zoraïde is the tempter of male desire: " 'La belle Zoraïde had eyes that were so dusky, so beautiful, that any man who gazed too long into their depths was sure to lose his head, and even his heart sometimes' " (*CW*, 304). But whereas white men have the option of losing head and heart, of lusting and even loving, Zoraïde (who is clearly a reference for Madame Delisle) does not.

Zoraïde's dilemma lies in the fact that she must choose between M'sieur Ambroise, a light-skinned body servant favored by her despotic mistress Madame Delarivière, and the black fieldhand Mézor. When Zoraïde takes Mézor as her lover and becomes pregnant, an angry Madame Delarivière arranges for Mézor to be sold and then snatches away the newborn baby. Believing her child to be dead, Zoraïde goes mad, clutching at a bundle of rags in place of her infant. Insanity saves her from marrying M'sieur Ambroise, but it also cuts her off from motherhood, since she refuses the child returned to her by a remorseful Madame Delarivière. At the story's end, Madame Delisle's only reaction is to moan " 'La pauv' piti! Mieux li mouri!' " ("The poor little one! Better had she died!") (*CW*, 307), in ambiguous response either to the fate of the child or to that of Zoraïde, with whom she perhaps identifies.

As Anna Shannon Elfenbein writes, Chopin's story suggests that "neither lady nor tragic octoroon can be free, since one is forced to live vicariously through tales of romance, and the other forced to escape the realities of her lot by going mad."[66] Certainly Madame Delisle suggests the tragedy of self-repression for white women, while Zoraïde suggests the tragedy of slavery: both conditions produce a loss of female potential in terms of sexuality and motherhood. But while Zoraïde's fate mirrors that of Madame Delisle's, their stories are not analogous. Zoraïde instead becomes the final index of female hysteria, the real symbol of excess in female behavior, an excess that is at least hinted at by the fact that Zoraïde is akin to the white supremacist stereotype of the oversexed black who reproduces.

Zoraïde also becomes a referent for the story's subtextual flirtation with miscegenation as a corrupting social practice. At the start of the story Madame Delisle is figured as a lonely picture of dormant white sexual energy lying sensually "in her sumptuous mahogany bed," an energy answered by the ministrations of Manna-Loulou: "The old negress . . . bathed her mistress's pretty white feet and kissed them lovingly, one, then the other. She . . . brushed her mistress's beautiful hair" (*CW*, 303). Borrowing from Sander L. Gilman's analysis of eighteenth- and nineteenth-century visual representation of race and womanhood, where in paintings such as Manet's *Olympia* "the figures of the black servants mark the presence of illicit sexual activity," I would argue that the juxtaposition of Madame Delisle and Manna-Loulou references nineteenth-century white fears of the detrimental connection between masters and slaves, especially since Manna-Loulou's protection of the seemingly helpless Madame Delisle figures as a corruption, her "soothing" bedtime story perhaps inciting the chaste female mind to lust and infidelity.[67] Manna-Loulou even lends a dangerously "Sapphic" air to the scene with her caresses, actions made more riveting by the contrast of the servant's skin, "black as the night" (*CW*, 303) with Delisle's blond paleness.[68] Ultimately the physical separation of black and white is reengaged in the story of Zoraïde herself. With her " '*café-au-lait* " skin and a figure envied by " 'half the ladies who visited her mistress' " (*CW*, 304), Zoraïde is a fantasy of desirable blackness and desirable black female passion. Thus Chopin seems to defy and confirm the need for Jim Crow laws, which were well established by the time of the story's publication.

The connection between Zoraïde and Madame Delisle is clear: both are petted; both are fair; both are oppressed by similar rules of social behavior. But in contrast to Madame Delisle, who senses Sépincourt's desire in a "glance that penetrated her own" yet refuses to act upon her "awakening," Zoraïde at first reverses the process of female objectification by tapping into her own sensual feelings: " 'Poor Zoraïde's heart grew sick in her bosom with love for le beau Mézor from the moment she saw the fierce gleam of his eye' " (*CW*, 299, 304). The octoroon whose body excites white male lust is herself capable of lust; but because of the story's framing, she must become the conduit for frustrated white desire, rather than a subject in her own right. Madame Delisle—and Chopin's white readers—can still fantasize about sex in comfort and safety: the spectacle of Zoraïde's sexual transgression furnishes the reader/listener with a moment of distanced sexual pleasure, and the punishment for that pleasure (insanity and social exclusion) is distanced within the black body. In a sense Chopin rewrites black sexual criminality (Mézor is not the black rapist, but rather the desired lover; Zoraïde is not the prostitute, but rather the desiring lover) to speak for white sexual lack, without necessarily disrupting the white supremacist linkage of blackness to bodily excess.

Chopin's complicated play on stereotypes of black and white femininity—to gratify Delisle's longing and then absolve her character of that longing—further grapples with patriarchal notions of white desire by underscoring the excitement inspired by the stereotype of black male sexuality. As a possible sign of her rejection of "her white godmother's racist values," Zoraïde spurns the mulatto M'sieur Ambroise, "with his shining whiskers like a white man's, and his small eyes, that were cruel and false as a snake's" (*CW*, 304).[69] In "A Lady of Bayou St. John" Sépincourt's appearance is more appealing: darkened by the sun, he has "quicker and hotter blood in his veins" than his white neighbors. Though he has a "slim figure, a little bent" (*CW*, 298–99), he is still more desirable than Gustave Delisle's portrait, near which the dead man's impotent sword hangs.

But all three men are overshadowed by the sexually charged Mézor; if Sépincourt seduces with words, Mézor seduces with the promise of the black phallus: "Mézor was as straight as a cypress-tree and as proud looking as a king. His body, bare to the waist, was like a column of ebony and it glistened like oil" (*CW*, 304). As with the stereotype of the black rapist, in Chopin's and the reader's—and presumably Madame Delisle's—eyes, Mézor is finally the object of white desire instead of white terror. And more than Sépincourt, who wants Madame Delisle but cannot "comprehend that psychological enigma, a woman's heart," Mézor proves to be a compassionate lover, with "kindness" in his eyes and "only gentleness in his voice" (*CW*, 302, 305).

Despite such gentleness, Mézor also excites because of the danger implied by his presence. Zoraïde (and through her, the reader) first catches sight of him in New Orleans' Congo Square performing the Bamboula, one of a number of antebellum slave dances characterized by "a frenzied African beat" that whites found both disturbing and fascinating.[70] According to early white observers, dances like the Bamboula

> mounted from a slow, repetitious, and grimly deliberate opening phase
> . . . in an increasingly lascivious crescendo to a final frenzy of "fantastic
> leaps" in which "ecstasy rises to madness," and finally, suddenly, the danc-
> ers fell, exhausted and unconscious, "foam on their lips," and were
> "dragged out of the circle by their arms and legs" as new dancers took
> their place, the music never ceasing.[71]

As the symbol of racial regression in the story, Mézor functions doubly as the romantic connection to an exotic African past and as a forbidding reference to a "savage" black passion that, according to Chicago physician G. Frank Lydston, accounted for why "the Ashantee warrior knocks down his prospective bride with a club and drags her off into the woods." According to Lydston the primitive sexual feeling that marked the regressive African provided "an excellent prototype illustration of the criminal sexual acts of the negro in the United States."[72] But though he personifies the black phallus, as the potentially violent lover who restricts his animal passion to his dances, Mézor is made safe in Chopin's narrative, always tethered to the earth, under white control, "hoeing sugar-cane, barefooted and half naked" (*CW*, 305), the subdued African body.

Chopin's Mézor resembles the larger-than-life slave, African prince, and sometime dancer of the Bamboula, Bras-Coupé, who appears in George Washington Cable's historical novel set in 1803 New Orleans, *The Grandissimes: A Story of Creole Life* (1880).[73] Revered by the quadroon Palmyre but feared by whites, Bras-Coupé functions in *The Grandissimes* less as a character than as Cable's stereotype of enslaved black masculinity in all its passion and primitive power. A violent figure who showers curses on his master's family but bows down as a tributary before white women, Bras-Coupé is finally mutilated by exasperated slaveholders; and like the lynch victim of post–Civil War American culture, he casts his shadow over Yankees and Southerners struggling to achieve national reunion.

In Mézor, Chopin evacuates altogether the violence that distinguishes Cable's Bras-Coupé, but neither figure has a presence temporally coexistent with the principal white characters; instead they are written out of the national narrative as actors, to remain finally as symbols of white guilt and desire. Consequently Mézor's safeness is precisely what accounts for his usefulness as a device to stage the articulation of Madame Delisle's suppressed lust. Under the burden of the story's framing, Zoraïde is a frustrated octoroon out of control who must stand in for a white woman unable to imagine herself out of control. Mézor, on the other hand, as a black man is always in the narrator's grasp, trapped within the white idealization of the perfect lover, referencing finally white, not black social insurrection.

The criminalization of blackness that enforces distance is also underscored by the mingled discourses of failed maternity, eugenics, and racial regression invested in "La Belle Zoraïde." Within the story's late-nineteenth-century context, "[m]iscegenation . . . was a fear not merely of interracial sexuality but of its results, the decline of the population."[74] Zoraïde's black maternity highlights both Madame Delisle's and Madame Delarivière's barrenness: Delisle moves from immaturity to childless widowhood, while Delarivière can only manage a surrogate black daughter instead of a white one.

The play on black fecundity here as a sign of white disempowerment is further emphasized because the birth of Zoraïde's child in the story signifies the octoroon's disobedience to white law. By denying Zoraïde her child, Delarivière deprives her slave of any claim to a domestic identity, and here Chopin seems to be rejecting antebellum social relations much as she does in *At Fault*, because they allowed such abuses.[75] But though Chopin seems to be engaging in racial disloyalty by validating black female maternal rights, she sets into motion turn-of-the-century discourses about racial inferiority that deny black capacity to exercise those rights.[76] Zoraïde might reproduce, but she is ultimately unfit for parenting even when a regretful Madame Delarivière returns the child.

Nineteenth-century medical discourse would have attributed Zoraïde's madness not only to her grief over the loss of the child, but to her "impure" racial identity: an octoroon rendered inherently unstable by her heritage of racial interbreeding. The eugenicist language of the story casts M'sieur Ambroise as diminutive, imitative of whiteness, but finally deceitful and cruel, the product of racial refinement that does not improve physical or temperamental characteristics. In *The Grandissimes* Cable's quadroons are similarly afflicted: they suffer either from uncontrollable anger or from a failure of will. Thus at the moment of her rejection of white domination, Zoraïde proves herself to be a version of the "tragic mulatto" who goes mad at the restrictions set upon her identity.[77]

But whereas Zoraïde is trapped within madness and slavery because of the unchangeable features of race and blood, Madame Delisle is trapped by Southern tradition and history, conditions about to undergo radical change in the story because of its setting during the Civil War. Thus, Zoraïde finally exemplifies black sexuality but also black powerlessness, if we read Madame Delisle's "La pauv' piti! Mieux li mouri!" as a comment on the slave's hopeless condition. On the other hand, Delisle exemplifies white female empowerment precisely because of her race, and the frustration generated in the narrative by Zoraïde's tragedy as a black slave becomes finally a frustration at Madame Delisle, who does not exercise the choices Chopin implies are hers by virtue of her whiteness.[78]

It is worthwhile to return to Chopin's heroine in At Fault, Thérèse Lafirme, as a rewriting of women like Madame Delisle. Rousing herself from the stupor of the antebellum age, refusing to become a memorial for her husband, Thérèse actively inserts herself into Southern economic life and indeed harnesses and flirts with black sexuality. Like Madame Delisle, Thérèse possesses a black "mammy," Tante Marie Louise, who plies her with food and gentle massages, providing a haven of female sensuality for her weary white mistress. Thérèse is on similarly close terms with Joçint's mixed-blood father Morico, taking delight in combing "that exquisite white hair of his" (CW, 805). She does not proffer similar intimacies to Joçint, however; and her rejection of Joçint affirms her instinct for racial self-policing, even as she reorders the sinfulness of the black body with Marie Louise and Morico. Thus Thérèse's rebellious attraction to blackness, tempered by her maintenance of firm control over the latter, becomes a measure of her newly found power as Chopin's ideal of New South womanhood.

I have been arguing in this chapter for a reconsideration of Kate Chopin as neither disengaged from the racial politics of the late nineteenth century nor actively in resistance to white supremacist thought. Rather, Chopin's female characterizations are as much a response to stereotypes of race as they are a reaction to patriarchal domination. While traditional readings cast her as resistant to the gender conventions of her age, I would argue that Chopin's feminism worked in tandem with her investment in turn-of-the-century racist discourses. As such, her fiction offers an added site from which to consider the racialization of gender within turn-of-the-century white women's fiction. Her fiction also helps to decenter monolithic notions of white supremacist discursive patterns. Inasmuch as Chopin contributes to white supremacist thought with works such as At Fault, "In Sabine," and "La Belle Zoraïde," she revises the white supremacist association of the white female body to suggest a more affirming sexualization and a site for white female subjectivity. She does not address the problem of rape as a category of white racial violence against blacks, but she does register a sense of white anxiety with regard to lynching and mob rule, as exemplified in the behavior of characters such as the Santiens.

However troubling may be Chopin's failure to address fully in any politically meaningful way the horror of lynching, she critiques the balance of power within the gender relations prescribed by turn-of-the-century white supremacy in its restriction of female access to economic and sexual freedom. Chopin's work also registers tensions within "white" culture about the nature of whiteness itself and about the boundaries among ethnicity, race, and region in determining American enfranchisement. As a result, Chopin's work reveals the complex entanglement among white supremacist public discourses, "mainstream" white writing on regional and community development, and especially female "nonpolitical" fiction as she subtly evokes a vision of white supremacy that both liberates and confines.

# Cultural Memories
# and Critical Inventions

When these officers were first put on trial in Simi Valley, and when
the jury came back with its not guilty verdicts, what metaphoriza-
tion of the black male body had to have been already in place that
invoked a national historical memory (constructed by whites), a
code in which African Americans are nonetheless perfectly literate?

> Elizabeth Alexander,
> " 'Can you be BLACK and Look at This?':
> Reading the Rodney King Video(s)"

We give life and validity to our constructions of race, community
and politics by giving those constructions a history. Those who construct masculine notions of blackness and race progress and who
claim only some forms of violence as central to African American
liberation struggles are claiming/remembering a particular history.
. . . Before we can construct truly participatory discussions around
a fully democratic agenda where the history and struggles of women
and men are raised as issues of general interest necessary to the liberation of all, we have some powerful lot of remembering to do.

> Elsa Barkley Brown,
> "Negotiating and Transforming
> the Public Sphere"

I BEGAN in my introduction by evoking a few of the infamous
nineteenth- and twentieth-century cases of criminalized black masculinity: Sam
Hose, Emmett Till, Yusuf Hawkins, Rodney King. One could also add other
names that have come to public attention within the past five years: Justice
Clarence Thomas, Mike Tyson, O. J. Simpson.[1] Their cases do not reference
white violence, but they do reference the condition of possibility for that violence, because—the still-raging questions of their guilt or innocence aside—in
the minds of many Americans black and white, the stories of these men are
continually filtered through and in turn help to construct the coalescing race,
class, and gender anxieties that are expressed in the stereotype of black criminality. This accounts for Clarence Thomas's savvy (and some would argue reprehensible) move to rescue his nomination to the Supreme Court by claiming

before an all-white panel of male senators who were anxious not to appear racist that his confirmation hearing on Capitol Hill had turned into a high-tech lynching. This claim came despite the fact that he was accused of sexually harassing a *black* woman subordinate.

The twentieth-century figures I have enumerated must remain individual subjects for case studies to reveal how Americans have continued to reshape their thinking about gender, violence, and black criminality. What I am concerned with here are the ways in which the fantasy of a constructive dialogue about race is continually put forward as the goal of a public discourse in which all attempts at a so-called "clarification" of the issues can only be a partial possibility. From Daniel Patrick Moynihan's vilification of black matriarchy in his infamous 1965 study of the black family to the plethora of television and talk-show forums on the aftermath of the 1992 Los Angeles rebellion to 1994 CNN and National Public Radio reporters' queries to Brentwood, California, residents about whether or not the O. J. Simpson murder case was really about "race" or "class," general attempts to address the intersection of issues have often proved most effective as moments of mythification and mystification, rather than as opportunities for any rigorous public analyses in an era of proliferating "talk."[2]

In this afterword I want to offer a few remarks on the challenges of reading public discourse (and in this context I consider the literature of any age part of a public discourse) on race, sex, and violence, and on refining the nature of our own supposedly more self-conscious academic discourses of analysis. Elizabeth Alexander's discussion of the relationship between the kinds of mainstream knowledge about blackness that fuels "a national historical memory" and, for blacks especially, the "sometimes-subconscious collective memories which are frequently forged and maintained through a storytelling tradition" is particularly useful.[3] Thus far I have been tracing the very different kinds of stories about race, rape, and violence in an interracial context that are filtered through both "a national historical memory (constructed by whites)" to use Alexander's words and a black cultural memory, and I have been discussing the kinds of analyses and representations of racial violence the black male body generated in literature produced at the turn of the century. Here I see "historical" as referring to the accretion over time of a variety of cultural attitudes, beliefs, and interpretations of black criminality and white violence that come to be named as what Americans "think" of when they see a black man being beaten. I also agree generally with Alexander's point that within "historical memory," African Americans, through an invention of their own cultural narrative, are constantly "mitigat[ing] against a history of [white] narrative dominion which attempts to talk black people out of what they know."[4]

Exactly what is it that we assume blacks as well as whites come to "know" about alleged black criminality in particular and race, violence, and nation

more generally? Without ignoring their very different social arenas, their varying agendas, and their unequal access to power, I would locate the writers in
this study as participants in a late nineteenth- and early twentieth-century national memory-making, which situates historical and/or cultural "memory" as
a site of endless exchange, intervention, and reinvention, where what passes as
national or communal or individual "truth" becomes a dense composite of
social and political desires in constant power play. This reading of how cultural
knowledge is produced has encouraged me to reject the notion that the literary
"red record" on lynching in America is simply the squaring off of a dominant
white discourse proclaiming black criminality against a defensive black protest
tradition. I also reject the notion that a politicized literary discourse on
lynching could be conceivable without the presence of black and white women
as full-fledged subjects, however camouflaged their participation might be. In
this book I argue for a much more fluid, dynamic model of gendered, cultural
interaction that begins from the assumption that each "side" was anything but
uniform in terms of its goals, membership, and strategies. To assume such
uniformity is both to deny the incredibly dialectical (as opposed to merely
pluralist) nature of what we want to call "American" national culture and to
fail to acknowledge the ways in which racial and ethnic communities in the
United States have negotiated historical change as a series of retreats, advances,
and detours. Nation-building, in other words the building of myths about the
nation and its inhabitants, must be seen as a constant field of (often hostile)
negotiations and cultural appropriations between men and women and among
local populations.

   Although most of my discussion of white writers has been devoted to
Thomas Dixon, Jr., Mark Twain, and Kate Chopin, they along with the other
literary and political figures I have referenced—William Dean Howells, Thomas
Nelson Page, George Washington Cable, Ray Stannard Baker, Mary Johnston,
Frances Willard, Jane Addams, to name a few—give us some insight into how
the very precarious process Alexander calls white "narrative dominion" actually
works in practice. Taken as a whole, the differing images of black masculinity
surfacing in their works—the plantation darky, the savage post-Reconstruction
monster, potentially seductive African figures such as Bras-Coupé and Mézor—
function as a kind of imagistic register through which one might trace the self-
articulations of white communities north and south, rural and urban, under
the stress of post-Reconstruction economic, social, and artistic politics and in
the face of relentlessly shifting class and gender power relations. Indeed, books
such as Chopin's *At Fault* (1890), Howells's *An Imperative Duty* (1891), Dixon's
*The Leopard's Spots* (1902), and Baker's *Following the Color Line* (1908) are primarily about the conflicted conceptualization and deployment of the metaphor
of the gendered white body as a repository of white ambitions and fears that
play out in the tension between the local and the national, the individual and

the imagined group. The trope of the black rapist and its attendant violence function as part of the enabling language of that conceptualization and, ultimately, not as its central focus.

In comparison to their white counterparts, black writers and activists obviously had very different readings of alleged black male criminality and of whiteness itself, as evidenced by the work of Charles Chesnutt, Ida B. Wells, or David Bryant Fulton. (And, to move beyond the scope of this book, we could easily include the novelists Frances E. W. Harper and Sutton E. Griggs and the militant journalist John Edward Bruce.) However, we need to conceptualize African American responses to lynching and the stereotype of the black rapist as a similarly problematic, similarly conflicted process of trying, testing, and renegotiating black individual and community roles in the wake of slavery. The constant assault on black citizenship aside, there was undeniably a literal transformation of black bodies in the journey from slavery to freedom, where exslaves reinvented themselves by claiming the social and civic rights of marriage, by becoming property owners, by demanding the right to education. Yet, such acts not only challenged a racial status quo that had existed before the founding of the American republic, but they also challenged blacks to confront, in their own minds, the consequences of proclaiming themselves fully fledged members of American society.

From this standpoint, the question of how African Americans negotiated their status as Americans might encompass not only their survival and defiance of white supremacist violence but also their confrontation of internal cultural shifts as folk and urban, slave- and free-born subcultures mingled, and as African Americans appropriated and transformed white social codes of conduct. Because these shifts were not smooth, the process of black survival and community formation ushered in conflicts around questions of status, regional affiliation, personal history, and color, questions that erupt within the highly heterogeneous black world depicted in the novels of Pauline Hopkins, David Bryant Fulton, and Charles Chesnutt.

As I sought to demonstrate in the case of Charles Chesnutt's rendering and resolution of social conflict within *The Marrow of Tradition,* some of these strategies of community formation allowed African Americans to gain as well as sacrifice moral ground, because of the complicated structuring of authority within black communities. In Chapter 2, Chesnutt and Mark Twain are juxtaposed to highlight the compromises inherent in anti-racist fiction; at the same time, Chesnutt's enactment of black masculine recovery on the public stage stands against Ida B. Wells's struggle for agency in Chapter 3 and against the image of the black woman as public spectacle. In the cases of Chesnutt and Wells respectively, an evolving black communal negotiation of traditional gender roles enabled on the one hand and threatened to foreclose on the other radical reorientations of male and female access to power. Thus, African American writers provide a "record" of social transformations, reversals, and compromises, in which the artifice of novelistic closure speaks as much for the hunger for resolution as it does for the sheer uncontainability of so many divergent social processes at work in any one community. It is in providing such a record, I would argue, that ironically these writers might be seen to resemble their white counterparts.

The subject of turn-of-the-century white racial violence provides at least one historical event through which we might consider the kinds of similar and dissimilar processes whereby various Americans came to a racial knowledge of each other. On the subject of lynching and rape, turn-of-the-century writers produced a particular world of public discourse that challenges us to refine continuously our own evolving assumptions—our own particular brand of mythmaking, if you will—about literary history, gender, culture, and critical discourse.

Two critical moves informing my study have been what Shelley Fisher Fishkin recently called the twin projects of "interrogating 'whiteness' " and "complicating 'blackness.' "[5] In agreement with Fishkin I take these projects to mean necessarily linked analyses of, on the one hand, "how the imaginative construction of 'whiteness' [as an invisible category] has shaped American literature and American history" and, on the other, how "blackness" has been constructed and reified as the ultimate (and some would say ultimately monstrous) sign of race in American culture.[6] These are necessarily difficult projects that on every level still need to be theorized considerably, for a number of reasons.

In the first place, when we reference specifically Anglo-Americans and African Americans—two incredibly diverse populations—through the words "black" and "white," we automatically risk a dual homogenization of community histories, lived experiences, ideological forces, and cultural articulations that intersect and encompass the worlds of a Thomas Dixon, Jr., or a Pauline Hopkins. True, the more abstract terms "blackness" and "whiteness" focus our attention not on actual people but on the ideological constructs that structure American lives; yet, as terms that ultimately reference racial differences within the nation through the image of alternate "colorations," their crudeness still forces us to the brink of an oversimplification—even distortion—of the very processes we wish to describe. And what do we do with the obfuscation of other non-black or non-Anglo races and/or ethnicities that these terms encourage? And last, but certainly not least, within the racialized model, how do we avoid a displacement of class and gender as categories of analysis, categories that have to be necessarily recurring elements in any larger critiques of culture and history?

As an attempt to problematize the homogenizations of the blackness/whiteness model through the inclusion to greater and lesser extents of discussions of

gender, class, and ethnicity, my study highlights the kinds of theoretical questions that must be addressed and suggests the possible routes one might take
in that address. For me the possibilities of demystifying, critiquing, and learning from this critical enterprise can only come in the broadly comparative
methodology inherent in the complication of "blackness" and the interrogation
of "whiteness." And here I want to make it clear that I am arguing for the
model as a starting point, not as the goal of inquiry. One way to initiate the
conversation would be to tease out the complicated politics of canons, methodologies, and scholarly identity at the heart of any rethinking of the construction
of black and white. Certainly the call for an examination of these politics is not
original to my project. Yet given the deplorable lack of dialogue between the
scholars who use a race-based critical method and those who use a traditional
feminist methodology, and between Americanists and African-Americanists, it
seems to be worth constant public reiteration.

For the study of literature, race, and gender, the relevant questions seem to
be: 1) how do we integrate the study of race within the framing of United States
women's literatures; and, conversely, 2) how do we integrate the study of gender
within the framing of racialized culture? These questions are often more easily
enunciated than answered, but they are important in light of my resituation of
Kate Chopin from what has been generally thought of as a white feminist
literary canon into a discussion of race relations, rather than gender discourse,
the usual arena for discussions of Chopin's work. Yet must we assume that the
canon of (in this case white) women's writing is a stable entity, founded on
texts that speak of one common female relation to the larger social world, that
of oppression and rebellion? Must we assume that feminist readings are necessarily not about race, or vice versa, since race and gender are not analogous
categories but in fact are always in simultaneous operation? Must we assume
that traditional feminist analysis will automatically be done away with (as opposed to being made more sophisticated, and therefore more effective) if the
terms of that analysis are expanded and complicated by discussions of race?

On the question of race in reading white women's writing, if we consider
Harriet Jacobs's *Incidents in the Life of a Slave Girl* as not only the story of a
slave woman's experiences but also (as I often imagine Jacobs herself had intended it) as social criticism, we find the seeds of a helpful analysis. In describ-
ing her genealogy, the narrator Linda Brent speaks of troubled (and yet founda-
tional) moments in the conceptualization of black and white female
subjectivity:

> My mother's mistress was the daughter of my grandmother's mistress.
> She was the foster sister of my mother; they were both nourished at my
> grandmother's breast. In fact, my mother had been weaned at three
> months old, that the babe of the mistress might obtain sufficient food.

They played together as children; and, when they became women, my
mother was a most faithful servant to her white foster sister.[7]

The white woman described in the passage becomes the narrating Linda Brent's
surrogate mother/mistress who wills Brent to the Flints after her death, thereby
precipitating a harrowing downward journey for Brent into slavery's world of
emotional and physical abuse, even as, according to Lydia Maria Child, white
women appear to live in a world where "our ears are too delicate to listen" to
such a fate.[8]

The cutting irony here of course is the almost but not quite familial intimacy
between black and white, which deceptively displays the outward harmony of a
pro-slavery model of race relations even as it describes in visceral detail the
separation of black and white women in terms of both the literal and the
culturally symbolic. Yet *Incidents* also bears witness to the necessarily present
moments of intersection between black and white female experiences that
structure the kinds of power inequality and relation to public and private that
eventually determine profound differences in social identity. It is highly appropriate then that the rest of Brent's narrative speaks not only of the conditions
of her enslavement but also about how that enslavement contextualizes the
conditions of freedom for her white female audience, suggesting that black and
white bodies always operate (willingly or unwittingly) in tandem, to animate
the meaning of race in the American national consciousness.

If we think about the lessons put forth by Linda Brent, then, an assessment
of white women writers—in this case, Kate Chopin—should also provide an
opportunity for rethinking the narratives critics have constructed about the
rebelliousness of white feminist writers. Without denying the ways in which
white feminist discourse has virtually transformed the academic landscape, I
want to suggest that there is nothing to fear in fully examining both the poten-
tials—and the complications—that inhere uneasily in the female radicalism of
literary subjects such as Kate Chopin. Just as in *Incidents in the Life of a Slave
Girl* the first mistress's apparent ability to act in freedom is buttressed by the
division of power in a racialized context, Chopin's ability to imagine white
female rebellion within community politics in rural Louisiana is structured
through a pattern of racial imagining enabled by black subjugation.

I am less interested here in deliberately dethroning Chopin or implying that
she was a closet racist than in challenging the humanist notion (still very much
alive) that one of the things that makes literature worthwhile is its ability to
imagine a moral resolution for social dilemma. The founding moment in many
rereadings of white women's literature has been a recovery of rebelliousness
against patriarchy as a form of subversion, resolution, defeat, or transcendence
of social crises or power inequalities (and I must point out that in a similar
way, black texts are assumed—indeed at times solely judged on—their rebellion

against mainstream values in terms of both their content and textual strategies). Yet while outright rebellion or subversion is certainly a defining characteristic of many texts (by blacks and whites, men and women), it is hardly an uncomplicated subversion, as the examples of Chopin, Chesnutt, or Twain demonstrate. Kate Chopin's value is precisely the troublesomeness of her antipatriarchal stance that emerges, paradoxically, through her embrace of white privilege.

With respect to the question of how gender fits into analyses of race and culture, I find extremely useful Elsa Barkley Brown's comment that a focus on the masculine is merely "the claiming/remembering of a particular history."[9] Scholars have so often failed to interrogate the fact that what we call "national" literature or history has been produced or enacted by men. Thus the category of gender is rendered invisible, because (male) literature or history is read as universal literature or history. For some time feminist scholars have agitated against this dangerously obliterating collapse of categories, but it is still a persistent feature in cultural imaginings both inside and outside of the academy. Brown's statement implies that in fact communal/national history (and for my purposes literary culture) must be conceptualized as multiple narratives in simultaneous operation. As a result, the critic is challenged to imagine the ways in which narratives are deployed against or collide with each other, especially in the context of gendered and racialized power relations that structure access to the public. The reading of historical and literary "records," then, calls for a recognition of the ways in which critical discourses themselves are implicated in the apparent canceling out of alternative histories—in the case of this project (especially white) female commentary on lynching and rape—because the masculine as universal remains so uninterrogated as a general given.

Now let me now turn to the additional question of how a comparative method might complicate the role of both Americanist and African-Americanist scholarship in light of the recent expansion of literary histories. On the polarization of these two scholarly camps, I want to point out an important statement made by the scholar of African American literature Robert B. Stepto at the 1987 conference "The Study of Afro-American Literature: An Agenda for the 1990s." According to Stepto,

> any agenda for Afro-Americanist literary criticism in the next decade should include a call for more comparative Americanist discussion. Some of us have turned away from this work, possibly because it seemed to Americanize or "bleach" the black texts considered, or possibly because such acts of criticism seemed to promote consensus and/or accommodation. I have no doubt that some members of this conference might wish to question this agenda item exactly for these reasons. They might add that what this agenda is all about is the consolidation of power, and that

a call for comparative scholarship creates, however unintentionally, possibilities for power sharing, or worse, power dissipation. But I make this call nonetheless, if for no other reason than the sincere belief that the work of the future includes the tasks to which Afro-Americanists who are Americanists are attracted.[10]

Of course a number of critics, many of whom I have cited in this study (Elizabeth Ammons, Eric Sundquist, Dana Nelson, for example), have been engaged for some time in just this kind of comparative work. However, despite the presence of these individuals, Americanist and African-Americanist projects still seem to exist as entirely separate entities in the national academy, with only a small number of practitioners on either side attempting what would ultimately be a promising dialogue between fields. Stepto's analysis is useful because he identifies the particular politics behind such lack of conversation.

The comparative approach for which Stepto calls might be disturbing for some because it demands a reassessment of what exactly an "Americanist" versus an "African-Americanist" critical approach might look like, especially from the standpoint of interrogating essentialist assumptions about literature (and literary critics) that might lead some African Americanists to assume that a "black" text could be "bleached" or some Americanists to think that a "white" text could be "darkened," with too much emphasis on race. Indeed, we need to rethink the assumption that Americanist and African-Americanist projects are stable endeavors in the first place. The point here is not that we must all become generalists, but that in our own particular fields of scholarship we must pay more careful attention to the ways in which the very dialectical nature of the respective canons we study demand an attention to the inevitably present points of intersection. An exploration of these points of intersection might then encourage the necessary reassessments and reorientation any critical field needs to survive and adapt in the face of literary histories in a state of unending reconstruction.

In agreeing with Stepto on the need for more comparative approaches, I am not suggesting that black texts must necessarily be included in every American project in order to reference a discussion of "race."[11] Nor am I arguing that we embrace some romantic and unproblematized notion of a common ground or a shared culture between African American and mainstream American literatures. Rather, I am arguing for a recognition of a common ground of cultural struggle, where (in the case of my particular study) blacks and whites worked to reinvent themselves in different and distinct ways, even as they recognized or repudiated moments of connection. An awareness of such cultural struggles going on between and among any number of populations separated by class, race, and ethnicity needs to be the contextualizing moment in any examination of writing produced by the multiracial, multiethnic inhabitants of the United

States. Here I am rejecting simplistic models of multiculturalism or an unproblematized "opening up of the canon"; rather, I am speaking about the necessity of theorizing the next step in American literary and cultural studies in light of the burgeoning scholarship on African American and, for that matter, Asian American, Native American, and Chicano literatures.

Because of such scholarship, old theories of what constituted the national literature of the United States are rapidly being pushed aside, and academics are now scrambling (to borrow a few phrases from a recent article by Carolyn Porter) to imagine a world of American literary studies they did not know before.[12] As more and more texts are recovered and more histories retold, the earlier cry to expand the canon must now coexist with real efforts to assess the consequences of that expansion. For instance, in specific examples from African American literature, Charles Chesnutt, Ida B. Wells, David Bryant Fulton, and Pauline Hopkins wrote within a segregated national context, but they consistently claimed their legal and cultural American citizenship by demanding the public recognition of their presence and collective participation in national life. Given the far from coherent control of public discourse achieved by white Americans, the participation of African American, when more fully interrogated, must necessarily force a reconceptualization of the current unsatisfactory binary model of margin and center.

In reference to African American scholarship, let me state clearly that I am not arguing for a cessation in the continuing recovery and theorization of black literature. On the contrary, the African American scholarship that theorized the innovations, the internal connections, and particular politics at work in the traditions of African American literature have provided the vital prelude to my own reading of black writers in this study. And, as both Oxford University Press's Schomburg Library of Nineteenth-Century Black Women Writers and Frances Smith Foster's recent discovery of three lost novels of Frances E. W. Harper demonstrate, the mapping of African American literary history is hardly a project of the past.[13]

Yet, why should not comparative readings of black and white literature be a more consistent project within the purview of an African American critic, as a means of demonstrating more consistently the multiple traditions African American writers wrote within and against? Such critical models have existed for years, and they continue at the present time in the work of Richard Yarborough on black writing and the phenomenon of *Uncle Tom's Cabin*, for example; or in Frances Smith Foster's contextualization of the late-nineteenth-century writer Octavia Victoria Rogers Albert with both slave narratives and the white tradition of local color fiction; or more recently in Carla Peterson's contextualization of Charlotte Forten's journal against the tradition of nineteenth-century white middle-class adolescent girls' diaries.[14] In referencing white literary models as simply one of a number of critical strategies, such scholarly work does not "bleach" black texts, as African American texts are not essentially "black" (just as white literary ones are not essentially "white") but are in fact uniquely composite artifacts. Rather, a comparative approach could only continue to afford African American critics an opportunity to further develop already existing interpretive models; at the same time, it would allow us to challenge traditional readings of white texts as uncomplicated or unmotivated by the issues that seem to drive black writers.

In the end, a comparative approach is only achievable if we address directly the ongoing struggle for academic representation and power consolidation between fields, a struggle that underlies and nuances the critical choices we make and the texts we read, teach, and research. For one thing, we need to address more directly the concern—held by many black as well as white scholars—that a comparative approach would lead to the appropriation of African American literature by even the most well-meaning white Americanists. This fear also feeds the assumption that appropriation is doubly reprehensible because there is no guarantee that the white scholar would bother to educate him/herself in the field to begin with, but would merely be content to pick out a particular "specimen" text for analysis.[15] And in the case of the white scholar who has taken the project seriously enough to do the necessary reading, there is still the problem of how the current academy might value African Americanist work only after it has proved worthy of, and been validated by, white critical effort.

Certainly the production, circulation, and validation of inadequate scholarship is a danger that must be resisted at all costs. At the same time, we cannot afford to assume that such scholarship will naturally occur when the scholar is white, just as we cannot assume that better research on African American texts will occur when a black scholar is at the helm; such an belief is doubly racist and essentializing in its demand for an imagined cultural affinity between critic and text. And yet the reification of this belief has been widespread, given the fact that so many English departments overwhelmingly demand that Americanists automatically be white and African-Americanists automatically be black, a situation that Henry Louis Gates, Jr., has identified as a confusion of the requirements of affirmative action with the requirements of building African American literary studies as a scholarly field.[16]

Clearly, for black scholars who work on African American writing, the slow, painful emergence of the field within a national academy hardly exempt from institutionalized racism has meant the opening up of employment opportunities long denied. And in this age of shrinking university budgets and dwindling federal support for the humanities, battles continue to be won and lost over the nature and number of course offerings, the racial composition of the entering pool of graduate students in Ph.D programs, "target of opportunity" as opposed to "regular" funding sources for academic jobs, and, of course, the tenuring of black faculty. Yet what is lost when these battles are fought upon the bodies of texts themselves, when members of one group demand ownership of Harriet Jacobs or Frances E. W. Harper for example, or when members of another claim only they have the right or skills to interpret Herman Melville or Henry James? In the end scholars risk compromising much of the achievement of the last two decades in both affirmative action and the rearticulation of literary histories when they continue to make the text stand in for the critic.

The continued call to see writers such as Jacobs and Melville in dialogue cannot be ignored, because it points to a wealth of still unimagined opportunities for rethinking the relationship among American literary histories. At the same time, however, it must necessarily add fuel to the fire that rages around questions of critical identity and textual ownership. And yet because a comparative method demands that we ask questions about the politics of narrative, literary access, gender, and community struggle within literary history, it could also be the moment at which we confront questions of academic power, privilege, publishing, and professional status that circumscribe the roles of its practitioners.

The reading of literary histories together as a way of recovering and imagining a dialectic could potentially create a space for scholarly self-criticism, because such an approach would demand an interrogation of the familiar terms of argument. It would demand a reorientation and, if need be, a destablizing of long-held terms, beliefs, and even particular kinds of field categories that stop us from imagining new allegiances among different kinds of scholarship. As such, it might then aid us in disabling the conditions that make both real scholarly appropriation and careless research possible. Ultimately, a comparative approach in literary history and in literary theory, an approach which refigures the meaning of race and gender in the history of American literary culture, can only prove valuable if critics have the will to use such an approach as a starting point, not a substitute, for dialogue.

In *Race, Rape, and Lynching* I have been engaged with my own desires as a feminist, an African Americanist, and an Americanist to reshape notions of canon and methods of literary study, and my desires have been produced both in conflict with and as a result of the history of American literary studies in this country. To rephrase Elsa Barkley Brown's words once more, I have been claiming and remembering a particular literary history about racial violence and literature, and my critical discourse has had to partake in the kind of necessary and inevitable invention implied in the distance between staking out an area of study and generating new interpretations.[17]

The case studies and juxtapositions presented in this work are my attempts to use the possibilities of critical invention to interrogate the vexed trope of the black male as criminal as a sign of discursive contradiction that masks as much as it reveals about turn-of-the-century American racial subjectivities. I have posed questions about stereotypes of coherent white masculinity that come apart in white supremacist literature of this period, as well as the kinds of masculine discourse that draw commonalities between the literature of black and white men at the turn of the century. At the same time, the context of black and white male constructions of the very terms of national discourse on racial violence has encouraged me to rethink the ways in which the production of individual desire through the articulation of community desire enabled distinctly different figurations for black and white women's discussions of racial violence and rape. In so doing, I hope I have opened up or clarified more avenues for readers and researchers to reimagine literary and cultural divisions that we have generally taken for granted.

# Notes

INTRODUCTION

1. In *Exorcising Blackness: Historical and Literary Lynching and Burning Rituals* (Bloomington: Indiana Univ. Press, 1984), Trudier Harris generally limits her discussion to African American writing dealing with the lynching and castration of black men. In addressing the growth of nineteenth-century black female intellectual thought, Hazel V. Carby's *Reconstructing Womanhood: The Emergence of the Afro-American Woman Novelist* (New York: Oxford Univ. Press, 1987) provides valuable discussions of how black women writers addressed lynching and rape as products of white supremacist attitudes in America.

2. Breaking away from a long-standing trend of tokenizing black writers for the problematic purpose of *permitting* the sounding of "other voices" in the American literary canon, a number of scholars have recently begun to theorize the mutually constitutive relationships between black and white literary traditions. See, for example, Dana D. Nelson, *The Word in Black and White: Reading "Race" in American Literature 1638–1867* (New York: Oxford Univ. Press, 1992); Shelley Fisher Fishkin, *Was Huck Black? Mark Twain and African American Voices* (New York: Oxford Univ. Press, 1993); Eric J. Sundquist, *To Wake the Nations: Race in the Making of American Literature* (Cambridge, Mass.: Harvard Univ. Press, 1993); and Kenneth W. Warren, *Black and White Strangers: Race and American Literary Realism* (Chicago: Univ. of Chicago Press, 1993).

3. Bettina Aptheker, "Woman Suffrage and the Crusade Against Lynching, 1890–1920," in *Woman's Legacy: Essays on Race, Sex and Class in American History* (Amherst: Univ. of Massachusetts Press, 1982), p. 60. See also her introduction to *Lynching and Rape: An Exchange of Views* (New York: American Institute for Marxist Studies, 1977), pp. 1–21; and James Elbert Cutler, *Lynch-Law: An Investigation into the History of Lynching in the United States* [1905] (Montclair, N.J.: Patterson Smith, 1969).

4. As historian W. Fitzhugh Brundage suggests, anxiety over the black rapist was just one element in the larger phenomenon of epidemic racial violence in the latter half of the nineteenth century. My book is not intended as a historical study of these factors, but simply as a study of how a particular stereotype––that of the black rapist––functioned in turn-of-the-century American literature. See W. Fitzhugh Brundage, *Lynching in the New South: Georgia and Virginia, 1880–1930* (Urbana: Univ. of Illinois Press, 1993), pp. 8–15.

5. Thomas Nelson Page, "The Lynching of Negroes—Its Cause and Its Prevention," in *The Negro: The Southerner's Problem* (New York: Charles Scribner, 1904), pp. 99–100.

6. Ben Tillman, "Black Peril," reprinted in *Justice Denied: The Black Man in White America*, ed. William M. Chace and Peter Collier (New York: Harcourt, Brace & World, 1970), p. 182.

7. W[ilbur] J. Cash, *The Mind of the South* (New York: Alfred A. Knopf, 1941), p. 115.

8. The historical scholarship that has shaped my thinking for this book includes Thomas F. Gossett, *Race: The History of an Idea in America* (New York: Schocken, 1965); Forrest G. Wood, *Black Scare: The Racist Response to Emancipation and Reconstruction* (Berkeley: Univ. of California Press, 1970); George M. Fredrickson, *The Black Image in the White Mind: The Debate on Afro-American Character and Destiny, 1817–1914* [1971] (Middletown, Conn.: Wesleyan Univ. Press, 1987); Jacquelyn Dowd Hall, *Revolt Against Chivalry: Jesse Daniel Ames and the Women's Campaign Against Lynching* (New York: Columbia Univ. Press, 1974), and " 'The Mind That Burns in Each Body': Women, Rape and Racial Violence," in *Powers of Desire: The Politics of Sexuality*, ed. Ann Snitow, Christine Stansell, and Sharon Thompson (New York: Monthly Review Press, 1983), pp. 328–49; Lawrence Goodwyn, *The Populist Moment: A Short History of the Agrarian Revolt in America* (New York: Oxford Univ. Press, 1978); Ronald T. Takaki, *Iron Cages: Race and Culture in Nineteenth-Century America* (Seattle: Univ. of Washington Press, 1979); John Hope Franklin, *From Slavery to Freedom: A History of Negro Americans*, 5th ed. (New York: Alfred A. Knopf, 1980); Thomas Dyer, *Theodore Roosevelt and the Idea of Race* (Baton Rouge: Louisiana State Univ. Press, 1980); Angela Y. Davis, *Women, Race and Class* (New York: Vintage, 1983); Joel Williamson, *The Crucible of Race: Black-White Relations in the American South Since Emancipation* (New York: Oxford Univ. Press, 1984); Nell Irvin Painter, *Standing at Armageddon: The United States, 1877–1919* (New York: W. W. Norton, 1987); and Herbert Shapiro, *White Violence and Black Response: From Reconstruction to Montgomery* (Amherst: Univ. of Massachusetts Press, 1988).

9. In terms of racial stereotypes, I want to stress here that I am not arguing that the black rapist was *the* dominant figure of anxiety in this period, although it clearly operated in multiple arenas. Specifically in terms of race relations, the figure of mixed-race individual—in particular, the mulatto—as a threatening expression of the collapse of whiteness through miscegenation existed as a feature of American culture long before the invention of the black rapist, and it continued to serve as a symbol of racial anxiety during the late 1890s and early 1900s. Despite its long and complex history, the mulatto did not have a relationship to vigilante violence quite like that of the black rapist; but the two must be seen as operating in tandem as racial symbols, in the presence of a host of other stereotypes.

For notable discussions of the mulatto in American culture, see Judith R. Berzon, *Neither White nor Black: The Mulatto Character in American Fiction* (New York: New York Univ. Press, 1978); Joel Williamson, *New People: Miscegenation and Mulattoes in the United States* (New York: Free Press, 1980); Hortense J. Spillers, "Notes on an Alternative Model—Neither/Nor," in *The Difference Within: Feminism and Critical Theory*, ed. Elizabeth Meese and Alice Parker (Philadelphia: J. Benjamins, 1989), pp. 165–85; and Susan Gillman, "The Mulatto, Tragic or Triumphant? The Nineteenth-Century American Race Melodrama," in *The Culture of Sentiment: Race, Gender, and Sentimentality in Nineteenth-Century America*, ed. Shirley Samuels (New York: Oxford Univ. Press, 1992), pp. 221–43.

10. T. Thomas Fortune, "The Negro's Place in American Life at the Present Day," and Booker T. Washington, "Industrial Education for the Negro," both in *The Negro Problem: A Series of Articles by Representative American Negroes of To-day,* [ed. Booker T. Washington, 1903] (Miami: Mnemosyne Publishing, 1969), p. 229, 19.

11. Martha Hodes, "The Sexualization of Reconstruction Politics: White Women and Black Men in the South After the Civil War," *Journal of the History of Sexuality* 3 (1993): 415, 404. As her title indicates, Hodes's essay addresses racial violence specifically during Reconstruction, but she suggests that during this period "black male sexuality first became a major theme in white Southern politics, thereby commencing an era of terrorism and lynching" (p. 403).

12. In his study of the Emmett Till case, Stephen J. Whitfield suggests that the 1955 murder may have marked a turning point in the history of Southern white violence: although Till's murderers were acquitted by a local all-white male jury, they were ostracized by their neighbors. By the 1950s, according to Whitfield, traditional forms of violence against blacks were "becoming less impulsive and available, and the vast majority of Southern whites abstained from participation in the brutality that became the price of maintaining segregation." For Whitfield's comments, see his *A Death in the Delta: The Story of Emmett Till* (Baltimore: Johns Hopkins Univ. Press, 1988), p. 140.

13. Quoted in Shapiro, *White Violence and Black Response,* p. 66. While the riot was clearly the product of white resentment over black political participation, the excuse of black surliness toward white women did surface when the editor of the town's black newspaper, Alexander Manly, responded to the pro-lynching remarks of Georgia's Rebecca Latimer Felton that "[e]very negro lynched is called a Big Burly Black Brute, when, in fact many of those . . . were sufficiently attractive for white girls of culture and refinement to fall in love with them, as is well known to all." Manly's office was one of the first black buildings burned in the riot. The editorial is quoted in H. Leon Prather, Sr., *We Have Taken a City: Wilmington Racial Massacre and Coup of 1898* (Rutherford, N.J.: Fairleigh Dickinson Univ. Press, 1984), pp. 72–73.

14. Ida B. Wells, *A Red Record: Tabulated Statistics and Alleged Causes of Lynchings in the United States, 1892–1893–1894,* in *Selected Works of Ida B. Wells-Barnett,* comp. Trudier Harris (New York: Oxford Univ. Press, 1991), p. 141.

15. For an account of Wells's strategy, see Gail Bederman, " 'Civilization,' the Decline of Middle-Class Manliness, and Ida B. Wells's Antilynching Campaign (1892–94)," *Radical History Review* 52 (Winter 1992): 5–30.

16. Harris, *Exorcising Blackness.* Harris suggests that

> [b]lack writers from Charles Waddell Chesnutt to Sutton Griggs, from Paul Laurence Dunbar to James Weldon Johnson, from Richard Wright to James Baldwin, and from Langston Hughes to Ralph Ellison have all presented the tragic consequences, usually death by lynching and burning, which frequently awaited black men who found themselves accidentally or voluntarily in "questionable" circumstances with white women. This particular accusation and form of punishment point to another tradition within the literature—that which suggests that black people, by their very existence in American society, were emasculated because they were stripped of economic and political power, and of any kind of social status. (xi–xii)

17. This is of course the standard line taken by many discussions of lynching and rape. Among the notable exceptions is Davis, *Women, Race and Class.*

18. Robyn Wiegman, "The Anatomy of Lynching," *Journal of the History of Sexuality* 3 (1993): 446 n.1; p. 462.

19. Wiegman, "The Anatomy of Lynching," p. 462.

20. See Gerda Lerner's indispensable *Black Women in White America: A Documentary History* (New York: Vintage, 1973) for documentary accounts of sexual assault suffered by black women. For illuminating discussions of rape, race, and gender, see also Davis, *Women, Race and Class*; Valerie Smith, "Split Affinities: The Case of Interracial Rape," in *Conflicts in Feminism*, ed. Marianne Hirsch and Evelyn Fox Keller (New York: Routledge, 1990), pp. 271–87; and Nellie Y. McKay, "Alice Walker's 'Advancing Luna— and Ida B. Wells': A Struggle Towards Sisterhood," in *Rape and Representation*, ed. Lynn A. Higgins and Brenda R. Silver (New York: Columbia Univ. Press, 1991), pp. 248–60.

21. Carby, *Reconstructing Womanhood*, p. 22.

22. Aptheker, "Woman Suffrage and the Crusade against Lynching 1890–1920," in *Woman's Legacy*, pp. 53–76; Elizabeth Ammons, *Conflicting Stories: American Women Writers at the Turn into the Twentieth Century* (New York: Oxford Univ. Press, 1992); Claudia Tate, *Domestic Allegories of Political Desire: The Black Heroine's Text at the Turn of the Century* (New York: Oxford Univ. Press, 1992). More recently historian Elsa Barkley Brown has brought attention to the politics of gender and public space in African American culture during the Reconstruction and post-Reconstruction eras. Her arguments complicate in new and powerful ways the scholarly view of black women activists and gender convention. See her "Negotiating and Transforming the Public Sphere: African American Political Life in the Transition from Slavery to Freedom," *Public Culture* 7 (1994): 107–46.

23. Carby, *Reconstructing Womanhood*, p. 18. See also Sylvia Wynter's description of "*whiteness* . . . as a striking phenomenon calling for extensive research" in "Sambos and Minstrels," *Social Text* 1 (1979): 150; see also Carby, "The Canon: Civil War and Reconstruction" *Michigan Quarterly Review* 27 (Winter 1989): 35–43; and Toni Morrison, *Playing in the Dark: Whiteness and the Literary Imagination* (Cambridge, Mass.: Harvard Univ. Press, 1992).

For examples of writers and critics who have begun the kind of interrogation Wynter, Carby, and Morrison have called for, see Biddy Martin and Chandra Talpade Mohanty, "Feminist Politics: What's Home Got to Do with It?" in *Feminist Studies/Critical Studies*, ed. Teresa de Lauretis (Bloomington: Indiana Univ. Press, 1986), pp. 190–212; and more recently Elizabeth Abel, "Black Writing, White Reading: Race and the Politics of Feminist Interpretation," *Critical Inquiry* 19 (Spring 1993): 470–98. In attempting to consider how the intersection of gender and race codes white women's writing, Helen Taylor's *Gender, Race, and Region in the Writings of Grace King, Ruth McEnery Stuart, and Kate Chopin* (Baton Rouge: Louisiana State Univ. Press, 1989) and Anna Shannon Elfenbein's *Women on the Color Line: Evolving Stereotypes and the Writings of George Washington Cable, Grace King, Kate Chopin* (Charlottesville: Univ. of Virginia Press, 1989) may herald a significant shift in white feminist scholarship on turn-of-the-century white women's writing. Their analyses of Kate Chopin's cultural context first encouraged me to reconsider the impact of white violence and the myth of black criminality on this recently canonized white female author.

24. Both Fredrickson and Williamson stress the complex circulation of a variety of white supremacist attitudes toward blacks after the Civil War. For instance, Williamson distinguishes in the 1870s and 1880s between a predominantly "liberal" attitude toward

blacks that "flirted with the idea of equality in important categories—as in religion, in educational and economic opportunities, and civil rights"; and a "conservative" racist attitude which "always began and ended with the idea that Negroes were inferior to whites in every major way" (*The Crucible of Race,* p. 108). Williamson argues that, after 1889 and until World War I—during the period with which I am concerned in *Race, Rape, and Lynching*—the onset of a more "radical" racism ushered in the notion of the regressive black and centralized more vigorously the figure of the black rapist as a major threat to white peace and prosperity. See also Fredrickson, *The Black Image in the White Mind,* chapters 6–9.

25. Wiegman, "The Anatomy of Lynching," p. 445.

26. Wiegman, "The Anatomy of Lynching," p. 447.

27. See, for instance, Eric Sundquist's argument that "white American culture simply cannot be imagined apart from black American culture," in *To Wake the Nations,* p. 4.

### CHAPTER ONE

1. William Dean Howells, *A Boy's Town, Described For "Harper's Young People"* (New York: Harper, 1890), pp. 129–30, 230.

2. William Dean Howells, *The Shadow of a Dream* and *An Imperative Duty,* ed. Martha Banta (Austin: Univ. of Texas Press, 1970), pp. 89–90.

3. I have borrowed this very apt phrase from Martha Banta's introduction to *An Imperative Duty,* p. iv.

4. Houston A. Baker, Jr., *Workings of the Spirit: The Poetics of Afro-American Women's Writing* (Chicago: Univ. of Chicago Press, 1991), p. 13. See especially Baker's discussion of the display on the slave body before Northern abolitionist audiences.

5. I am using Eve Kosofsky Sedgwick's definition of desire as "the affective or social force, the glue, even when its manifestation is hostility or hatred or something less emotively charged, that shapes an important relationship." See her *Between Men: English Literature and Male Homosocial Desire* (New York: Columbia Univ. Press, 1985), p. 2.

6. Hortense J. Spillers, "Notes on an Alternative Model—Neither/Nor," in *The Difference Within: Feminism and Critical Theory,* ed. Elizabeth Meese and Alice Parker (Philadelphia: J. Benjamins, 1989), p. 168.

7. The black beast was of course the flip side of figure of the illiterate, often comical plantation black popularized by local color and plantation fiction writers.

8. Quoted in Allen W. Trelease, *White Terror: The Ku Klux Klan Conspiracy and Southern Reconstruction* [1971] (Westport, Conn.: Greenwood, 1979), p. xx.

9. For a study of the earlier moments in the development of such an attitude, see Forrest G. Wood, *Black Scare: The Racist Response to Emancipation and Reconstruction* (Berkeley: Univ. of California Press, 1970). See also George M. Fredrickson, *The Black Image in the White Mind: The Debate on Afro-American Character and Destiny, 1817–1914* [1971] (Middletown, Conn.: Wesleyan Univ. Press, 1987); and Joel Williamson, *The Crucible of Race: Black–White Relations in the American South Since Emancipation* (New York: Oxford Univ. Press, 1984).

10. Quoted in Williamson, *The Crucible of Race,* pp. 121–22.

11. George Washington Cable, *The Grandissimes: A Story of Creole Life* [1880] (Athens: Univ. of Georgia Press, 1988). References to this text are indicated by the abbreviation *G*.

12. Thomas Nelson Page, *Red Rock: A Chronicle of Reconstruction* (New York: Charles Scribner, 1898), p. 193.

13. Upton Sinclair, *The Jungle* [1906] (New York: Signet, 1960), pp. 270–71.

14. Though some of his contemporaries must clearly have disagreed with his reading of African Americans, Howells's study of race relations in *An Imperative Duty* suggests that after Emancipation the black presence within the white world could be regulated through the black's traditional role as servant; the pleasure in the continuance of a "natural" black subordination is articulated in Olney's association of comfort with the image of "the white linen jacket and apron of a black waiter" (*An Imperative Duty*, 5).

15. Ray Stannard Baker, *Following the Color Line: American Negro Citizenship in the Progressive Era* [1908] (New York: Harper, 1964), pp. xiii, 180.

16. See Gail Bederman's argument in her article " 'Civilization,' the Decline of Middle-Class Manliness, and Ida B. Wells's Antilynching Campaign (1892–94)," *Radical History Review* 52 (Winter 1992): 5–30.

17. Ida B. Wells, *A Red Record: Tabulated Statistics and Alleged Causes of Lynchings in the United States, 1892–1893–1894*, reprinted in *Selected Works of Ida B. Wells-Barnett*, comp. Trudier Harris (New York: Oxford Univ. Press, 1991), pp. 166–67.

18. Andrew Sledd, "The Negro: Another View," *Atlantic Monthly* 90 (July 1902): 70–71.

19. Theodore Dreiser, "Nigger Jeff," reprinted in *Free and Other Stories* (New York: Boni & Liveright, 1918).

20. E. D. Cope, "Two Perils of the Indo-European," *Open Court* 3(127) (1890): 2071.

21. Quoted in Barbara Ehrenreich and Deirdre English, *For Her Own Good: 150 Years of the Experts' Advice to Women* (Garden City, N.Y.: Doubleday, 1978), p. 190.

Clyde Griffen's recent assertion that the frequently argued "crisis" of late nineteenth-century (white) masculinity can lead to oversimplifications and misleading generalizations about the variety of masculine self-definitions worked out by American white men in this period is important. However, without trying to argue that Cope or Roosevelt spoke for all white men, I do want to point out that in particular the ideology of race management justified by the "existence" of the black rapist is partly produced by an anxiety over changing definitions of white femininity. See Griffen, "Reconstructing Masculinity from the Evangelical Revival to the Waning of Progressivism: A Speculative Synthesis," in *Meanings for Manhood: Constructions of Masculinity in Victorian America*, ed. Mark C. Carnes and Clyde Griffen (Chicago: Univ. of Chicago Press, 1990), pp. 183–204, 265–71.

22. Wells, *Selected Works*, p. 14.

23. Jacquelyn Dowd Hall, " 'The Mind That Burns in Each Body': Women, Rape, and Racial Violence," in *Powers of Desire: The Politics of Sexuality*, ed. Ann Snitow, Christine Stansell, and Sharon Thompson (New York: Monthly Review Press, 1983), p. 337.

24. Quoted in Anna Shannon Elfenbein, *Women on the Color Line: Evolving Stereotypes and the Writings of George Washington Cable, Grace King, Kate Chopin* (Charlottesville: Univ. Press of Virginia, 1989), p. 19.

25. Kathleen M. Blee, *Women of the Klan: Racism and Gender in the 1920s* (Berkeley: Univ. of California Press, 1991), p. 13. See also Martha Hodes, "The Sexualization of Reconstruction Politics: White Women and Black Men in the South after the Civil War," *Journal of the History of Sexuality* 3 (1993): 409.

26. Williamson, *The Crucible of Race*, p. 141.

27. For information on Griffith and Dixon, I am relying on Raymond Allen Cook, *Fire from the Flint: The Amazing Careers of Thomas Dixon* (Winston-Salem, N.C.: John F. Blair, 1968), chapters 7 and 8.

After *The Birth of a Nation*, Dixon was convinced that motion pictures would "shape the destiny of humanity," and for a time he tried his hand at filmmaking. He established the short-lived Dixon Studios in Los Angeles and tried unsuccessfully to produce movie versions of his other novels, including a sequel to Griffith's saga, called *The Fall of a Nation*, which was a complete failure.

28. Cook, *Fire from the Flint*, p. 168.

29. Russell Merritt, "Dixon, Griffith, and the Southern Legend," *Cinema Journal* 12 (1972): 27 n.2. On *The Birth of a Nation* and the rebirth of the Klan, see John Hope Franklin, " 'Birth of a Nation'—Propaganda as History," *Massachusetts Review* 20 (1979): 430–31.

30. Quoted in Cook, *Fire from the Flint*, p. 170.

31. Maxwell Bloomfield, "Dixon's *The Leopard's Spots*: A Study in Popular Racism," *American Quarterly* 16 (1964): 390–91. See also Cook, *Fire from the Flint*.

32. Cook, *Fire from the Flint*, p. 112.

33. Lilian Lida Bell, "The Leopard's Spots," *Saturday Evening Post* (12 April 1902): 15.

34. John Hope Franklin, *From Slavery to Freedom: A History of Negro Americans*, 5th ed. (New York: Alfred A. Knopf, 1980), pp. 268–80; Gilbert Osofsky, "Progressivism and the Negro: New York, 1900–1915," *American Quarterly* 16 (1964): 155.

35. Thomas Dixon, Jr., "Booker T. Washington and the Negro," *Saturday Evening Post* (19 August 1905): 2, 1.

36. Quoted in Thomas Dyer, *Theodore Roosevelt and the Idea of Race* (Baton Rouge: Louisiana State Univ. Press, 1980), p. 140.

37. Michael Rogin, " 'The Sword Became a Flashing Vision': D. W. Griffith's *The Birth of a Nation*," *Representations* 9 (1985): 153, 153–54. Some aspects of my argument about Dixon's novels are complemented by Rogin's discussion of Griffith's film.

38. Quoted in Durant Da Ponte, "The Greatest Play of the South," *Tennessee Studies in Literature* 2 (1957): 17.

39. Dixon, "Booker T. Washington," pp. 1, 2.

40. Hazel V. Carby, *Reconstructing Womanhood: The Emergence of the Afro-American Woman Novelist* (New York: Oxford Univ. Press, 1987), 25.

41. Thomas Dixon, Jr., *The Leopard's Spots: A Romance of the White Man's Burden— 1865–1900* [1902] (Ridgewood, N.J.: Gregg, 1967). References to this text are indicated by the abbreviation *LS*.

42. "Thomas Dixon Talks of The Clansman," *Atlanta Constitution* (29 October 1905). As for the New York scene, years later Dixon would incorporate this anecdote in his novel *The Root of Evil* (Garden City, N.Y.: Doubleday, 1911). Here the young Southern hero James Stuart, adrift in the urban North, encounters the same pair. This time doing what Dixon perhaps wanted to do, Stuart assaults the black man and beats him unconscious. The girl, properly penitent and grateful for her release, is then cloistered within a fallen women's shelter. See also F. Garvin Davenport, Jr., "Thomas Dixon's Mythology of Southern History," *Journal of Southern History* 36 (1970): 359–60, for another view of the novelistic incident.

43. Eve Kosofsky Sedgwick's "The Beast in the Closet: James and the Writing of Homosexual Panic" in *Sex, Politics, and Science in the Nineteenth-Century Novel*, ed.

Ruth Bernard Yeazell [Selected Papers from the English Institute, 1983–84] (Baltimore: Johns Hopkins Univ. Press, 1986), pp. 148–86, proves useful here. Sedgwick suggests that, since nineteenth-century "paths of male entitlement . . . required certain intense male bonds that were not readily distinguishable from the most reprobated bonds, an endemic and ineradicable state . . . [of] male homosexual panic became the normal condition of male heterosexual entitlement" (151). If, as Sedgwick suggests,

> such compulsory relationships as male friendships, mentorship, admiring identification, bureaucratic subordination, and heterosexual rivalry all involve forms of investment that force men into the arbitrarily mapped, self-contradictory, and anathema-riddled quicksands of the middle distance of male homosocial desire, then . . . men enter into adult masculine entitlement only through acceding to the permanent threat that the small space they have cleared for themselves on this terrain may always, just as arbitrarily and with just as much justification, be punitively and retroactively foreclosed. (152)

One result of the fearful but inevitably produced "arbitrariness" says Sedgwick is "a reservoir of potential for *violence*" (152), which, in a racially homogeneous situation, can fuel homophobia as a means of regulating "compulsory" male bonds. Sedgwick's argument might be extended to the interracial fantasy of the white hero and the black beast, since violence does function in this context to define a white heterosexual masculinity put in jeopardy by the "rivalry" (to put it mildly) between black and white men.

44. Leslie A. Fiedler, "Come Back to the Raft Ag'in, Huck Honey!" in *An End to Innocence: Essays on Culture and Politics* [1948] (New York: Stein & Day, 1972), p. 147.

45. The threat of the homosocial triangle's transformation into a homosexual pairing between black and white men is also fueled by the iconography of race, since, according to Robert K. Martin, to "embrace . . . the Dark African, [is] to accept, symbolically at least, anal penetration (entry into the darkness within), and thus to make oneself over as female, a commodity to be exchanged." See his "Knights-Errant and Gothic Seducers: The Representation of Male Friendship in Mid-Nineteenth-Century America" in *Hidden from History: Reclaiming the Gay and Lesbian Past*, ed. Martin Duberman, Martha Vicinus and George Chauncey, Jr. (New York: New American Library, 1989), p. 178.

46. Rogin, "The Sword Becomes a Flashing Vision": pp. 170–71.

47. Thomas Dixon, Jr., *The Clansman: An Historical Romance of the Ku Klux Klan* [1905] (Lexington: Univ. Press of Kentucky, 1970). References to this text are indicated by the abbreviation *C*.

48. For an excellent recent discussion of the theme of heroic manhood in turn-of-the-century fiction, see Amy Kaplan, "Romancing the Empire: The Embodiment of American Masculinity in the Popular Historical Novel of the 1890s," *American Literary History* 2 (Winter 1990): 659–90.

49. For an account of the real-life Dick, see Cook, *Fire in the Flint*, pp. 18–19. Dixon's biographer seems delighted by Dixon's love of his black friend but does not speculate as to the meaning of Dixon's decision to transform the beloved Dick into the rapist in *The Leopard's Spots*.

50. For a reading of Dixon's childhood reaction to his own mother's illness, see Williamson, *The Crucible of Race*, chapter 5.

51. Dixon in fact does reincarnate Little Eva in the dramatic version of *The Clansman*. In the play, little Eva is raped by Gus.

52. Bloomfield, "Dixon's *The Leopard's Spots,*" p. 393; see also Davenport, "Thomas Dixon's Mythology," pp. 355, 360–61.

53. Dixon's distinction is of course idealized. While many whites, including Ray Stannard Baker, assumed that lynch mobs were composed of poor whites, most riots, as in the case of the 1898 race riot in Wilmington, North Carolina, were composed of a cross-section of the community and often were led by important men of the town. For discussion of the Wilmington Riot, see H. Leon Prather, Sr., *We Have Taken a City: Wilmington Racial Massacre and Coup of 1898* (Rutherford, N.J.: Fairleigh Dickinson Univ. Press, 1984); Herbert Shapiro, *White Violence and Black Response: From Reconstruction to Montgomery* (Amherst: Univ. of Massachusetts Press, 1988); and Eric J. Sundquist, *To Wake the Nations: Race in the Making of American Literature* (Cambridge, Mass.: Harvard Univ. Press, 1993), chapter 4.

54. Dixon claimed that he owed allegiance only to the early Klan and that its subsequent revivals were never in touch with the original goal of white self-protection. Strangely, both Raymond Allen Cook, Dixon's biographer, and Maxwell Bloomfield seem to see this as a positive attribute in Dixon, as if the original Klan were not itself a white terrorist organization. See Cook, *Fire in the Flint;* and Bloomfield, "Dixon's *The Leopard's Spots,*" p. 395.

55. Quoted in Bertram Wyatt-Brown, *Southern Honor: Ethics and Behavior in the Old South* (New York: Oxford Univ. Press, 1982), p. 455.

56. Rogin, "The Sword Became a Flashing Vision," p. 180.

57. Thomas Dixon, Jr., *The Sins of the Father: A Romance of the South* (New York: Grosset & Dunlap, 1912). References to this text are indicated by the abbreviation *S.*

## CHAPTER TWO

1. Ben Tillman, "The Black Peril," reprinted in *Justice Denied: The Black Man in White America,* ed. William M. Chace and Peter Collier (New York: Harcourt, Brace & World, 1970), p. 181. I thank Stephanie A. Smith for suggesting this reading of Tillman's words.

2. Theodore Dreiser, "Nigger Jeff," in *Free and Other Stories* (New York: Boni & Liveright, 1918). References to this text will be indicated by the abbreviation *N.*

3. Anna Julia Cooper, "Womanhood a Vital Element in the Regeneration and Progress of a Race," in *A Voice From the South* [1892] (New York: Oxford Univ. Press, 1988), p. 31. For a discussion of black attempts at self-representation in the post-Reconstruction context, see Henry Louis Gates, Jr., "The Trope of a New Negro and the Reconstruction of the Image of the Black," *Representations* 24 (1988): 129–55.

4. Claudia Tate, *Domestic Allegories of Political Desire: The Black Heroine's Text at the Turn of the Century* (New York: Oxford Univ. Press, 1992), pp. 59, 56.

5. Sutton E. Griggs, *Imperium in Imperio* [1899] (New York: Arno Press, 1969), p. 62. Griggs of course refers to an earlier conception of the "New Negro" than that promulgated by Alain Locke during the Harlem Renaissance. For a discussion of the concept of the New Negro and its various applications for turn-of-the-century and Harlem Renaissance blacks, see Eric J. Sundquist, *To Wake the Nations: Race in the Making of American Literature* (Cambridge, Mass.: Harvard Univ. Press, 1993), 334–36.

6. Frederick Douglass, "Lynch Law in the South," *North American Review* 155 ( July 1892): 22.

7. Bruce quoted in Herbert Shapiro, *White Violence and Black Response: From Reconstruction to Montgomery* (Amherst: Univ. of Massachusetts Press, 1988), p. 42. For a general discussion of black responses to lynching, see Shapiro's chapter 2. Ida B. Wells, *Southern Horrors: Lynch Law in All Its Phases,* reprinted in *Selected Works of Ida B. Wells-Barnett,* comp. Trudier Harris (New York: Oxford Univ. Press, 1991), p. 42.

8. See, for instance, Tourgée's work as an attorney in the 1896 *Plessy v. Ferguson* decision, and his earlier attempts in fiction to challenge American thinking on race and sectional issues, in novels such as *A Fool's Errand* (1879) and *Bricks Without Straw* (1880). Cable became famous for his nonfictional responses in favor of black civil rights, as in the case of his essay "The Freedman's Case in Equity" (1884). Through his journalism, Baker attempted to track what he thought was a narrative of race relations more reasonable than that promulgated by radical racists. His essays on black and white life North and South were published in the *American Magazine* between 1906 and 1908, and reissued in book form as *Following the Color Line* (1908).

9. Paula A. Treichler, "Feminism, Medicine, and the Meaning of Childbirth," in *Body/Politics: Women and the Discourses of Science,* ed. Mary Jacobus, Evelyn Fox Keller, and Sally Shuttleworth (New York: Routledge, 1990), p. 132.

10. Michael Rogin, "Francis Galton and Mark Twain: The Natal Autograph in *Pudd'nhead Wilson,*" in *Mark Twain's Pudd'nhead Wilson: Race, Conflict and Culture,* ed. Susan Gillman and Forrest G. Robinson (Durham, N.C.: Duke Univ. Press, 1990), p. 74. For some examples of the lively critical debate over racism in *Pudd'nhead Wilson,* see Philip S. Foner, *Mark Twain: Social Critic* (New York: International Publishers, 1958); Leslie A. Fiedler, *Love and Death in the American Novel* [1960] rev. ed. (New York: Stein & Day, 1966); Philip Butcher, "Mark Twain Sells Roxy Down the River," *CLA Journal* 8 (1965): 225–33; Arthur G. Pettit, *Mark Twain and the South* (Lexington: Univ. Press of Kentucky, 1974); James Kinney, *Amalgamation! Race, Sex and Rhetoric in the Nineteenth-Century American Novel* (Westport, Conn.: Greenwood, 1985); and Lee Clark Mitchell, " 'De Nigger in You': Race or Training in *Pudd'nhead Wilson,*" *Nineteenth-Century Literature* 42 (1987): 295–312.

More recently, the debate over Twain's entanglements on the subject of race in *Pudd'nhead Wilson* has been greatly expanded in the collection *Mark Twain's Pudd'nhead Wilson: Race, Conflict and Culture,* ed. Susan Gillman and Forrest G. Robinson, in which Rogin's essay appears. In this volume, see especially Susan Gillman's " 'Sure Identifiers': Race, Science and the Law in *Pudd'nhead Wilson,*" pp. 86–104; Myra Jehlen, "The Ties That Bind: Race and Sex in *Pudd'nhead Wilson,*" pp. 105–20; and Carolyn Porter, "Roxana's Plot," 121–36. See also Eric J. Sundquist, "Mark Twain and Homer Plessy," pp. 46–72; a longer version of this essay also appears in Sundquist's *To Wake the Nations.* My own reading of Twain's novel has been greatly influenced by Sundquist's work, as well as by the collection edited by Gillman and Robinson.

11. From *Europe and Elsewhere,* in *The Portable Mark Twain,* ed. Bernard DeVoto (New York: Viking, 1946), p. 592.

12. Susan Gillman, "The Mulatto, Tragic or Triumphant? The Nineteenth-Century American Race Melodrama," in *The Culture of Sentiment: Race, Gender, and Sentimentality in Nineteenth-Century America,* ed. Shirley Samuels (New York: Oxford Univ. Press, 1992), p. 222. Gillman categorizes the mulatto-centered text at the turn of the century as "race melodrama," a subgenre that consistently treats issues of race, family, and national identity. According to Gillman, such a subgenre would encompass not only

Twain's *Pudd'nhead Wilson* but also work by figures as diverse as Pauline Hopkins, Thomas Dixon, and W. E. B. DuBois. Unlike my usage of her term, she specifically stresses that the race melodrama "focuses broadly on the situation of the black family . . . as a means of negotiating the social tensions surrounding the formation of racial, national, and sexual identity in the post-Reconstruction years" (222). This idea of the "situation of the black family" might need further clarification, if she wants to argue for the inclusion of novels such as Dixon's *The Leopard's Spots*.

13. Frances Richardson Keller, *An American Crusade: The Life of Charles Waddell Chesnutt* (Provo, Utah: Brigham Young Univ. Press, 1978), p. 213.

14. The teasing question of how this disorder arises, both because and in spite of Twain's acute awareness of social issues, has been widely addressed. See, for instance, the essays collected in *Mark Twain's Pudd'nhead Wilson: Race, Conflict and Culture*.

15. Quoted in Arthur John, *The Best Years of the Century: Richard Watson Gilder, Scribner's Monthly, and Century Magazine, 1870–1909* (Urbana: Univ. of Illinois Press, 1981), p. 126. See also John Tebbel and Mary Ellen Zuckerman, *The Magazine in America, 1741–1990* (New York: Oxford Univ. Press, 1991). For an important assessment of the role of magazines like the *Century* in mediating discussions of race, white supremacy, and citizenship after Reconstruction, see Kenneth W. Warren, *Black and White Strangers: Race and American Literary Realism* (Chicago: Univ. of Chicago Press, 1993), especially chapter 2. For a discussion of the phenomenon of sectional reunion, see Nina Silbers, *The Romance of Reunion: Northerners and the South, 1865–1900* (Chapel Hill: Univ. of North Carolina Press, 1993).

16. Mark Twain, *Pudd'nhead Wilson and Those Extraordinary Twins*, [1894], ed. Malcolm Bradbury (Harmondsworth, G.B.: Penguin, 1986). References to this text will be indicated by the abbreviation *PW*.

17. James M. Cox, "*Pudd'nhead Wilson*: The End of Mark Twain's American Dream," *South Atlantic Quarterly* 58 (1959): 355.

18. See Eric Lott, "Love and Theft: The Racial Unconscious of Blackface Minstrelsy," *Representations* 39 (Summer 1992): 23–50, for a valuable discussion of minstrelsy's engagement with white attraction to black sexuality.

19. The element of Tom's characterization is of course a remnant of the earlier plot of the dark and light Siamese twins in *Those Extraordinary Twins*, the story out of which *Pudd'nhead Wilson* arose.

20. Sundquist, *To Wake the Nations*, p. 394.

21. In "Roxana's Plot" Carolyn Porter argues differently for Roxy's power as a black woman out of control in Twain's narrative.

22. Rogin, "Francis Galton and Mark Twain," p. 76.

23. Richard Yarborough, "Violence, Manhood and Black Heroism: The Wilmington Riot in Two Turn-of-the-Century Afro-American Novels" (unpublished manuscript, 1990), p. 2. For an account of the riot itself, see H. Leon Prather, Sr., *We Have Taken a City: Wilmington Racial Massacre and Coup of 1898* (Rutherford, N.J.: Fairleigh Dickinson Univ. Press, 1984). For recent discussions of *The Marrow of Tradition* and the 1898 Wilmington riot, see William Gleason, "Voices at the Nadir: Charles Chesnutt and David Bryant Fulton," *American Literary Realism* 24 (Spring 1992): 22–41; and Sundquist, *To Wake the Nations*, chapter 4. Importantly, both Gleason and Yarborough discuss Chesnutt's novel in relation to the considerably lesser known *Hanover; or The Persecution of*

*the Lowly: A Story of the Wilmington Massacre,* published in 1900 by black journalist David Bryant Fulton. See my Chapter 3 for a full discussion of Fulton's novel.

24. Quoted in Prather, *We Have Taken a City,* p. 71; for Manly's response to Felton, see pp. 72–73.

25. Charles W. Chesnutt, *The Journals of Charles W. Chesnutt,* ed. Richard Brodhead (Durham: Duke Univ. Press, 1993), pp. 139–40. Chesnutt was actually born in Cleveland, Ohio, but spent his formative years in Fayetteville, North Carolina. He taught there until 1883, then returned to Ohio to pursue careers in writing, the law, and court reporting.

My focus on Chesnutt for the purposes of this chapter precludes my addressing his long career as a biographer, essayist, novelist, and short-story writer in the context of both African American and American literary traditions. For general discussions of Chesnutt as a writer, see William L. Andrews, *The Literary Career of Charles W. Chesnutt* (Baton Rouge: Louisiana State Univ. Press, 1980); Sundquist, *To Wake the Nations,* chapter 4; and Richard H. Brodhead, *Cultures of Letters: Scenes of Reading and Writing in Nineteenth-Century America* (Chicago: Univ. of Chicago Press, 1993).

26. John Edgar Wideman, "Charles W. Chesnutt: *The Marrow of Tradition,*" *American Scholar* 42 (1972): 128.

27. Charles W. Chesnutt, *The Marrow of Tradition* [1901] (Ann Arbor: Univ. of Michigan Press, 1969). References to this text are indicated by the abbreviation *MT.*

28. It is quite tempting here to imagine that, in the context of Chesnutt's knowledge of the well-publicized Manly–Felton clash, Ochiltree's rabid pronouncements of violence to save white privilege might be drawn on some levels from Felton's public statements about the need for white men to be much more active in thwarting the rise of blacks in the South. See Joel Williamson, *The Crucible of Race: Black–White Relations in the American South Since Emancipation* (New York: Oxford Univ. Press, 1984), p. 128. I offer further discussions of Felton and Manly in Chapters 3 and 4.

29. While there is no evidence to suggest that *The Marrow of Tradition* is in any way a direct response to *Pudd'nhead Wilson,* this refiguration of white womanhood challenges Twain's negative construction of Roxy.

30. Sundquist, *To Wake the Nations,* p. 446.

31. See also William L. Andrews's discussion in *The Literary Career of Charles W. Chesnutt,* pp. 192–93.

32. Arlene A. Elder, " 'The Future American Race': Charles W. Chesnutt's Utopian Illusion," *MELUS* 15 (Fall 1988): 122. The problem of Chesnutt's validation of color is of course a thorny issue. Elder reads Chesnutt's favoring of the mulatto as an indication of his "awareness of the legal and social power inherent in assimilation rather than . . . [his valuation of] ethnic diversity, an understandable, if unfortunate, position for a mulatto writer living during the racially-turbulent turn-of-the-century" (123). For an alternative view of Chesnutt and color, see SallyAnn H. Ferguson, "Chesnutt's Genuine Blacks and Future Americans," *MELUS* 15 (Fall 1988): 109–19.

A middle-class black writer who was light-skinned enough to pass, and who at one point in his life even considered this possibility, Chesnutt takes a position on color that is indeed problematic. Yet his own attitudes notwithstanding, I find extremely provocative Hazel V. Carby's reading of how the mulatto in turn-of-the-century African American fiction might have been used "as a mediating device" that "enabled an exploration of the social relations between races" as well as "an expression of the sexual relations between races" (Introduction to *Iola Leroy, or Shadows Uplifted* [Boston: Beacon Press, 1987], pp. xxi–xxii). Instead of simply reading Chesnutt's use of the mulatto as his attempt to create a realistic character, I would prefer to consider the metaphoric implications of this figure as a site for Chesnutt to reimagine race conflicts and their resolution.

Still, the interplay between fictional uses of the figure of the mulatto and the intersection of class and race issues with the historical presences of light-skinned people of color have yet to be fully addressed. Useful recent historical scholarship toward this end includes Willard B. Gatewood, *Aristocrats of Color: The Black Elite, 1880–1920* (Bloomington: Indiana Univ. Press, 1990); on Chesnutt and the context of black folk culture, see Sundquist, *To Wake the Nations,* chapter 4.

33. In 1900 Chesnutt set out his views on racial admixture in a series of articles suggesting that a realistic approach to amalgamation would reveal "pure" racial whiteness to be already a thing of the past. In his article "What is a White Man," Chesnutt remarks "it is evident that where the intermingling of the races has made such progress as it has in this country, the line which separates the races must in many instances have been practically obliterated" (*Independent* 51 [1889]: 5–6). This is an ironic and brave statement, given the great deal of blood being spilled at the time to preserve the notion of racial purity and separation of the races. See his writings on "The Future American," reprinted as "Charles W. Chesnutt's Future American," *MELUS* 15 (Fall 1988): 95–107.

34. Sundquist, *To Wake the Nations,* pp. 444–45. The contradiction between Josh and Miller has sparked much debate about Chesnutt's attitude toward black male violence. See Andrews, Gleason, and Yarborough for important commentaries.

35. Griggs, *Imperium in Imperio,* p. 43. Both Griggs's *Imperium in Imperio,* and his *The Hindered Hand: or, The Reign of the Repressionist* (1905) offer important commentaries on the same question of black male retaliation.

36. William Dean Howells, "A Psychological Counter-Current in Recent Fiction," *North American Review* 173 (December 1901): 882. For the dual review of the novels by Chesnutt and Dixon, see "The Leopard's Spots," *Independent* 54 (1902): 1548.

### CHAPTER THREE

1. Hazel V. Carby, *Reconstructing Womanhood: The Emergence of the Afro-American Woman Novelist* (New York: Oxford Univ. Press, 1987), p. 18. See also Paula Giddings, *When and Where I Enter: The Impact of Black Women on Race and Sex in America* (New York: Bantam, 1984), chapter 5.

In a recent ground-breaking article, historian Elsa Barkley Brown has argued that "one of the most neglected areas of Reconstruction history and of African American history in general, is that of violence against women." She also laments in modern scholarship a general "emphasis on lynching as the major form of racial violence, and the limited historical attention to the black women who were lynched," ("Negotiating and Transforming the Public Sphere: African American Political Life in the Transition from Slavery to Freedom," *Public Culture* 7 [1994]: 112 n.8). Without losing sight of the actual lynching of black women, I am specifically dealing in this chapter with the rape of black women in the political context of post-Reconstruction. For information on the rape of black women in the context of white supremacist violence, see Gerda Lerner, "The Rape of Black Women as a Weapon of Terror," in *Black Women in White America:*

*A Documentary History* (New York: Vintage, 1973), pp. 172–93; on black women, rape, and Reconstruction, see Laura F. Edwards, "Sexual Violence, Gender, Reconstruction, and the Extension of Patriarchy in Granville County, North Carolina," *North Carolina Historical Review* 68 (July 1991): 237–60.

2. Quoted in Giddings, *When and Where I Enter*, p. 82.

3. In his attempt to refigure the image of black women, Chesnutt joined a long line of African American male activists that extended throughout the nineteenth century, from Frederick Douglass to Alexander Crummell to black minister and writer Sutton E. Griggs. Late-nineteenth-century black journalists Calvin Chase of the *Washington Bee* and T. Thomas Fortune of the *New York Age* also agitated for the reconceptualization of black womanhood. See Rosalyn Terborg-Penn, "Black Male Perspectives on the Nineteenth-Century Woman," in *The Afro-American Woman: Struggles and Images*, ed. Sharon Harley and Rosalyn Terborg-Penn (Port Washington, N.Y.: Kennikat, 1978), pp. 28–42. See also Crummell's 1883 address, "The Black Woman of the South: Her Neglects and Her Needs," in *Destiny and Race: Selected Writings, 1840–1898*, ed. Wilson Jeremiah Moses (Amherst: Univ. of Massachusetts Press, 1992), 211–23.

4. Anna Julia Cooper, 1893 Address to the Congress of Representative Women, reprinted in *Black Women in Nineteenth-Century American Life: Their Words, Their Thoughts, Their Feelings*, ed. Bert James Loewenberg and Ruth Bogin (Univ. Park: Pennsylvania State Univ. Press, 1976), p. 329.

5. See, for instance, *Maria W. Stewart, America's First Black Woman Political Writer: Essays and Speeches*, ed. Marilyn Richardson (Bloomington: Indiana Univ. Press, 1987); Harriet Jacobs, *Incidents in the Life of a Slave Girl*, [1861], ed. Jean Fagan Yellin (Cambridge, Mass.: Harvard Univ. Press, 1987); and *Narrative of Sojourner Truth; A Bondswoman of Olden Time, With a History of Her Labors and Correspondence Drawn from Her "Book of Life*," ed. Olive Gilbert [1878] (New York: Oxford Univ. Press, 1991). In "Negotiating and Transforming the Public Sphere," Elsa Barkley Brown argues convincingly that, in particular, African American women "were seeking in the late-nineteenth century not a new authority but rather a lost authority, one they now often sought to justify on a distinctively female basis." According to Barkley Brown, "these women were attempting to regain space they traditionally had held in the post-emancipation period" (108).

6. Fannie Barrier Williams, "The Woman's Part in a Man's Business," *Voice of the Negro* 1 (11) (November 1904): 547. See Barkley Brown, "Negotiating and Transforming the Public Sphere," pp. 137–41, for an important discussion of the historical specificities that dictated the particular kinds of black female activism undertaken at the turn of the century.

7. Wilson Jeremiah Moses, *The Golden Age of Black Nationalism, 1850–1925* [1978] (New York: Oxford Univ. Press, 1988), p. 104; see also Bettina Aptheker, "Woman Suffrage and the Crusade against Lynching, 1890–1920," in *Woman's Legacy: Essays on Race, Sex, and Class in American History* (Amherst: Univ. of Massachusetts Press, 1982), pp. 53–76. See especially Giddings, *When and Where I Enter*.

8. The motto of the National Association of Colored Women was "Lifting as We Climb," an ideal both heroic and problematic, since it flew in the face of racist ideology while at the same time embracing aspects of American middle-class ideology. The question of whether late-nineteenth-century black women activists and writers made radical challenges to the status quo is of course determined by how one defines "radical chal-

lenges." In line with many critics of African American literature before him, Houston A. Baker, Jr., makes a negative judgment of their efforts:

> Taking up residence in the North, the departed daughters . . . attempted to avoid the weight of an "old oligarchy" by founding a new voice and image. Unfortunately, their articulations echoed preeminently the didactic embodiments of white abolitionism, ignoring black southern soundings, preferring instead a soothing mulatto utopianism. Economics, politics, sociology, and even religion were left out of account. In their place the daughters inserted a bright Victorian morality in whiteface. (*Workings of the Spirit: The Poetics of Afro-American Women's Writing* [Chicago: Univ. of Chicago Press, 1991], pp. 32–33.)

The work of Giddings and Carby argues against this view, with Giddings suggesting that black women who had achieved some status did not separate themselves "along class lines from other women" (85). Certainly, the intersection of class and race with respect to black women's culture at the turn of the century needs to be explored more seriously by Baker; yet, the same could be said of Giddings, since her study does not address fractures within black female activity along regional, class, and color lines.

Recent studies that have begun to contextualize turn-of-the-century black women's goals in conjunction with their cultural and historical setting include Claudia Tate, *Domestic Allegories of Political Desire: The Black Heroine's Text at the Turn of the Century* (New York: Oxford Univ. Press, 1992); Elizabeth Ammons, *Conflicting Stories: American Women Writers at the Turn into the Twentieth Century* (New York: Oxford Univ. Press, 1992); and Ann duCille, *The Coupling Convention: Sex, Text, and Tradition in Black Women's Fiction* (New York: Oxford Univ. Press, 1993).

9. Frances Smith Foster, " 'In Respect to Females . . .': Differences in the Portrayals of Women by Male and Female Narrators," *Black American Literature Forum* 15 (1981): 66. For further discussion of the earlier context of black female representation, see Ronald G. Walters, "The Erotic South: Civilization and Sexuality in American Abolitionism," *American Quarterly* 25 (1973): 177–201; Jean Fagan Yellin, *Women and Sisters: The Antislavery Feminists in American Culture* (New Haven, Conn.: Yale Univ. Press, 1989); and Karen Sánchez-Eppler, "Bodily Bonds: The Intersecting Rhetorics of Feminism and Abolition," and Carolyn L. Karcher, "Rape, Murder, and Revenge in 'Slavery's Pleasant Homes': Lydia Maria Child's Antislavery Fiction and the Limits of Genre," both in *The Culture of Sentiment: Race, Gender, and Sentimentality in Nineteenth-Century America*, ed. Shirley Samuels (New York: Oxford Univ. Press, 1992), pp. 92–114 and 58–72, respectively.

10. Loewenberg and Bogin, *Black Women in Nineteenth-Century American Life*, pp. 273, 274, 274–75.

11. Giddings, *When and Where I Enter*, p. 86.

12. Lynn A. Higgins and Brenda R. Silver, introduction to *Rape and Representation* (New York: Columbia Univ. Press, 1991), p. 4.

13. As Elizabeth Ammons details in *Conflicting Stories*, novels like Harper's *Iola Leroy* did address "the connection among institutionalized violence, the sexual exploitation of women, and female muteness" (20). But as Ammons points out, part of the challenge facing Harper was one of form and decorum: "how could she make a novel capable of embracing the huge complex of issues, obvious and hidden—even taboo—that had to go into the telling of even the most middle-class or 'respectable' black woman's story in

late nineteenth-century America?" (27). For Ammons's discussion of *Iola Leroy*, see *Conflicting Stories*, chapter 2.

14. Mildred I. Thompson, *Ida B. Wells-Barnett: An Exploratory Study of an American Black Woman, 1893–1930* (*Black Women in United States History*, vol. 15; Brooklyn: Carlson, 1990), p. 17. The article has recently been reprinted, along with other material, in *The Memphis Diary of Ida B. Wells*, ed. Miriam DeCosta-Willis (Boston: Beacon Press, 1995).

15. Thompson, *Ida B. Wells-Barnett*, p. 22. See David M. Tucker, "Miss Ida B. Wells and Memphis Lynching," *Phylon* 32 (Summer 1971): 112–22, for a useful discussion of Wells's activities as an editor for the *Free Speech*.

16. Ida B. Wells, *Crusade for Justice: The Autobiography of Ida B. Wells*, ed. Alfreda M. Duster (Chicago: Univ. of Chicago Press, 1970). Wells's autobiography was published posthumously. References to this text are indicated by the abbreviation *C*.

17. Ida B. Wells, *Southern Horrors: Lynch Law in All Its Phases*, reprinted in *Selected Works of Ida B. Wells-Barnett*, comp. Trudier Harris (New York: Oxford Univ. Press, 1991), p. 42. References to this text are indicated by the abbreviation *SH*.

Wells's position on self-defense did not diminish with marriage and motherhood. When her young sons were harassed by white boys in their Chicago neighborhood, Wells, "[i]n a voice that carried far down the street," "let everyone know that she owned a pistol and would use it if necessary." See Dorothy Sterling, *Black Foremothers: Three Lives* (Old Westbury, N.Y.: Feminist Press, 1979), p. 103 for this anecdote.

18. This is part of Gail Bederman's argument in her article " 'Civilization,' the Decline of Middle-Class Manliness, and Ida B. Wells's Antilynching Campaign (1892–94)," *Radical History Review* 52 (Winter 1992): 5–30.

19. For important discussions of Wells's lynching analysis, see Thomas C. Holt, "The Lonely Warrior: Ida B. Wells-Barnett and the Struggle for Black Leadership," in *Black Leaders of the Twentieth Century*, ed. John Hope Franklin and August Meier (Urbana: Univ. of Illinois Press, 1982), pp. 39–61; Hazel V. Carby, " 'On the Threshold of Woman's Era': Lynching, Empire, and Sexuality in Black Feminist Theory," *Critical Inquiry* 12 (Autumn 1985): 262–77, as well as her *Reconstructing Womanhood*, chapter 5; Bederman " 'Civilization,' the Decline of Middle-Class Manliness," pp. 5–30.

20. Quoted in Thompson, *Ida B. Wells-Barnett*, pp. 22, 18.

21. As Joanne M. Braxton has suggested, Wells eventually used her autobiography as a means of settling accounts with those who had charged her with immodest behavior. Thus, in "decrying the evils of lynching and the moral decay at its root," Wells could locate herself historically as a noble black woman "who did her Christian duty." Braxton, *Black Women Writing Autobiography: A Tradition Within a Tradition* (Philadelphia: Temple Univ. Press, 1989), p. 118.

22. Her speech before the New York gathering of black women and the subsequent meetings her presentation generated had the effect of affirming and extending the power of Wells's critique of racial violence. Indeed the event in New York contributed to the general movement afoot to organize black women into national social and political clubs; and on her visits to newly organized Boston clubs, Wells made her first contacts with white sympathizers, eventually influencing white Boston papers to carry the stories she had been reporting in the *New York Age*. See Wells's autobiography, *Crusade For Justice*, chapter 9.

23. On the subject of white women, Wells was not unique in her beliefs. Numerous

African American male writers and journalists, including the newspaperman Alexander Manly of Wilmington, North Carolina, suggested that white women were often attracted to black men.

24. The white male citizens of Memphis may have assumed that Wells's business partner J. L. Fleming was responsible for the editorial; hence the orientation of their threats.

25. This is not to suggest of course that they would not have lynched Wells. Novelist Frances E. W. Harper's 1869 serialized novel, *Minnie's Sacrifice,* includes a brief account of a black woman lynched "for saying 'cendiary words." See *Minnie's Sacrifice; Sowing and Reaping; Trial and Triumph: Three Rediscovered Novels by Frances E. W. Harper,* ed. Frances Smith Foster (Boston: Beacon Press, 1994), p. 88.

26. My discussion here is not meant to imply that Wells saw *Southern Horrors* as simply an account of black victimhood. As mentioned earlier in this chapter, the pamphlet is an appeal to white justice, but equally a call to arms aimed at black men.

27. See P. Gabrielle Foreman, "The Spoken and the Silenced in *Incidents in the Life of a Slave Girl* and *Our Nig,*" *Callaloo* 13(2) (Spring 1990): 313–24 for a similar discussion of selective referencing of sexual details in black women's narratives.

28. Karlyn Kohrs Campbell, "Style and Content in the Rhetoric of Early Afro-American Feminists," *Quarterly Journal of Speech* 72 (1986): 436. See also Shirley W. Logan, "Rhetorical Strategies in Ida B. Wells's 'Southern Horrors: Lynch Law in All Its Phases,' " *Sage* 8 (Summer 1991): 3–9.

29. In *Domestic Allegories of Political Desire* Claudia Tate raises the important point that the "aesthetic value" of post-Reconstruction novels by black women "initially resided in their ability to gratify a distinct audience of ambitious black Americans who sought to live fully, despite their commonly experienced racial oppression" (7). Certainly Hopkins's *Contending Forces* and to some extent Fulton's *Hanover* attempt to resolve more directly the dilemmas in the lives of black women described by *Southern Horrors.*

30. Richard Yarborough, "Violence, Manhood, and Black Heroism: The Wilmington Riot in Two Turn-of-the-Century Afro-American Novels" (unpublished manuscript, 1990), p. 18. For the dedication to Wells, see Jack Thorne [David Bryant Fulton], *Hanover; or The Persecution of the Lowly: A Story of the Wilmington Massacre* [1900] (New York: Arno, 1969), p. 2. Future references to this novel will be indicated by the abbreviation *H.*

Fulton must have felt a special affinity to Wells, since he saw himself as persecuted by whites for voicing his protests ("because of my bold defense of my people I became the object of the spleen of those who possessed the power to rob me of the means of support"), and he registered a sense of disappointment that some of his black friends were not more supportive: "It was said to me one day . . . that I was an eccentric on the Race question. This taunt from the lips of one of my own people, a man who had my confidence . . . ." See his "Introductory Note" in *"Eagle Clippings" by Jack Thorne, Newspaper Correspondent and Story Teller: A Collection of His Writings to Various Newspapers* (Brooklyn: D. B. Fulton, 1907), pp. 4, 3.

31. Jack Thorne [David Bryant Fulton], *"Eagle Clippings",* pp. 29, 53.

32. Jack Thorne [David Bryant Fulton], *A Plea for Social Justice for the Black Woman* (Yonkers, N.Y.: Negro Society for Historical Research, 1912), pp. 2–3.

33. Apart from Yarborough's unpublished article (which makes the comparison between Fulton's *Hanover* and Chesnutt's *The Marrow of Tradition*), materials on Fulton

are scarce: Thomas R. Cripps's introduction to *Hanover*, pp. i-vii; William L. Andrews, "Jack Thorne [David Bryant Fulton]," in *Dictionary of American Negro Biography*, ed. Rayford W. Logan and Michael R. Winston (New York: Norton, 1982), pp. 589–90; and William Gleason, "Voices at the Nadir: Charles Chesnutt and David Bryant Fulton," *American Literary Realism* 24 (Spring 1992): 22–41. Fulton himself provides some commentary on the public reception of *Hanover* in *Eagle Clippings*, pp. 3–4. I have drawn heavily from Andrews's biographical sketch for my own background discussion of Fulton.

34. Andrews, "Jack Thorne," p. 590.

35. H. Leon Prather, Sr., *We Have Taken a City: Wilmington Racial Massacre and Coup of 1898* (Rutherford, N.J.: Fairleigh Dickinson Univ. Press, 1984), 71, 72–73. Not surprisingly, in their reprinting of Manly's editorial white papers always managed to include the section about white female desire but omitted his comments about white male engagement with miscegenation. During the Wilmington Riot of 1898, Manly's newspaper establishment was burned to the ground by an organized white mob, and the journalist himself barely escaped physical harm. Thomas Dixon includes a depiction of Manly as an unruly anonymous black editor in *The Leopard's Spots* (1902), albeit from a very different perspective.

36. I do not mean to imply here that Fulton does not talk about black masculinity and the riot. Indeed, in their articles both Yarborough and Gleason center their discussions largely on the novel's depiction of black male characters.

For a discussion of the relationship between Stowe's novel and later African-American literature, see Richard Yarborough, "Strategies of Black Characterization in *Uncle Tom's Cabin* and the Early Afro-American Novel," in *New Essays on Uncle Tom's Cabin*, ed. Eric J. Sundquist (New York: Cambridge Univ. Press, 1986), pp. 45–84. See also Cripps's introduction to *Hanover*, p. vii.

37. Fulton was especially distressed by black prostitutes who catered to white clients: "The heart of a REAL MAN bleeds when he sees girls of tender age beautiful to look upon, buttonholing old, vermin-eaten white men upon the streets of our cities. To these ignorant creatures and their sympathizers this is 'social equality' for they will turn and stare with amazement if rebuked by a man or woman of the race" (Fulton, *A Plea for Social Justice for the Black Woman*, p. 7).

38. See [Gilbert], *Narrative of Sojourner Truth*.

39. Or at least, as Claudia Tate might argue, personal desire in turn-of-the-century domestic black female novels functions as an expression of political involvement. See the general thesis in Tate's *Domestic Allegories*.

40. Deborah E. McDowell, " 'The Changing Same': Generational Connections and Black Women Novelists," *New Literary History* 18 (1987): 284.

41. Earlier negative readings of *Contending Forces* can be found in Vernon Loggins, *The Negro Author: His Development in America to 1900* [1931] (Port Washington, N.Y.: Kennikat, 1964), and Gwendolyn Brooks, Afterword to *Contending Forces* [1900] (Carbondale: Southern Illinois Univ. Press, 1978). For a shift in criticism, see Ann Allen Shockley, "Pauline Elizabeth Hopkins: A Biographical Excursion into Obscurity," *Phylon* 33 (1972): 22–26; Jane Campbell, *Mythic Black Fiction: The Transformation of History* (Knoxville: Univ. of Tennessee Press, 1986); Carby, *Reconstructing Womanhood*; Mary Helen Washington, "Uplifting the Women and the Race: The Forerunners—Harper and Hopkins," in *Invented Lives: Narratives of Black Women 1860–1960* (Garden City, N.Y.:

Doubleday, 1987); Ammons, *Conflicting Stories;* and Claudia Tate, "Pauline Hopkins: Our Literary Foremother," in *Conjuring: Black Women, Fiction and Literary Tradition,* ed. Marjorie Pryse and Hortense J. Spillers (Bloomington: Indiana Univ. Press, 1985), pp. 53–66, and *Domestic Allegories.*

42. [W. E. B. Du Bois?], "The Colored American Magazine in America," *Crisis* 5 (November 1912): 33. See especially Richard Yarborough's introduction to *Contending Forces* [1900] (New York: Oxford Univ. Press, 1988), pp. xxvii–xlviii.

43. William Stanley Braithwaite, "Negro America's First Magazine," *Negro Digest* 6 (1947): 25. According to Braithwaite, "Miss Hopkins regarded herself as a national figure, in the company of Charles W. Chesnutt and Paul Lawrence Dunbar and as such felt free to impose her views and opinions upon her associates in the conduct of both the book and the magazine publications" (25).

44. Yarborough, introduction, pp. xlii–xliii. After her tenure at the *Colored American Magazine,* Hopkins worked briefly for Atlanta's *Voice of the Negro* between 1904 and 1905. After 1916 she ceased publishing and worked as a stenographer at MIT until her tragic death in a fire in 1930. For further biographical detail, see Dorothy B. Porter's entry on Hopkins in *Dictionary of American Negro Biography,* pp. 325–26.

45. [Pauline E. Hopkins], "Women's Department," *Colored American Magazine* 1 (June 1900): 121, 122.

46. Pauline E. Hopkins, *Contending Forces: A Romance Illustrative of Negro Life North and South* [1900] (Miami: Mnemosyne, 1969). References to this text will be indicated by the abbreviation *CF.*

47. See Carby, *Reconstructing Womanhood,* p. 132.

48. See Eric J. Sundquist "Mark Twain and Homer Plessy," in *Mark Twain's Pudd'n-head Wilson: Race, Conflict and Culture,* ed. Susan Gillman and Forrest G. Robinson (Durham, N.C.: Duke Univ. Press, 1990), pp. 46–72.

49. Tate, *Domestic Allegories,* p. 161.

50. See also Tate, *Domestic Allegories,* pp. 148–49.

51. For a useful discussion of the function of such scenes of protective domestication in black women's novels of this period, see Tate, *Domestic Allegories,* pp. 83–87. For their function in white women's texts, see Jane Tompkins, *Sensational Designs: The Cultural Work of American Fiction 1790–1860* (New York: Oxford Univ. Press, 1985), chapter 6.

52. Iola Leroy in Frances Harper's novel of the same name survives her own grim past as a quadroon sold into slavery. In her novel however, Harper never gives the kind of horrific details that Hopkins provides about Sappho.

53. Hazel V. Carby, introduction to Frances E. W. Harper, *Iola Leroy, or Shadows Uplifted* [1893] (Boston: Beacon Press, 1987), pp. xxi–xxii.

54. Nicole Albert, "Sappho Mythified, Sappho Mystified or the Metamorphoses of Sappho in Fin de Siècle France," *Journal of Homosexuality* 25 (1993): 100, 91. See also Joan DeJean, *Fictions of Sappho, 1546–1937* (Chicago: Univ. of Chicago Press, 1989). My thanks to Yopie Prins for her valuable suggestions about the symbolic usages of Sappho in Hopkins's text and for further readings on the changing image of Sappho.

55. In the United States, Thomas Wentworth Higginson reshaped Sappho into a less sensationalized nurturer of female art, in the vein of Margaret Fuller. On early-twentieth-century women writers and Sappho, see Susan Gubar, "Sapphistries," in *The Lesbian Issue: Essays from Signs,* ed. Estelle B. Freedman (Chicago: Univ. of Chicago Press, 1985), pp. 91–110; on Higginson and Sappho, see Gloria Shaw Duclos, "Thomas

Wentworth Higginson's Sappho," *New England Quarterly* 57 (September 1984): 403–11.

56. On Sappho Clark as the silenced artist, see Ammons, *Conflicting Stories*, p. 80.

57. See, for instance, Washington, *Invented Lives*.

58. Here I am indebted to Ann duCille's reading of the Smith household in *The Coupling Convention*, p. 38.

59. While excellent work on early black female political and social culture continues to be done, there has been little focus on the internal class and color politics among black women. Clearly, as the numerous articles by and about black women in a 1904 issue of Atlanta's *Voice of the Negro* demonstrate, African American female leaders recognized the need to be judged on moral character, not class or skin color. Yet their language of progress, though revisionary in its attack on racial stereotypes, is sometimes structured curiously within class terms.

Speaking no doubt of her own generation, one of the contributors to the special issue of the *Voice* on black women, a Mrs. Addie Hunton, acknowledged that "there is hardly a daughter of a slave mother who has not heard of the sublime and heroic soul of some maternal ancestor that went home to the God that gave it rather than live a life of enforced infamy" ("Negro Womanhood Defended," *Voice of the Negro* 1(7) [July 1904]: 281). At the same time, however, the motto of the National Association of Colored Women—"Lifting as We Climb"—and the frequent focus on such signs of progress as education and economic prosperity undoubtedly fostered a sense of hierarchy. As another contributor, a Sylvanie Francaz Williams, argues,

> We could not, nor would not feel aggrieved if in citing the immorality of the Negro, the accusation was limited to the pauperized and brutalized members of the race. But it is that broad condemnation without exception; that uncharitableness of thought and deed that casts a shadow of distrust over the women of an entire race, that offends.   ("The Social Status of the Negro Woman" *Voice* 1(7) [July 1904]: 299.)

Clearly, although she saw her fate tied to that of other black women, Williams envisioned a differentiation based on class.

60. The character of Mrs. Willis has occasioned a variety of critical readings. See Washington, *Invented Lives*, p. 81; Yarborough, "Introduction," p. xl; Tate, *Domestic Allegories*, pp. 162–65.

61. I am not implying that rape was only a problem faced by Southern black women, of course, but I am suggesting that Hopkins is pointing to the problem of articulating a sense of community among a black population that at times included members with vastly different backgrounds. For instance, although Ida B. Wells remained thoroughly committed to the black women's club movement she helped to found, her autobiography *Crusade for Justice* is full of tales of intraracial female rivalries and bitter battles between herself and women such as Mary Church Terrell. Color and class tensions must surely have been a factor in their less than smooth relationship: Wells was the daughter of impoverished ex-slaves, whereas Terrell was from a considerable more established well-to-do black middle-class background. Thus, our reading of black women's narratives must certainly pay tribute to the power of black female unity, but it must also recognize internal tensions.

62. Tate, *Domestic Allegories*, pp. 160–66, 132, 175; duCille, *The Coupling Convention*, p. 43.

63. Fulton of course had the same concern in *A Plea for Social Justice for the Bl Woman.*

64. duCille, *The Coupling Convention,* p. 45.

### CHAPTER FOUR

1. For general studies on white female activism in the nineteenth-century public arena, see Aileen S. Kraditor, *The Ideas of the Woman Suffrage Movement, 1890–1920* (1965; New York: W. W. Norton, 1981); Ellen Carol DuBois, *Feminism and Suffrage: The Emergence of an Independent Women's Movement in America, 1848–1869* (Ithaca, N.Y.: Cornell Univ. Press, 1978); Carroll Smith-Rosenberg, *Disorderly Conduct: Visions of Gender in Victorian America* (New York: Oxford Univ. Press, 1985); Jean Fagan Yellin, *Women and Sisters: The Antislavery Feminists in American Culture* (New Haven, Conn.: Yale Univ. Press, 1989); and Paula Baker, "The Domestication of Politics: Women and American Political Society, 1780–1920," in *Unequal Sisters: A Multicultural Reader in U.S. Women's History,* ed. Ellen Carol DuBois and Vicki L. Ruiz (New York: Routledge, 1990), pp. 66–91.

2. Quoted in Joel Williamson, *The Crucible of Race: Black–White Relations in the American South Since Emancipation* (New York: Oxford Univ. Press, 1984), p. 128. See also John E. Talmadge, *Rebecca Latimer Felton: Nine Stormy Decades* (Athens: Univ. of Georgia Press, 1960), especially chapter 13.

3. Quoted in Ida B. Wells, *Crusade for Justice: The Autobiography of Ida B. Wells,* ed. Alfreda M. Duster (Chicago: Univ. of Chicago Press, 1970), 151–152. For more information on Willard, Wells, and lynching, see Ruth Bordin, *Frances Willard: A Biography* (Chapel Hill: Univ. of North Carolina Press, 1986); and Vron Ware, " 'To Make the Facts Known': Racial Terror and the Construction of White Femininity," in *Beyond the Pale: White Women, Racism and History* (London: Verso, 1992), pp. 167–244, especially 198–205.

4. Ware, *Beyond the Pale,* p. 203.

5. Jane Addams, "Respect for Law" [1901], reprinted in *Lynching and Rape: An Exchange of Views,* ed. Bettina Aptheker (New York: American Institute for Marxist Studies, 1977), pp. 24, 25, 26. See also Aptheker's "Introduction," p. 12.

6. Ida B. Wells, "Lynching and the Excuse for It," reprinted in *Lynching and Rape,* pp. 29, 34.

7. Quoted in Angela Y. Davis, "Racism in the Woman Suffrage Movement," in *Women, Race and Class* (New York: Vintage, 1983), p. 72. See especially her chapter "Woman Suffrage at the Turn of the Century: The Rising Influence of Racism", pp. 110–126; and Paula Giddings, *When and Where I Enter: The Impact of Black Women on Race and Sex in America* (New York: Bantam, 1984), chapter 7.

8. Jacquelyn Dowd Hall, " 'The Mind That Burns in Each Body': Women, Rape, and Racial Violence," in *Powers of Desire: The Politics of Sexuality,* ed. Ann Snitow, Christine Stansell, and Sharon Thompson (New York: Monthly Review Press, 1983), p. 338. See also Hall's book-length study, *Revolt Against Chivalry: Jessie Daniel Ames and the Women's Campaign Against Lynching* (New York: Columbia Univ. Press, 1974).

Ames's movement did not by any means suggest a national shift in white women's racial alliances. For information on the campaign to increase white female enrollment in the revived Ku Klux Klan during this same period, see Kathleen M. Blee, *Women of the Klan: Racism and Gender in the 1920s* (Berkeley: Univ. of California Press, 1991).

9. In her memoir *The Walls Came Tumbling Down* (New York: Harcourt, Brace, 1947), the white NAACP activist Mary White Ovington includes her riveting short story "The White Brute" (pp. 88–99), in which a black newlywed couple traveling southward encounter trouble in a small town. While they wait for the arrival of their homebound train, two white men (one of whom turns out to be the son of the local sheriff) kidnap the bride for the purpose of rape, keeping the horrified groom at bay with the threat of lynching. The story was originally published by Max Eastman in *The Masses* in 1916. I am indebted to Steve Gray for bringing the Ovington piece to my attention.

10. Mary Johnston, "Nemesis," in *The Collected Short Stories of Mary Johnston*, ed. Annie Woodbridge and Hensley C. Woodbridge (Troy, N.Y.: Whitston, 1982), p. 61.

11. Vernon Loggins, *The Negro Author: His Development in America to 1900* [1931] (Port Washington, N.Y.: Kennikat, 1964), p. 326.

12. For an important discussion of Northern publishers and their reluctance to engage in radical discussions of race and reform in the aftermath of slavery, see Kenneth W. Warren, *Black and White Strangers: Race and American Literary Realism* (Chicago: Univ. of Chicago Press, 1993), chapter 2.

13. With regard to Chopin and turn-of-the-century racialized discourses on gender, modern white feminist scholarship on Chopin is undergoing a long overdue change. Two recent studies that link the concerns of white feminist critics (that is, a study of Chopin's feminism) with the impact of region and race are Anna Shannon Elfenbein, *Women on the Color Line: Evolving Stereotypes and the Writings of George Washington Cable, Grace King, Kate Chopin* (Charlottesville: Univ. Press of Virginia, 1989), and Helen Taylor, *Gender, Race, and Region in the Writings of Grace King, Ruth McEnery Stuart, and Kate Chopin* (Baton Rouge: Louisiana State Univ. Press, 1989). Neither of these studies has "failed to recognize how Chopin's feminism is mediated through her implicit positions on race and regionalism" (Taylor, p. 139), and I am indebted to them for shaping my own thinking about Chopin's creole stories. See also Wai-chee Dimock, "Rightful Subjectivity," *Yale Journal of Criticism* 4 (1990): 25–51; and Elizabeth Ammons, *Conflicting Stories: American Women Writers at the Turn into the Twentieth Century* (New York: Oxford Univ. Press, 1992). For a consideration of race and sex in *The Awakening*, see Michele A. Birnbaum, " 'Alien Hands': Kate Chopin and the Colonization of Race," *American Literature* 66 (June 1994): 301–23.

Notable early exceptions to the dehistoricizing and deracialization of Chopin's work include Robert D. Arner, "Landscape Symbolism in Kate Chopin's 'At Fault', " *Louisiana Studies* 9 (1970): 142–53; Richard H. Potter, "Negroes in the Fiction of Kate Chopin," *Louisiana History* 12 (Winter 1971): 41–58; Joyce Coyne Dyer, "Bright Hued Feathers and Japanese Jars: Objectification of Character in Kate Chopin's *At Fault*," *Revue de Louisiane/Louisiana Review* 9 (1980): 27–35; Joyce Coyne Dyer and Robert Emmett Monroe, "Texas and Texans in the Fiction of Kate Chopin," *Western American Literature* 20 (1985): 3–15; and Anne Goodwyn Jones, *Tomorrow Is Another Day: The Woman Writer in the South, 1859–1936* (Baton Rouge: Louisiana State Univ. Press, 1981).

Ironically, Cyrille Arnavon's 1953 introduction to the French translation of *The Awakening* (entitled *Edna*) spends more time contextualizing the novel in its historical and regional setting than many American feminist readings of the past two decades. For a translation of the Arnavon introduction, see *A Kate Chopin Miscellany*, ed. Per Seyersted and Emily Toth (Oslo and Natchitoches, La.: Universitetsforlaget and Northwestern State Univ. Press, 1979), pp. 168–88.

14. Jones, *Tomorrow Is Another Day*, p. 149.

15. I am especially guided here by two early articles on the context of Chopin's local color fiction: Donald A. Ringe, "Cane River World: *At Fault* and Related Stories," in *Modern Critical Views: Kate Chopin*, ed. Harold Bloom (New York: Chelsea House, 1987), pp. 25–33; and Patricia Hopkins Lattin, "Kate Chopin's Repeating Characters," *Mississippi Quarterly* 33 (1979–80): 19–37.

16. Taylor, *Gender, Race and Region*, pp. 155, 157.

17. Hazel V. Carby, "The Canon: Civil War and Reconstruction," *Michigan Quarterly Review* 27 (1989): 39.

18. Per Seyersted, *Kate Chopin: A Critical Biography* (Oslo and Natchitoches, La.: Universitetsforlaget and Northwestern State Univ. Press, 1969), p. 14. For information on the O'Flaherty slaves, see Emily Toth, *Kate Chopin* (New York: William Morrow, 1990), p. 57.

19. Toth, *Kate Chopin*, p. 64.

20. Seyersted and Toth, *A Kate Chopin Miscellany*, pp. 115–16. See also a letter written by Kate Chopin's mother Eliza to her Louisiana relatives towards the close of the war, *Miscellany*, 103–4.

21. John W. Blassingame, *Black New Orleans, 1860–1880* (Chicago: Univ. of Chicago Press, 1973), 15–22. See also chapter 7 of Blassingame's book for a discussion of race relations after the war.

22. Ted Tunnell, *Crucible of Reconstruction: War, Radicalism and Race in Louisiana, 1862–1877* (Baton Rouge: Louisiana State Univ. Press, 1984), p. 67.

23. Blassingame, *Black New Orleans*, p. 174.

24. Taylor, *Gender, Race and Region*, p. 145.

25. Toth, *Kate Chopin*, pp. 122–23.

26. Toth, *Kate Chopin*, pp. 134–36. At the time of the Battle of Liberty Place, Kate Chopin was away visiting her family in St. Louis.

27. Allen W. Trelease, *White Terror: The Ku Klux Klan Conspiracy and Southern Reconstruction* [1971] (Westport, Conn.: Greenwood, 1979), p. 93. According to Trelease, voter intimidation, election fraud, murder, and violence against politically active blacks and white Republicans became the norm in the early years after the war. During the 1868 election year, "[i]t was reported that in the course of a month at least twenty-five or thirty [n]egro bodies floated down the Red River past Shreveport" (130).

28. Trelease, *White Terror*, p. 131.

29. Emily Toth, "Kate Chopin's New Orleans Years," *New Orleans Review* 15 (1988): 58.

30. Herbert Shapiro, *White Violence and Black Response: From Reconstruction to Montgomery* (Amherst: Univ. of Massachusetts Press, 1988), pp. 61–63. Ida B. Wells discusses the incident in her third pamphlet *Mob Rule in New Orleans: Robert Charles and His Fight to the Death* (1900), reprinted in *Selected Works of Ida B. Wells-Barnett*, comp. Trudier Harris (New York: Oxford Univ. Press, 1991).

31. For a startling account of the intense violence during Reconstruction in the Red River area of Louisiana, see especially Ted Tunnell's incredible chapter 9, "Showdown on the Red River," in *Crucible of Reconstruction*. White supremacists viciously attacked blacks as well as white Northerners who came to "reconstruct" these areas.

32. For the full text of Breazeale's memoir, see Seyersted and Toth, *A Kate Chopin Miscellany*, pp. 157–66. Helen Taylor is one of the first critics to consider the importance

172    *Notes*

of this document for providing clues to the social and racial world Chopin inhabited in Natchitoches Parish. See her discussion on racial tensions in *Gender, Race and Region,* pp. 144–45.

33. Seyersted and Toth, *A Kate Chopin Miscellany,* p. 159.

34. See Toth, *Kate Chopin,* pp. 323–4, 177, for information on Chopin's friendship with Breazeale, and for a description of characters like the Santien brothers.

Chopin seems destined to have her name associated with the most violent men in Cloutierville. Toth has suggested that after Oscar's death, Chopin had an affair with her neighbor Albert Sampite. Handsome, charming, and wealthy, Sampite was nevertheless a reincarnation of the Chopin-McAlpin myth, since he was cruel to his black workers and would beat his wife with a leather strap. See Toth, *Kate Chopin,* pp. 165–66, 171. For an earlier reference, see Seyersted's introduction to *The Complete Works of Kate Chopin* (Baton Rouge: Louisiana State Univ. Press, 1969), p. 26.

35. Gwendolyn Midlo Hall, "The Formation of Afro-Creole Culture," in *Creole New Orleans: Race and Americanization,* ed. Arnold R. Hirsch and Joseph Logsdon (Baton Rouge: Louisiana State Univ. Press, 1992), p. 60.

36. L'Isle des Mulâtres was of course the real-life Isle Brevelle in Natchitoches Parish. For the history of the black creole settlement on the island, see Gary B. Mills, *The Forgotten People: Cane River's Creoles of Color* (Baton Rouge: Louisiana State Univ. Press, 1977).

37. *The Complete Works of Kate Chopin,* ed. Per Seyersted (Baton Rouge: Louisiana State Univ. Press, 1969). All references to Chopin's fiction come from this two-volume set, and are indicated in the text by the abbreviation *CW.*

38. Here I am relying especially on Donald A. Ringe's "Cane River World" for an important early discussion of Chopin's possible attitude toward creole violence and the post–Civil War South.

39. I am indebted here to Lattin's "Kate Chopin's Repeating Characters," pp. 21–25, for her discussion of the Santien brothers.

40. Joseph G. Tregle, Jr., "Creoles and Americans," in *Creole New Orleans,* p. 135.

41. "A No-Account Creole" was based on one of Chopin's first short stories. Variously titled in her notes "Euphrasie," "A Maid and Her Lovers," and "Euphrasie's Lovers," the story was eventually pared down and published in its present form in the *Century* in 1894. See Toth, *Kate Chopin,* pp. 177–78.

42. Robert D. Arner identifies some of the same qualities in Joçint but does not contextualize him within the postwar context of racism that provided the background to Chopin's literary production. See Arner, "Landscape Symbolism," p. 152.

43. Ringe, "Cane River World," p. 29.

44. Taylor, *Gender, Race and Region,* p. 170. My reading of *At Fault* is informed by Taylor's perceptive commentary. See her discussion of the novel in *Gender, Race and Region,* pp. 166–70.

45. Taylor, *Gender, Race and Region,* p. 170.

46. Thomas Dixon, Jr., "Booker T. Washington and the Negro," *Saturday Evening Post* (19 August 1905): 2.

47. See also Taylor, *Gender, Race and Region,* pp. 167–69.

48. Wilbur Fisk Tillett, "Southern Womanhood as Affected by the War," *Century Magazine* 43 (November 1891): 12. For an illuminating discussion of white female management during the Civil War, see Drew Gilpin Faust, " 'Trying to Do a Man's Business':

Slavery, Violence and Gender in the American Civil War," *Gender and History* 4 (Summer 1992): 197–214.

49. Henry W. Grady, *The Race Problem* [1889] (Philadelphia: John D. Morris, 1900), p. 546.

50. Grady, *The Race Problem*, p. 542.

51. Henry W. Grady, *The New South* (New York: Robert Bonner, 1890), p. 146.

52. Place-du-Bois is based on the old Chopin estate, and McFarlane is the renamed Robert McAlpin, the land's previous owner who was allegedly the model for Harriet Beecher Stowe's Simon Legree.

53. See Thomas Nelson Page, *In Ole Virginia: Or, Marse Chan and Other Stories* [1887] (Nashville: J. S. Sanders, 1991), and *Red Rock: A Chronicle of Reconstruction* (New York: Charles Scribner, 1898).

54. This point is made by Donald Ringe, though from a different perspective. See his "Cane River World," pp. 29–30.

55. A similar incident occurs in "In and Out of Old Natchitoches" (1893), when the planter Alphonse Laballière loses his temper and tries to force a young creole school teacher to integrate her classroom.

56. Arnavon, "Introduction" to *Edna* in Seyersted and Toth, *A Kate Chopin Miscellany*, p. 174.

57. Aiken's ethnic identity is especially important, since Chopin is much more generous in her portraits of lower-class whites of French background (the cajun characters). The bumbling but kindhearted Bobinôt in "At the 'Cadian Ball" and "The Storm" and the gallant Telèsphore in "A Night in Acadie" offer examples of romantic portrayals of lower-class cajun chivalry. On the other hand, when Chopin wants to hint at unbridled sexual energy, class and ethnicity come into play with half-Spanish, half-French characters such as Calixta in "At the 'Cadian Ball" and "The Storm" and Mariequita in *The Awakening*.

58. Elfenbein, *Women on the Color Line*, p. 119.

59. Tregle, "Creoles and Americans," p. 173.

60. Tregle, "Creoles and Americans," p. 132. See also Dyer and Monroe, "Texas and Texans in the Fiction of Kate Chopin" for a discussion of cajun or 'Cadian balls (where Grégoire would have met 'Tite Reine), as places frequented by "sensual, 'disreputable' women who threaten domesticity and monogamy" (6). Dyer and Monroe offer an entirely different reading of ethnicity from my own.

61. Thomas Dixon, Jr., *The Leopard's Spots: A Romance of the White Man's Burden—1865–1900* [1902] (Ridgewood, N.J.: Gregg, 1967), p. 372. Ironically, in white supremacist fiction of the period, usually the middle-class white hero embodied an ennobling racial hatred that expressed itself in justifiable and retributive white violence. Any obvious excesses of white brutality were usually construed as the acts of lower-class whites who were invariably thought to make up the undisciplined mobs that wreaked havoc during the numerous race riots of the 1890s and early 1900s. See, for instance, the stereotypes of white violence represented in Dixon's Ku Klux Klan trilogy of *The Leopard's Spots*, *The Clansman* (1905), and *The Traitor* (1907).

62. Dyer and Monroe, "Texas and Texans," pp. 1, 5–7.

63. Dyer and Monroe, "Texas and Texans," p. 6.

64. See Joyce Coyne Dyer's useful but strangely uncritical description of Chopin's invocation of race to distance and connect her white readers with the sexual desire

demonstrated by the black characters in "Techniques of Distancing in the Fiction of Kate Chopin," *Southern Studies* 24 (1985): 69–81. See also Michele A. Birnbaum's reading of the quadroon nursemaid in Chopin's *The Awakening*, in her article " 'Alien Hands': Kate Chopin and the Colonization of Race."

65. Cynthia Griffin Wolff makes an excellent point about the historical resonance that "Désirée's Baby" might have had for Southern readers in its subtle references to causes of the Civil War, but she fails to recognize that Southern (and Northern) readers in the 1890s were just as concerned about miscegenation as the story's main character, Armand. See Wolff, "The Fiction of Limits: 'Désirée's Baby', " in *Modern Critical Views: Kate Chopin*, ed. Harold Bloom (New York: Chelsea House, 1987), p. 38.

66. Elfenbein, *Women on the Color Line*, p. 131.

67. Sander L. Gilman, "Black Bodies, White Bodies: Toward an Iconography of Female Sexuality in Late Nineteenth-Century Art, Medicine, and Literature," *Critical Inquiry* 12 (Autumn 1985): p. 209. The specific idea of black corruption of whiteness is not new, of course. Northern white abolitionists had long feared that part of slavery's danger was the potential moral contamination achieved through associations with uncivilized black slaves. See, for example, Ronald G. Walter's extremely useful article "The Erotic South: Civilization and Sexuality in American Abolitionism," *American Quarterly* 25 (1973): 177–201.

68. See Gilman's reading of blackness, female sexuality, and disease in "Black Bodies, White Bodies," especially at p. 237. For a useful discussion of the metaphoric uses of Sappho as an emblem of corrupting lesbian relations in medical discourse, see Nicole Albert, "Sappho Mythified, Sappho Mystified or the Metamorphoses of Sappho in Fin de Siècle France," *Journal of Homosexuality* 25 (1993): 87–104.

69. Elfenbein, *Women on the Color Line*, p. 133.

70. Blassingame, *Black New Orleans*, p. 3. See also Jerah Johnson, "New Orleans's Congo Square: An Urban Setting for Early Afro-American Culture Formation," *Louisiana History* 32 (Spring 1991): 117–57.

71. Johnson, "New Orleans's Congo Square," pp. 143–44.

72. Hunter McGuire and G. Frank Lydston, *Sexual Crimes Among the Southern Negroes* (Louisville: Renz & Henry, 1893), p. 7.

73. George Washington Cable, *The Grandissimes: A Story of Creole Life* [1880] (Athens: Univ. of Georgia Press, 1988).

74. Gilman, "Black Bodies, White Bodies," p. 237. White fears of black and European immigrant overpopulation were of course widespread in the post–Civil War era, and white supremacists anxiously countered reports of the decline in the birthrate among whites with the notion that, without slavery, blacks were heading for extinction by the end of the nineteenth century. For a discussion of the issue of black/white population growth, see George M. Fredrickson, *The Black Image in the White Mind: The Debate on Afro-American Character and Destiny, 1817–1914* (Middletown, Conn.: Wesleyan Univ. Press, 1971), chapter 8. For advice given to women to avoid what Theodore Roosevelt termed "race suicide," see Barbara Ehrenreich and Deirdre English, *For Her Own Good: 150 Years of the Experts' Advice to Women* (Garden City, N.Y.: Anchor, 1978), pp. 134–37.

75. The context here, of course, would be Harriet Beecher Stowe's *Uncle Tom's Cabin* (1852).

76. It is important to note that black female claims to equality with white women had been argued in the nineteenth century through the figure of the maternal. See, for

instance, Harriet Jacobs in *Incidents in the Life of a Slave Girl* (1861) and, at the very moment of Chopin's stories, the numerous domestic novels by black women that stressed black female capacity for responsible motherhood and racial uplift.

77. For a discussion of blackness and madness in nineteenth-century thought see Gilman, *Difference and Pathology: Stereotypes of Sexuality, Race and Madness* (Ithaca, N.Y.: Cornell Univ. Press, 1985), chapter 5. There was of course a separate discourse on womanhood and madness; and my argument here is that, as a racial hybrid and a woman, Zoraïde bears the burden of a body doubly inscribed as the site of madness.

78. See also Birnbaum's discussion of race and female empowerment in *The Awakening* in " 'Alien Hands', " p. 304.

AFTERWORD

1. In 1991, during hearings on the confirmation of the Bush administration's black nominee Clarence Thomas for appointment to the United States Supreme Court, charges were raised by Thomas opponents that he had sexually harassed black law professor Anita Hill during the time she worked for him at the Equal Employment Opportunity Commission in the early 1980s. The charges did little to affect his confirmation but did, and still do, arouse great consternation among blacks and whites, men and women. In 1992 the black boxing heavy weight champion Mike Tyson was convicted of raping Desiree Washington, a black beauty pageant contestant, and he was sentenced to six years in prison; Tyson has since been released and has resumed his boxing career. At the time of this writing, the celebrated black football star O. J. Simpson has been acquitted in Los Angeles of the murder of his white ex-wife Nicole Brown Simpson and her acquaintance Ronald Goldman.

2. This is particularly striking in the case of how Americans variously assessed the meaning of Anita Hill's testimony against Clarence Thomas on Capitol Hill in 1991. While Thomas supporters still suggest her accusations of sexual harassment were the fantasy of a diseased brain, white feminists never tire in proclaiming Hill a hero for her stand against the abuse of all working women. But the story of what the Hill-Thomas spectacle really meant, and how their story is as much about the compromised quality of American justice and class privilege as it is about feminism and race, is just now being described. See, among other efforts, Nancy Fraser, "Sex, Lies, and the Public Sphere: Some Reflections on the Confirmation of Clarence Thomas," *Critical Inquiry* 18 (Spring 1992): 595–612; and the useful volume *Race-ing Justice, and En-gendering Power: Essays on Anita Hill, Clarence Thomas, and the Construction of Social Reality*, ed. Toni Morrison (New York: Pantheon, 1992).

3. Elizabeth Alexander, "Can you be BLACK and Look at This?': Reading the Rodney King Video(s)," *Public Culture* 7 (1994): 79, 80.

4. Alexander, " 'Can you be BLACK,' " pp. 92–93.

5. Shelley Fisher Fishkin, "Interrogating 'Whiteness,' Complicating 'Blackness': Remapping American Culture," *American Quarterly* 47 (September 1995): 428–466. In this invaluable review article, Fishkin surveys not just studies in literature but also history, linguistics, popular culture, and sociology. Yet despite the welcomed rise in scholarship problematizing race in this way, I would argue that such a methodology is very much in its infancy.

6. Fishkin, "Remapping American Culture," 430.

7. Harriet A. Jacobs, *Incidents in the Life of a Slave Girl Written by Herself* (1861), ed. Jean Fagan Yellin (Cambridge, Mass.: Harvard Univ. Press, 1987), pp. 6–7.

8. Lydia Maria Child, "Introduction by the Editor," *Incidents*, p. 4.

9. Elsa Barkley Brown, "Negotiating and Transforming the Public Sphere: African American Political Life in the Transition from Slavery to Freedom," *Public Culture* 7 (1994): 146.

10. Robert B. Stepto, Response to Richard Yarborough's "The First Person in Afro-American Fiction," in the conference proceedings published as *Afro-American Literary Study in the 1990s*, ed. Houston A. Baker, Jr., and Patricia Redmond (Chicago: Univ. of Chicago Press, 1989), p. 126.

11. Indeed, the move away from a reliance on the presence of black figures and black texts to reference racial discussion is a primary tenet of the critical stance of interrogating whiteness. For instance, as black critic Kenneth Warren has demonstrated, Henry James is as much a referent for race as Charles Chesnutt might be. See Warren, *Black and White Strangers: Race and American Literary Realism* (Chicago: Univ. of Chicago Press, 1993).

12. For an excellent review of and response to a variety of growing trends and resulting new issues arising from reconceptualizations of American literature (among others: the globalization of American studies in the move to see U.S. texts as postcolonial; the rethinking of historical periodization as an increasingly bankrupt method for conceptualizing the relationship between texts and traditions; the place of multicultural studies and women's writing in the new scramble to "remap" the terrain of American literary studies), see Carolyn Porter, "What We Know That We Don't Know: Remapping American Literary Studies," *American Literary History* 6 (3) (Fall 1994): 467–526.

13. See Frances E. W. Harper, *Minnie's Sacrifice; Sowing and Reaping; Trial and Triumph; Three Rediscovered Novels by Frances E. W. Harper*, ed. Frances Smith Foster (Boston: Beacon Press, 1994).

14. Richard Yarborough, "Strategies of Black Characterization in *Uncle Tom's Cabin* and the Early Afro-American Novel," in *New Essays on Uncle Tom's Cabin*, ed. Eric J. Sundquist (New York: Cambridge Univ. Press, 1986), pp. 45–84; Frances Smith Foster, *Written by Herself: Literary Production by African American Women, 1746–1892* (Bloomington: Indiana Univ. Press, 1993), chapter 9; Carla L. Peterson, *"Doers of the Word": African-American Women Speakers and Writers in the North (1830–1880)* (New York: Oxford Univ. Press, 1995), chapter 7.

15. Current favorites remain the novels of Toni Morrison and Zora Neale Hurston and Harriet Jacobs's *Incidents in the Life of a Slave Girl.*

16. Henry Louis Gates, Jr., "Introduction: 'Tell Me Sir, . . . What *Is* "Black" Literature?,' " (Special Issue on African and African American Literatures), *PMLA* 105 (1990): 12.

17. Brown, "Negotiating and Transforming the Public Sphere," p. 146.

# Bibliography

PRIMARY SOURCES

Addams, Jane. "Respect for Law." [1901.] Reprinted in *Lynching and Rape: An Exchange of Views*, ed. Bettina Aptheker, pp. 22–27. New York: American Institute for Marxist Studies, 1977.

Baker, Ray Stannard. *Following the Color Line: American Negro Citizenship in the Progressive Era*. [1908.] New York: Harper & Row, 1964.

Bell, Lilian Lida. "The Leopard's Spots." *Saturday Evening Post* (12 April 1902): 15.

Braithwaite, William Stanley. "Negro America's First Magazine." *Negro Digest* 6 (1947): 21–26.

Cable, George Washington. *The Grandissimes: A Story of Creole Life*. [1880.] Athens: Univ. of Georgia Press, 1988.

———. *The Negro Question: A Selection of Writing on Civil Rights in the South*, ed. Arlin Turner. Garden City, N.Y.: Doubleday, 1958.

Chesnutt, Charles W. "The Future American." [Three-article series, 1901.] Reprinted as "Charles Chesnutt's 'Future American.'" *MELUS* 15 (Fall 1988): 95–107.

———. *The Journals of Charles W. Chesnutt*, ed. Richard Brodhead. Durham, N.C.: Duke Univ. Press, 1993.

———. *The Marrow of Tradition*. [1901.] Ann Arbor: Univ. of Michigan Press, 1969.

———. "What Is a White Man?" *Independent* 51 (1889): 5–6.

Chopin, Kate. *The Complete Works of Kate Chopin*, ed. Per Seyersted. 2 vols. Baton Rouge: Louisiana State Univ. Press, 1969.

Cooper, Anna Julia. *A Voice from the South*. [1892.] New York: Oxford Univ. Press, 1988.

———. "1893 Address to the Congress of Representative Women." Reprinted in *Black Women in Nineteenth-Century American Life: Their Words, Their Thoughts, Their Feelings*, ed. Bert Loewenberg and Ruth Bogin, pp. 329–31. University Park: Pennsylvania State Univ. Press, 1976.

Cope, E. D. "Two Perils of the Indo-European." *Open Court* 3(126, 127) (1890): 2052–54, 2070–71.

Crummell, Alexander. "The Black Woman of the South: Her Neglects and Her Needs." [1883.] Reprinted in *Destiny and Race: Selected Writings, 1840–1898*, ed. Wilson Jeremiah Moses, pp. 211–23. Amherst: Univ. of Massachusetts Press, 1992.

Cutler, James Elbert. *Lynch-Law: An Investigation into the History of Lynching in the United States.* [1905.] Montclair, N.J.: Patterson Smith, 1969.

Dixon, Thomas, Jr. "Booker T. Washington and the Negro." *Saturday Evening Post* (19 August 1905): 1–2.

————. *The Clansman: An Historical Romance of the Ku Klux Klan.* [1905.] Lexington: Univ. Press of Kentucky, 1970.

————. *The Leopard's Spots: A Romance of the White Man's Burden—1865–1900.* [1902.] Ridgewood, N.J.: Gregg, 1967.

————. *The One Woman: A Story of Modern Utopia.* New York: Doubleday, 1903.

————. *The Root of Evil.* Garden City, N.Y.: Doubleday, 1911.

————. *The Sins of the Father: A Romance of the South.* New York: Grosset & Dunlap, 1912.

————. "Why I Wrote 'The Clansman.' " *Theatre* 6 (1906): 20–22.

Douglass, Frederick. "Lynch Law in the South." *North American Review* 155 ( July 1892): 17–24.

————. *Narrative of the Life of Frederick Douglass, an American Slave.* [1845.] Ed. Houston A. Baker, Jr. Harmondsworth, G.B.: Penguin, 1982.

Dreiser, Theodore. "Nigger Jeff." In *Free and Other Stories,* pp. 76–111. New York: Boni & Liveright, 1918.

[DuBois, W.E.B. ?] "The Colored American Magazine in America." *Crisis* 5 (November 1912): 33–35.

Fortune, T. Thomas. "The Negro's Place in American Life at the Present Day." In *The Negro Problem: A Series of Articles by Representative American Negroes of To-day,* [ed. Booker T. Washington. 1903.] Miami: Mnemosyne, 1969.

Grady, Henry W. *The New South.* New York: Robert Bonner, 1890.

————. *The Race Problem.* [1889.] Philadelphia: John D. Morris, 1900.

Griggs, Sutton E. *The Hindered Hand; or, The Reign of the Repressionist.* Nashville: Orion, 1905.

————. *Imperium in Imperio.* [1899.] New York: Arno, 1969.

Harper, Francis E. W. *Iola Leroy, or Shadows Uplifted.* [1892.] Boston: Beacon Press, 1987.

————. *Minnie's Sacrifice; Sowing and Reaping; Trial and Triumph: Three Rediscovered Novels by Frances E. W. Harper,* ed. Frances Smith Foster. Boston: Beacon Press, 1994.

Hopkins, Pauline E. *Contending Forces: A Romance Illustrative of Negro Life North and South.* [1900.] Miami: Mnemosyne, 1969.

[————.] "Women's Department." *Colored American Magazine* 1 ( June 1900): 118–23.

Howells, William Dean. *A Boy's Town, Described for "Harper's Young People."* New York: Harper, 1890.

————. "A Psychological Counter-Current in Recent Fiction." *North American Review* 173 (December 1901): 872–88.

————. *The Shadow of a Dream* and *An Imperative Duty,* ed. Martha Banta. Bloomington: Indiana Univ. Press, 1970.

Hunton, Addie. "Negro Womanhood Defended." *Voice of the Negro* 1 (7) ( July 1904): 280–82.

Jacobs, Harriet A. *Incidents in the Life of a Slave Girl.* [1861.] Ed. Jean Fagan Yellin. Cambridge, Mass.: Harvard Univ. Press, 1987.

Johnston, Mary. "Nemesis." In *The Collected Short Stories of Mary Johnston,* ed. Annie

Woodbridge and Hensley C. Woodbridge, pp. 35–62. Troy, N.Y.: Whitston, 1982.

"The Leopard's Spots," *Independent* 54 (1902): 1548–49.

McGuire, Hunter, and G. Frank Lydston. *Sexual Crimes Among the Southern Negroes.* Louisville: Renz & Henry, 1893.

Ovington, Mary White. "The White Brute." In *The Walls Came Tumbling Down,* pp. 88–99. New York: Harcourt, Brace, 1947.

Page, Thomas Nelson. *In Ole Virginia: Or, Marse Chan and Other Stories.* [1887.] Nashville: J. S. Sanders, 1991.

———. *The Negro: The Southerner's Problem.* New York: Charles Scribner, 1904.

———. *Red Rock: A Chronicle of Reconstruction.* New York: Charles Scribner, 1898.

Sinclair, Upton. *The Jungle.* [1906.] New York: Signet, 1960.

Sledd, Andrew. "The Negro: Another View." *Atlantic Monthly* 90 (July 1902): 65–73.

Stewart, Maria W. *Maria W. Stewart, America's First Black Woman Political Writer: Essays and Speeches,* ed. Marilyn Richardson. Bloomington: Indiana Univ. Press, 1987.

Stowe, Harriet Beecher. *Uncle Tom's Cabin; or Life Among the Lowly.* [1852.] New York: Harper, 1965.

"Thomas Dixon Talks of *The Clansman*." *Atlanta Constitution* (29 October 1905).

Thorne, Jack [David Bryant Fulton]. *"Eagle Clippings" by Jack Thorne, Newspaper Correspondent and Story Teller: A Collection of His Writings to Various Newspapers.* Brooklyn: D. B. Fulton, 1907.

———. *Hanover; or The Persecution of the Lowly: A Story of the Wilmington Massacre.* [1900.] Ed. Thomas R. Cripps. New York: Arno, 1969.

———. *A Plea for Social Justice for the Black Woman.* Yonkers, New York: Negro Society for Historical Research, 1912.

Tillett, Wilbur Fisk. "Southern Womanhood as Affected by the War." *Century Magazine* 43 (November 1891): 9–16.

Tillman, Ben. "The Black Peril." Reprinted in *Justice Denied: The Black Man in White America,* ed. William M. Chace and Peter Collier, pp. 180–85. New York: Harcourt, Brace & World, 1970.

Tourgée, Albion W. *Bricks Without Straw.* New York: Fords, Howard & Hulbert, 1880.

———. *A Fool's Errand: By One of the Fools.* [1879.] Ed. John Hope Franklin. Cambridge, Mass.: Harvard Univ. Press, 1961.

Truth, Sojourner. *Narrative of Sojourner Truth; A Bondwoman of Olden Time, With a History of Her Labors and Correspondence Drawn from Her "Book of Life,"* ed. Olive Gilbert. [1878.] New York: Oxford University Press, 1991.

Twain, Mark. *Pudd'nhead Wilson and Those Extraordinary Twins.* [1894.] Ed. Malcolm Bradbury. Harmondsworth, G.B.: Penguin, 1986.

———. "The United States of Lyncherdom." [1901.] Reprinted in *The Portable Mark Twain,* ed. Bernard DeVoto, pp. 584–93. New York: Viking, 1946.

Washington, Booker T. "Industrial Education for the Negro." In *The Negro Problem: A Series of Articles by Representative American Negroes of To-Day,* [ed. Booker T. Washington. 1903]. Miami: Mnemosyne, 1969.

[———, ed.] *The Negro Problem: A Series of Articles by Representative American Negroes of To-Day.* [1903.] Miami: Mnemosyne, 1969.

Wells, Ida B. *Crusade for Justice: The Autobiography of Ida B. Wells,* ed. Alfreda M. Duster. Chicago: Univ. of Chicago Press, 1970.

———. "Lynching and the Excuse for It." [1901.] Reprinted in *Lynching and Rape: An*

*Exchange of Views,* ed. Bettina Aptheker, pp. 28–34. New York: American Institute for Marxist Studies, 1977.

———. *The Memphis Diary of Ida B. Wells,* ed. Miriam DeCosta-Willis. Boston: Beacon Press, 1995.

———. *Selected Works of Ida B. Wells-Barnett,* comp. Trudier Harris. New York: Oxford Univ. Press, 1991.

Williams, Fannie Barrier. "The Woman's Part in a Man's Business." *Voice of the Negro* 1 (11) (November 1904): 543–47.

Williams, Sylvanie Francaz. "The Social Status of the Negro Woman." *Voice of the Negro* 1 (7) (July 1904): 298–300.

Wright, Richard. *Native Son.* [1940.] New York: Harper, 1969.


SECONDARY SOURCES

Abel, Elizabeth. "Black Writing, White Reading: Race and the Politics of Feminist Interpretation." *Critical Inquiry* 19 (Spring 1993): 470–98.

Albert, Nicole. "Sappho Mythified, Sappho Mystified or the Metamorphoses of Sappho in Fin de Siècle France." *Journal of Homosexuality* 25 (1993): 87–104.

Alexander, Elizabeth. " 'Can you be BLACK and Look at This?': Reading the Rodney King Video(s)." *Public Culture* 7 (1994): 77–94.

Ammons, Elizabeth. *Conflicting Stories: American Women Writers at the Turn into the Twentieth Century.* New York: Oxford Univ. Press, 1992.

Andrews, William L. "Jack Thorne, [David Bryant Fulton]." In *Dictionary of American Negro Biography,* ed. Rayford W. Logan and Michael R. Winston, pp. 589–90. New York: W. W. Norton, 1982.

———. *The Literary Career of Charles W. Chesnutt.* Baton Rouge: Louisiana State Univ. Press, 1980.

Aptheker, Bettina. Introduction to *Lynching and Rape: An Exchange of Views,* ed. Bettina Aptheker, pp. 1–21. New York: The American Institute for Marxist Studies, 1977.

———. "Woman Suffrage and the Crusade Against Lynching, 1890–1920." In *Woman's Legacy: Essays on Race, Sex, and Class in American History,* pp. 53–76. Amherst: Univ. of Massachusetts Press, 1982.

Arnavon, Cyrille. "Introduction to Kate Chopin, *Edna.*" [Paris, 1953.] Translated by Bjφrn Braaten and Emily Toth, and reprinted in *A Kate Chopin Miscellany,* ed. Per Seyersted and Emily Toth, pp. 168–88. Oslo and Natchitoches, La.: Universitetsforlaget and Northwestern State Univ. Press, 1979.

Arner, Robert D. "Landscape Symbolism in Kate Chopin's *At Fault.*" *Louisiana Studies* 9 (1970): 142–53.

Baker, Houston A., Jr. *Workings of the Spirit: The Poetics of Afro-American Women's Writing.* Chicago: Univ. of Chicago Press, 1991.

Baker, Paula. "The Domestication of Politics: Women and American Political Society, 1780–1920." In *Unequal Sisters: A Multicultural Reader in U.S. Women's History,* ed. Ellen Carol DuBois and Vicki L. Ruiz, pp. 66–91. New York: Routledge, 1990.

Banta, Martha. Introduction to William Dean Howells, *The Shadow of a Dream* and *An Imperative Duty,* pp. iii–xii. Bloomington: Indiana Univ. Press, 1970.

Bederman, Gail. " 'Civilization,' the Decline of Middle-Class Manliness, and Ida B.

Wells's Antilynching Campaign (1892–94)." *Radical History Review* 52 (Winter 1992): 5–30.

Berzon, Judith R. *Neither White nor Black: The Mulatto Character in American Fiction.* New York: New York Univ. Press, 1978.

Birnbaum, Michele A. " 'Alien Hands': Kate Chopin and the Colonization of Race." *American Literature* 66 (June 1994): 301–23.

Blassingame, John W. *Black New Orleans, 1860–1880.* Chicago: Univ. of Chicago Press, 1973.

Blee, Kathleen M. *Women of the Klan: Racism and Gender in the 1920s.* Berkeley: Univ. of California Press, 1991.

Bloom, Harold, ed. *Modern Critical Views: Kate Chopin.* New York: Chelsea House, 1987.

Bloomfield, Maxwell. "Dixon's *The Leopard's Spots:* A Study in Popular Racism." *American Quarterly* 6 (1964): 387–401.

Bordin, Ruth. *Frances Willard: A Biography.* Chapel Hill: Univ. of North Carolina Press, 1986.

Braxton, Joanne M. *Black Women Writing Autobiography: A Tradition Within a Tradition.* Philadelphia: Temple Univ. Press, 1989.

Brodhead, Richard H. *Cultures of Letters: Scenes of Reading and Writing in Nineteenth-Century America.* Chicago: Univ. of Chicago Press, 1993.

Brooks, Gwendolyn. Afterword to Pauline E. Hopkins, *Contending Forces: A Romance Illustrative of Negro Life North and South,* pp. 403–9. Carbondale: Southern Illinois Univ. Press, 1978.

Brown, Elsa Barkley. "Negotiating and Transforming the Public Sphere: African American Political Life in the Transition from Slavery to Freedom." *Public Culture* 7 (1994): 107–46.

Brundage, W. Fitzhugh. *Lynching in the New South: Georgia and Virginia, 1880–1930.* Urbana: Univ. of Illinois Press, 1993.

Butcher, Philip. "Mark Twain Sells Roxy Down the River." *CLA Journal* 8 (1965): 225–33.

Campbell, Jane. *Mythic Black Fiction: The Transformation of History.* Knoxville: Univ. of Tennessee Press, 1986.

Campbell, Karlyn Kohrs. "Style and Content in the Rhetoric of Early Afro-American Feminists." *Quarterly Journal of Speech* 72 (1986): 434–45.

Carby, Hazel V. "The Canon: Civil War and Reconstruction." *Michigan Quarterly Review* 27 (1989): 35–43.

———. Introduction to Frances E. W. Harper, *Iola Leroy; or Shadows Uplifted,* pp. ix–xxvi. [1892.] Boston: Beacon Press, 1987.

———. " 'On the Threshold of Woman's Era': Lynching, Empire, and Sexuality in Black Feminist Theory." *Critical Inquiry* 12 (Autumn 1985): 262–77.

———. *Reconstructing Womanhood: The Emergence of the Afro-American Woman Novelist.* New York: Oxford University Press, 1987.

Carnes, Mark C., and Clyde Griffen, eds. *Meanings for Manhood: Constructions of Masculinity in Victorian America.* Chicago: Univ. of Chicago Press, 1990.

Cash, W[ilbur] J. *The Mind of the South.* New York: Alfred A. Knopf, 1941.

Chace, William M., and Peter Collier, eds. *Justice Denied: The Black Man in White America.* New York: Harcourt, Brace & World, 1970.

Chalmers, David M. *Hooded Americanism: The History of the Ku Klux Klan.* 1965. New York: Franklin Watts, 1981.

Cook, Raymond Allen. *Fire from the Flint: The Amazing Careers of Thomas Dixon.* Winston-Salem, N.C.: John F. Blair, 1968.

Cox, James M. *"Pudd'nhead Wilson:* The End of Mark Twain's American Dream." *South Atlantic Quarterly* 58 (1959): 351–63.

Cripps, Thomas R. Introduction to Jack Thorne [David Bryant Fulton], *Hanover; or The Persecution of the Lowly: A Story of the Wilmington Massacre,* pp. i–vii. New York: Arno, 1969.

Da Ponte, Durant. "The Greatest Play of the South." *Tennessee Studies in Literature* 2 (1957): 15–24.

Davenport, F. Garvin, Jr. "Thomas Dixon's Mythology of Southern History." *Journal of Southern History* 36 (1970): 350–67.

Davis, Angela Y. *Women, Race and Class.* New York: Vintage, 1983.

DeJean, Joan. *Fictions of Sappho, 1546–1937.* New York: Univ. of Chicago Press, 1989.

de Lauretis, Teresa. *Feminist Studies/Critical Studies.* Bloomington: Indiana Univ. Press, 1986.

Dimock, Wai-chee. "Rightful Subjectivity." *Yale Journal of Criticism* 4 (1990): 25–51.

Duberman, Martin; Martha Vicinus; and George Chauncey, Jr., eds. *Hidden from History: Reclaiming the Gay and Lesbian Past.* New York: New American Library, 1989.

DuBois, Ellen Carol. *Feminism and Suffrage: The Emergence of an Independent Women's Movement in America, 1848–1869.* Ithaca, N.Y.: Cornell Univ. Press, 1978.

DuBois, Ellen Carol, and Vicki L. Ruiz, eds. *Unequal Sisters: A Multicultural Reader in U.S. Women's History.* New York: Routledge, 1990.

duCille, Ann. *The Coupling Convention: Sex, Text, and Tradition in Black Women's Fiction.* New York: Oxford Univ. Press, 1993.

Duclos, Gloria Shaw. "Thomas Wentworth Higginson's Sappho." *New England Quarterly* 57 (September 1984): 403–11.

Dyer, Joyce Coyne. "Bright Hued Feathers and Japanese Jars: Objectification of Character in Kate Chopin's *At Fault.*" *Revue de Louisiane/Louisiana Review* 9 (1980): 27–35.

———. "Techniques of Distancing in the Fiction of Kate Chopin." *Southern Studies* 24 (1985): 69–81.

Dyer, Joyce Coyne, and Robert Emmett Monroe. "Texas and Texans in the Fiction of Kate Chopin." *Western American Literature* 20 (1985): 3–15.

Dyer, Thomas. *Theodore Roosevelt and the Idea of Race.* Baton Rouge: Louisiana State Univ. Press, 1980.

Edwards, Laura F. "Sexual Violence, Gender, Reconstruction, and the Extension of Patriarchy in Granville County, North Carolina." *North Carolina Historical Review* 68 (July 1991): 237–60.

Ehrenreich, Barbara, and Deirdre English. *For Her Own Good: 150 Years of Experts' Advice to Women.* Garden City, N.Y.: Anchor, 1978.

Elder, Arlene A. " 'The Future American Race': Charles W. Chesnutt's Utopian Illusion." *MELUS* 15 (Fall 1988): 121–29.

Elfenbein, Anna Shannon. *Women on the Color Line: Evolving Stereotypes and the Writings of George Washington Cable, Grace King, Kate Chopin.* Charlottesville: Univ. Press of Virginia, 1989.

Ellison, Ralph. "Change the Joke and Slip the Yoke," pp. 45–59. [1949.] Reprinted in *Shadow and Act.* New York: Vintage, 1972.

Faust, Drew Gilpin. " 'Trying to Do a Man's Business': Slavery, Violence and Gender in the American Civil War." *Gender and History* 4 (Summer 1992): 197–214.

Ferguson, SallyAnn. "Chesnutt's Genuine Blacks and Future Americans." *MELUS* 15 (Fall 1988): 109–19.

Fiedler, Leslie A. "Come Back to the Raft Ag'in, Huck Honey!" In Fiedler, *An End to Innocence: Essays on Culture and Politics*, pp. 142–51. [1948.] New York: Stein & Day, 1972.

———. *Love and Death in the American Novel.* [1960.] Revised ed. New York: Stein & Day, 1982.

Fishkin, Shelley Fisher. "Interrogating 'Whiteness,' Complicating 'Blackness': Remapping American Culture." *American Quarterly* 47 (September 1995): 428–466.

———. *Was Huck Black? Mark Twain and African American Voices.* New York: Oxford Univ. Press, 1993.

Foner, Philip S. *Mark Twain: Social Critic.* New York: International Publishers, 1958.

Foreman, P. Gabrielle. "The Spoken and the Silenced in *Incidents in the Life of a Slave Girl* and *Our Nig.*" *Callaloo* 13 (2) (Spring 1990): 313–24.

Foster, Frances Smith. " 'In Respect of Females . . .': Differences in the Portrayals of Women by Male and Female Narrators." *Black American Literature Forum* 15 (1981): 66–70.

———. *Written by Herself: Literary Production by African American Women, 1746–1892.* Bloomington: Indiana Univ. Press, 1993.

Franklin, John Hope. " 'Birth of a Nation'—Propaganda as History." *Massachusetts Review* 20 (1979): 417–434.

———. *From Slavery to Freedom: A History of Negro Americans.* 5th ed. New York: Alfred A. Knopf, 1980.

Franklin, John Hope, and August Meier, eds. *Black Leaders of the Twentieth Century.* Urbana: Univ. of Illinois Press, 1982.

Fraser, Nancy. "Sex, Lies, and the Public Sphere: Some Reflections on the Confirmation of Clarence Thomas." *Critical Inquiry* 18 (Spring 1992): 595–612.

Fredrickson, George M. *The Black Image in the White Mind: The Debate on Afro-American Character and Destiny, 1817–1914.* Middleton, Conn.: Wesleyan Univ. Press, 1971.

Freedman, Estelle B., ed. *The Lesbian Issue: Essays from Signs.* Chicago: Univ. of Chicago Press, 1985.

Gates, Henry Louis, Jr. "Introduction: 'Tell Me, Sir, . . . What *Is* "Black" Literature?' " Special Issue on African and African American Literature. *PMLA* 105 (January 1990): 11–22.

———. "The Trope of a New Negro and the Reconstruction of the Image of the Black." *Representations* 24 (Fall 1988): 129–55.

Gatewood, Willard B. *Aristocrats of Color: The Black Elite, 1880–1920.* Bloomington: Indiana Univ. Press, 1990.

Giddings, Paula. *When and Where I Enter: The Impact of Black Women on Race and Sex in America.* New York: Bantam, 1984.

Gillman, Susan. " 'Sure Identifiers': Race, Science, and the Law in *Pudd'nhead Wilson.*" In *Mark Twain's Pudd'nhead Wilson: Race, Conflict and Culture*, ed. Susan Gillman and Forrest G. Robinson, pp. 86–104. Durham, N.C.: Duke Univ. Press, 1990.

———. "The Mulatto, Tragic or Triumphant? The Nineteenth-Century American Race

Melodrama." In *The Culture of Sentiment: Race, Gender and Sentimentality in Nineteenth-Century America,* ed. Shirley Samuels, pp. 221–43. New York: Oxford Univ. Press, 1992.

Gillman, Susan, and Forrest G. Robinson, eds. *Mark Twain's Pudd'nhead Wilson: Race, Conflict and Culture.* Durham, N.C.: Duke Univ. Press, 1990.

Gilman, Sander L. "Black Bodies, White Bodies: Towards an Iconography of Female Sexuality in Late Nineteenth-Century Art, Medicine and Literature." *Critical Inquiry* 12 (Autumn 1985): 204–42.

———. *Difference and Pathology: Stereotypes of Sexuality, Race, and Madness.* Ithaca, N.Y.: Cornell Univ. Press, 1985.

Gleason, William. "Voices at the Nadir: Charles Chesnutt and David Bryant Fulton." *American Literary Realism* 24 (Spring 1992): 22–41.

Goodwyn, Lawrence. *The Populist Moment: A Short History of the Agrarian Revolt in America.* New York: Oxford Univ. Press, 1978.

Gossett, Thomas F. *Race: The History of an Idea in America.* New York: Schocken, 1965.

Griffen, Clyde. "Reconstructing Masculinity from the Evangelical Revival to the Waning of Progressivism: A Speculative Synthesis." In *Meanings for Manhood: Constructions of Masculinity in Victorian America,* ed. Mark C. Carnes and Clyde Griffen, pp. 183–204, 265–71. Chicago: Univ. of Chicago Press, 1990.

Gubar, Susan. "Sapphistries." In *The Lesbian Issue: Essays from Signs,* ed. Estelle B. Freedman, pp. 91–110. Chicago: Univ. of Chicago Press, 1985.

Hall, Gwendolyn Midlo. "The Formation of Afro-Creole Culture." In *Creole New Orleans: Race and Americanization,* ed. Arnold R. Hirsch and Joseph Logsdon, pp. 58–87. Baton Rouge: Louisiana State Univ. Press, 1992.

Hall, Jacquelyn Dowd. " 'The Mind That Burns in Each Body': Women, Rape, and Racial Violence." In *Powers of Desire: The Politics of Sexuality,* ed. Ann Snitow, Christine Stansell, and Sharon Thompson, pp. 328–49. New York: Monthly Review Press, 1983.

———. *Revolt Against Chivalry: Jessie Daniel Ames and the Women's Campaign Against Lynching.* New York: Columbia Univ. Press, 1974.

Harley, Sharon, and Rosalyn Terborg-Penn, eds. *The Afro-American Woman: Struggles and Images.* Port Washington, N.Y.: Kennikat, 1978.

Harris, Trudier. *Exorcising Blackness: Historical and Literary Lynching and Burning Rituals.* Bloomington: Indiana Univ. Press, 1984.

Higgins, Lynn A. and Brenda R. Silver, eds. *Rape and Representation.* New York: Columbia Univ. Press, 1991.

Hirsch, Arnold R., and Joseph Logsdon, eds. *Creole New Orleans: Race and Americanization.* Baton Rouge: Louisiana State Univ. Press, 1992.

Hirsch, Marianne, and Evelyn Fox Keller, eds. *Conflicts in Feminism.* New York: Routledge, 1990.

Hodes, Martha. "The Sexualization of Reconstruction Politics: White Women and Black Men in the South after the Civil War." *Journal of the History of Sexuality* 3 (1993): 402–17.

Holt, Thomas C. "The Lonely Warrior: Ida B. Wells-Barnett and the Struggle for Black Leadership." *Black Leaders of the Twentieth Century,* ed. John Hope Franklin and August Meier, pp. 39–61. Urbana: Univ. of Illinois Press, 1982.

Jacobus, Mary; Evelyn Fox Keller; and Sally Shuttleworth, eds. *Body/Politics: Women and the Discourses of Science.* New York: Routledge, 1990.

Jehlen, Myra. "The Ties That Bind: Race and Sex in *Pudd'nhead Wilson.*" In *Mark Twain's Pudd'nhead Wilson: Race, Conflict and Culture,* ed. Susan Gillman and Forrest G. Robinson, pp. 105–20. Durham, N.C.: Duke Univ. Press, 1990.

John, Arthur. *The Best Years of the Century: Richard Watson Gilder, Scribner's Monthly, and Century Magazine, 1870–1909.* Urbana: Univ. of Illinois Press, 1981.

Johnson, Jerah. "New Orleans's Congo Square: An Urban Setting for Early Afro-American Culture Formation." *Louisiana History* 32 (Spring 1991): 117–57.

Jones, Anne Goodwyn. *Tomorrow Is Another Day: The Woman Writer in the South, 1859–1936.* Baton Rouge: Louisiana State Univ. Press, 1981.

Kaplan, Amy. "Romancing the Empire: The Embodiment of American Masculinity in the Popular Historical Novel of the 1890s." *American Literary History* 2 (Winter 1990): 659–90.

Karcher, Carolyn L. "Rape, Murder, and Revenge in 'Slavery's Pleasant Homes': Lydia Maria Child's Antislavery Fiction and the Limits of Genre." In *The Culture of Sentiment: Race, Gender and Sentimentality in Nineteenth-Century America,* ed. Shirley Samuels, pp. 58–72. New York: Oxford Univ. Press, 1992.

Keller, Frances Richardson. *An American Crusade: The Life of Charles Waddell Chesnutt.* Provo, Utah: Brigham Young Univ. Press, 1978.

Kinney, James. *Amalgamation! Race, Sex and Rhetoric in the Nineteenth-Century American Novel.* Westport, Conn.: Greenwood, 1985.

Kraditor, Aileen S. *The Ideas of the Woman Suffrage Movement, 1890–1920.* [1965.] New York: W. W. Norton, 1981.

Lattin, Patricia Hopkins. "Kate Chopin's Repeating Characters." *Mississippi Quarterly* 33 (1979–1980): 19–37.

Lerner, Gerda, ed. *Black Women in White America: A Documentary History.* New York: Vintage, 1973.

Loewenberg, Bert James, and Ruth Bogin, eds. *Black Women in Nineteenth-Century American Life: Their Words, Their Thoughts, Their Feelings.* University Park: Pennsylvania State Univ. Press, 1976.

Logan, Rayford W., and Michael R. Winston. *Dictionary of American Negro Biography.* New York: W. W. Norton, 1982.

Logan, Shirley W. "Rhetorical Strategies in Ida B. Wells's 'Southern Horrors: Lynch Law in All Its Phases.' " *Sage* 8 (Summer 1991): 3–9.

Loggins, Vernon. *The Negro Author: His Development in America to 1900.* [1931.] Port Washington, N.Y.: Kennikat, 1964.

Lott, Eric. "Love and Theft: The Racial Unconscious of Blackface Minstrelsy." *Representations* 39 (Summer 1992): 23–50.

Martin, Biddy, and Chandra Talpade Mohanty. "Feminist Politics: What's Home Got to Do with It?" In *Feminist Studies/Critical Studies,* ed. Teresa de Lauretis, pp. 190–212. Bloomington: Indiana Univ. Press, 1986.

Martin, Robert K. "Knights-Errant and Gothic Seducers: The Representation of Male Friendship in Mid-Nineteenth-Century America." In *Hidden from History: Reclaiming the Gay and Lesbian Past,* ed. Martin Duberman, Martha Vicinus and George Chauncey, Jr., pp. 169–82. New York: New American Library, 1989.

McDowell, Deborah E. " 'The Changing Same': Generational Connections and Black Women Novelists." *New Literary History* 18 (1987): 281–302.

McKay, Nellie Y. "Alice Walker's 'Advancing Luna—and Ida B. Wells': A Struggle Towards Sisterhood." In *Rape and Representation,* ed. Lynn A. Higgins and Brenda R. Silver, pp. 248–60. New York: Columbia Univ. Press, 1991.

Meese, Elizabeth, and Alice Parker, eds. *The Difference Within: Feminism and Critical Theory.* Philadelphia: J. Benjamins, 1989.

Merritt, Russell. "Dixon, Griffith, and the Southern Legend." *Cinema Journal* 12 (1972): 26–45.

Mills, Gary B. *The Forgotten People: Cane River Creoles of Color.* Baton Rouge: Louisiana State Univ. Press, 1977.

Mitchell, Lee Clark. " 'De Nigger in You': Race or Training in *Pudd'nhead Wilson.*" *Nineteenth-Century Literature* 42 (1987): 295–312.

Morrison, Toni. *Playing in the Dark: Whiteness and the Literary Imagination.* Cambridge, Mass.: Harvard Univ. Press, 1992.

———, ed. *Race-ing Justice, and En-gendering Power: Essays on Anita Hill, Clarence Thomas, and the Construction of Social Reality.* New York: Pantheon, 1992.

Moses, Wilson Jeremiah. *The Golden Age of Black Nationalism 1850–1925.* [1978.] New York: Oxford Univ. Press, 1988.

Nelson, Dana D. *The Word in Black and White: Reading "Race" in American Literature 1638–1867.* New York: Oxford Univ. Press, 1992.

Neverdon-Morton, Cynthia. "The Black Woman's Struggle for Equality in the South, 1895–1925." In *The Afro-American Woman: Struggles and Images,* ed. Sharon Harley and Rosalyn Terborg-Penn, pp. 43–57. Port Washington, N.Y.: Kennikat, 1978.

Osofsky, Gilbert. "Progressivism and the Negro: New York, 1900–1915." *American Quarterly* 16 (1964): 153–68.

Painter, Nell Irvin. *Standing at Armageddon: The United States, 1877–1919.* New York: W. W. Norton, 1987.

Peterson, Carla L. *Doers of the Word: African-American Women Speakers and Writers in the North (1830–1880).* New York: Oxford Univ. Press, 1995.

Pettit, Arthur G. *Mark Twain and the South.* Lexington: Univ. Press of Kentucky, 1974.

Porter, Carolyn. "Roxana's Plot." In *Mark Twain's Pudd'nhead Wilson: Race, Conflict and Culture,* ed. Susan Gillman and Forrest G. Robinson, pp. 121–36. Durham, N.C.: Duke Univ. Press, 1990.

———. "What We Know That We Don't Know: Remapping American Literary Studies." *American Literary History* 6 #3 (Fall 1994): 467–526.

Porter, Dorothy B. "Pauline Elizabeth Hopkins." In *Dictionary of Literary Biography,* ed. Rayford W. Logan and Michael R. Winston, pp. 325–26. New York: W. W. Norton, 1982.

Potter, Richard H. "Negroes in the Fiction of Kate Chopin." *Louisiana History* 12 (Winter 1971): 41–58.

Prather, H. Leon, Sr. *We Have Taken a City: Wilmington Racial Massacre and Coup of 1898.* Rutherford, N.J.: Fairleigh Dickinson Univ. Press, 1984.

Pryse, Majorie, and Hortense J. Spillers, eds. *Conjuring: Black Women, Fiction and Literary Tradition.* Bloomington: Indiana Univ. Press, 1985.

Ringe, Donald A. "Cane River World: *At Fault* and Related Stories." In *Modern Critical Views: Kate Chopin,* ed. Harold Bloom, pp. 25–33. New York: Chelsea House, 1987.

Rogin, Michael. "Francis Galton and Mark Twain: The Natal Autograph in *Pudd'nhead Wilson.*" In *Mark Twain's Pudd'nhead Wilson: Race, Conflict and Culture,* ed. Susan Gillman and Forrest G. Robinson, pp. 73–85. Durham, N.C.: Duke Univ. Press, 1990.

————. " 'The Sword Became a Flashing Vision': D. W. Griffith's *The Birth of a Nation.*" *Representations* 9 (Winter 1985): 150–95.

Samuels, Shirley, ed. *The Culture of Sentiment: Race, Gender and Sentimentality in Nineteenth-Century America.* New York: Oxford Univ. Press, 1992.

Sánchez-Eppler, Karen. "Bodily Bonds: The Intersecting Rhetorics of Feminism and Abolition." In *The Culture of Sentiment: Race, Gender and Sentimentality in Nineteenth-Century America,* ed. Shirley Samuels, pp. 92–114. New York: Oxford Univ. Press, 1992.

Sedgwick, Eve Kosofsky. "The Beast in the Closet: James and the Writing of Homosexual Panic." In *Sex, Politics, and Science in the Nineteenth-Century Novel,* ed. Ruth Bernard Yeazell, pp. 148–86. Selected Papers from the English Institute, 1983–1984. Baltimore: Johns Hopkins Univ. Press, 1986.

————. *Between Men: English Literature and Male Homosocial Desire.* New York: Columbia Univ. Press, 1985.

Seyersted, Per. Introduction to *The Complete Works of Kate Chopin,* pp. 21–33. Baton Rouge: Louisiana State Univ. Press, 1969.

————. *Kate Chopin: A Critical Biography.* Oslo and Baton Rouge: Universitetsforlaget and Louisiana State Univ. Press, 1969.

Seyersted, Per, and Emily Toth, eds. *A Kate Chopin Miscellany.* Oslo and Natchitoches, La.: Universitetsforlaget and Northwestern State Univ. Press, 1979.

Shapiro, Herbert. *White Violence and Black Response: From Reconstruction to Montgomery.* Amherst: Univ. of Massachusetts Press, 1988.

Shockley, Ann Allen. "Pauline Elizabeth Hopkins: A Biographical Excursion into Obscurity." *Phylon* 33 (1972): 22–26.

Silber, Nina. *The Romance of Reunion: Northerners and the South, 1865–1900.* Chapel Hill: Univ. of North Carolina Press, 1993.

Smith, Valerie. "Split Affinities: The Case of Interracial Rape." In *Conflicts in Feminism,* ed. Marianne Hirsch and Evelyn Fox Keller, pp. 271–87. New York: Routledge, 1990.

Smith-Rosenberg, Carroll. *Disorderly Conduct: Visions of Gender in Victorian America.* New York: Oxford Univ. Press, 1985.

Snitow, Ann; Christine Stansell; and Sharon Thompson, eds. *Powers of Desire: The Politics of Sexuality.* New York: Monthly Review Press, 1983.

Spillers, Hortense J. "Notes on an Alternative Model—Neither/Nor." In *The Difference Within: Feminism and Critical Theory,* ed. Elizabeth Meese and Alice Parker, pp. 165–85. Philadelphia: J. Benjamins, 1989.

Stepto, Robert B. Response to Richard Yarborough, "The First Person in Afro-American Literature," pp. 121–28. In *Afro-American Literary Study in the 1990s.* Ed. Houston A. Baker, Jr., and Patricia Redmond. Chicago: Univ. of Chicago Press, 1989.

Sterling, Dorothy. *Black Foremothers: Three Lives.* Old Westbury, N.Y.: Feminist Press, 1979.

Sundquist, Eric J. "Mark Twain and Homer Plessy." In *Mark Twain's Pudd'nhead Wilson: Race, Conflict and Culture,* ed. Susan Gillman and Forrest G. Robinson, pp. 46–72. Durham, N.C.: Duke Univ. Press, 1990.

————. *To Wake the Nations: Race in the Making of American Literature.* Cambridge, Mass.: Harvard Univ. Press, 1993.

Takaki, Ronald T. *Iron Cages: Race and Culture in Nineteenth-Century America.* Seattle: Univ. of Washington Press, 1979.

Talmadge, John E. *Rebecca Latimer Felton: Nine Stormy Decades.* Athens: Univ. of Georgia Press, 1960.

Tate, Claudia. *Domestic Allegories of Political Desire: The Black Heroine's Text at the Turn of the Century.* New York: Oxford Univ. Press, 1992.

————. "Pauline Hopkins: Our Literary Foremother." In *Conjuring: Black Women, Fiction and Literary Tradition,* ed. Marjorie Pryse and Hortense J. Spillers, pp. 53–66. Bloomington: Indiana Univ. Press, 1985.

Taylor, Helen. *Gender, Race, and Region in the Writings of Grace King, Ruth McEnery Stuart, and Kate Chopin.* Baton Rouge: Louisiana State Univ. Press, 1989.

Tebbel, John, and Mary Ellen Zuckerman. *The Magazine in America, 1741–1990.* New York: Oxford Univ. Press, 1991.

Terborg-Penn, Rosalyn. "Black Male Perspectives on the Nineteenth-Century Woman." In *The Afro-American Woman: Struggles and Images,* ed. Sharon Harley and Rosalyn Terborg-Penn, pp. 28–42. Port Washington, N.Y.: Kennikat, 1978.

Thompson, Mildred I. *Ida B. Wells-Barnett: An Exploratory Study of an American Black Woman, 1893–1930. Black Women in United States History,* vol. 15. Brooklyn: Carlson, 1990.

Tompkins, Jane. *Sensational Designs: The Cultural Work of American Fiction 1790–1860.* New York: Oxford Univ. Press, 1985.

Toth, Emily. *Kate Chopin.* New York: William Morrow, 1990.

————. "Kate Chopin's New Orleans Years." *New Orleans Review* 15 (1988): 53–60.

Tregle, Joseph G. Jr., "Creoles and Americans." In *Creole New Orleans: Race and Americanization,* ed. Arnold R. Hirsch and Joseph Logsdon, pp. 131–185. Baton Rouge: Louisiana State Univ. Press, 1992.

Treichler, Paula A. "Feminism, Medicine, and the Meaning of Childbirth." In *Body/Politics: Women and the Discourses of Science,* ed. Mary Jacobus, Evelyn Fox Keller, and Sally Shuttleworth, pp. 113–38. New York: Routledge, 1990.

Trelease, Allen W. *White Terror: The Ku Klux Klan Conspiracy and Southern Reconstruction.* [1971.] Westport, Conn.: Greenwood, 1979.

Tucker, David M. "Miss Ida B. Wells and Memphis Lynching." *Phylon* 32 (Summer 1971): 112–22.

Tunnell, Ted. *Crucible of Reconstruction: War, Radicalism, and Race in Louisiana 1862–1877.* Baton Rouge: Louisiana State Univ. Press, 1984.

Walters, Ronald G. "The Erotic South: Civilization and Sexuality in American Abolitionism." *American Quarterly* 25 (1973): 177–201.

Ware, Vron. *Beyond the Pale: White Women, Racism and History.* London: Verso, 1992.

Warren, Kenneth W. *Black and White Strangers: Race and American Literary Realism.* Chicago: Univ. of Chicago Press, 1993.

Washington, Mary Helen. "Uplifting the Women and the Race: The Forerunners—Harper and Hopkins." In *Invented Lives: Narratives of Black Women 1860–1960,* pp. 73–86. Garden City, N.Y.: Doubleday, 1987.

Whitfield, Stephen J. *A Death in the Delta: The Story of Emmett Till.* Baltimore: Johns Hopkins Univ. Press, 1988.

Wideman, John Edgar. "Charles W. Chesnutt: *The Marrow of Tradition*." *American Scholar* 42 (1972): 128–34.

Wiegman, Robyn. "The Anatomy of Lynching." *Journal of the History of Sexuality* 3 (1993): 445–67.

Williamson, Joel. *The Crucible of Race: Black-White Relations in the American South Since Emancipation.* New York: Oxford Univ. Press, 1984.

——. *New People: Miscegenation and Mulattoes in the United States.* New York: Free Press, 1980.

Wolff, Cynthia Griffin. "The Fiction of Limits: 'Désirée's Baby'." In *Modern Critical Views: Kate Chopin*, ed. Harold Bloom, pp. 35–42. New York: Chelsea House, 1987.

Wood, Forrest G. *Black Scare: The Racist Response to Emancipation and Reconstruction.* Berkeley: Univ. of California Press, 1970.

Wyatt-Brown, Bertram. *Southern Honor: Ethics and Behavior in the Old South.* New York: Oxford Univ. Press, 1982.

Wynter, Sylvia. "Sambos and Minstrels." *Social Text* 1 (1979): 149–56.

Yarborough, Richard. Introduction to Pauline E. Hopkins, *Contending Forces: A Romance Illustrative of Negro Life North and South.* [1900.] New York: Oxford Univ. Press, 1988.

——. "Strategies of Black Characterization in *Uncle Tom's Cabin* and the Early Afro-American Novel." In *New Essays on Uncle Tom's Cabin*, ed. Eric J. Sundquist, pp. 45–84. New York: Cambridge Univ. Press, 1986.

——. "Violence, Manhood, and Black Heroism: The Wilmington Riot in Two Turn-of-the-Century Afro-American Novels." Unpublished manuscript, 1990.

Yeazell, Ruth Bernard, ed. *Sex, Politics, and Science in the Nineteenth-Century Novel.* Selected Papers from the English Institute, 1983–1984. Baltimore: Johns Hopkins Univ. Press, 1986.

Yellin, Jean Fagan. *Women and Sisters: The Antislavery Feminists in American Culture.* New Haven, Conn.: Yale Univ. Press, 1989.

# Index

*Incidents in the Life of a Slave Girl* (Jacobs), 102, 141–42
*Independent*, 74, 109, 110
*Iola Leroy* (Harper), 79, 163n. 13, 167n. 52

Jacobs, Harriet A., 102, 141–42, 147
James, Henry, 54, 147
Jefferson, Thomas, 19
Johnston, Mary, 111, 138
Jones, Anne Goodwyn, 112,
*Jungle, The* (Sinclair), 24–25

King, Grace, 108
King, Rodney, 3, 136
Knights of the White Camellia, 115
Ku Klux Klan, the, 13, 35, 44, 69, 113, 115, 120, 121, 123; early, 24, 28–29, 41, 157n. 54; revival of, in the twentieth century, 29; white female membership in, 169n. 8

"Lady of Bayou St. John, A" (Chopin), 16, 128, 129
*Leopard's Spots, The* (Dixon), 12, 14, 29–34, 35, 36–41, 42, 43, 44, 47, 51, 53, 74, 127, 138, 166n. 35
Literature: African Americanist approaches to, 144–48; Americanist approaches to, 144–48; Asian American, 145; black female approaches to, 8, 9, 11, 47, 143, 148, 149n. 1; black male approaches to, 9, 11, 12, 13; Chicano, 145; gendered nature of, 11–12, 16, 111–12, 138, 141; humanist readings of, 13, 142; Native American, 145; and politics of narrative, 8–9; and race, 3, 12, 16–17, 22, 47, 141; and tradition, 4; white female approaches to, 3, 8, 9, 11, 47, 111–12, 143, 148; white male approaches to, 9, 11, 12. *See also* Domestic novel; Local color fiction; Melodrama; Plantation fiction; Seduction novel; Sentimental novel; *specific authors*
"Little Free Mulatto, A," 117
Local color fiction, 13, 16, 112, 114, 117, 145
Locke, Alain, 157n. 5
Los Angeles, 137
Louisiana, 13, 16, 114–17, 126, 142
Louisiana Purchase, 126
Lydston, G. Frank, 132
"Lynch Law in the South" (Douglass), 48
Lynching, 3–11, 12, 14, 15, 16, 19, 25, 28, 31, 40, 46, 47, 49, 52, 76, 98, 106, 108, 112, 115, 116, 122, 137, 138, 139, 140, 151n. 16; and black men, 6, 9, 22, 26, 34, 35, 37, 42, 66, 67, 89, 104–5, 116, 126; and black women, 6, 8, 9–10, 16, 77, 78, 79–80, 81–82, 83–85, 87, 98, 161n. 1, 165n. 25; and castration, 5, 85, 151n. 16; effects on white participants, 5, 12, 13, 14, 26, 34, 39–40, 49, 68–69; of Italians in New

Orleans, 115; and mob rule, 5, 7, 15, 115; as punishment for rape, 6, 8, 9, 19, 26, 33, 34, 39–40; rise of, after the Civil War, 3; ritual of, 5, 10, 14, 42–43, 49, 123; and white unity, 7, 28, 13, 31, 111; white women's attitude toward, 11, 63, 85, 95, 108–11, 120, 121, 126, 135, 143. *See also* Black men; Ku Klux Klan; Race riots; Rape; White men; White supremacists
"Lynching and the Excuse For It" (Wells), 110
*Lynching in the New South* (Brundage), 5

"Ma'ame Pélagie" (Chopin), 118
Manly, Alexander, 63, 66, 73, 90, 95, 109, 151n. 13, 160n. 28, 164n. 23, 166n. 35
"Mark Twain and Homer Plessy" (Rogin), 52
*Marrow of Tradition, The* (Chesnutt), 13, 14, 15, 51, 52–53, 62–76, 78, 89, 95, 139
Martin, Robert K., 156n. 45
McDowell, Calvin, 81
Melodrama, 15, 52, 158n. 12
Melville, Herman, 147
Minstrelsy, 58, 68
Miscegenation, 9, 32, 33, 34, 35, 40, 45, 53, 54, 55, 62, 63, 64, 65, 67, 75, 99, 112, 113, 114, 117, 128, 130, 174n. 65; and black men, 9, 13, 27, 32, 56; and white men, 27, 33, 34, 35, 44, 47, 54, 60, 62, 72, 90, 100; and white women, 7, 9, 13, 32, 85–86, 95
Mob rule. *See* Race riots
*Mob Rule in New Orleans* (Wells), 25, 82
"Model Woman, The," (Wells), 81
Monroe, Robert Emmett, 127
Moss, Thomas, 81
Moynihan, Daniel Patrick, 137
Mulattoes, 15, 20, 21, 32, 34, 46, 75, 117, 128, 150n. 9, 160n. 32. *See also* Octoroons; Quadroons
Multiculturalism, 145

*Narrative of the Life of Frederick Douglass*, 102
Natchitoches Parish, Louisiana, 114, 116, 125
Nation, 8, 9, 22, 25, 51, 138, 143; and imperialism, 31; and nationalism, 7; in racial danger, 6, 31, 52, 75; racial identity of, 24, 32, 35; renewal and unity of 6, 31, 48, 52, 53, 54, 57, 60, 64, 75, 125, 133; white woman as symbol of, 7, 75, 121
National Association for the Advancement of Colored People, 5, 20, 30
National Association of Colored Women, 162n. 8, 168n. 59
National League on Urban Conditions Among Negroes, 30
National Public Radio, 137
Native Americans, 23
*Native Son* (Wright), 9

Printed in the United States
99754LV00002B/70-84/A